HATS

THE ANIMAL TURN

HATS

A Very UNnatural History

Malcolm Smith

Michigan State University Press
East Lansing

♾ The paper used in this publication meets the minimum requirements
of ANSI/NISO Z39.48-1992 (R 1997) (Permanence of Paper).

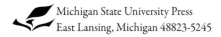 Michigan State University Press
East Lansing, Michigan 48823-5245

LIBRARY OF CONGRESS CATALOGING-IN-PUBLICATION DATA
Names: Smith, Malcolm, 1949 March 11– author. | Michigan State University Press.
Title: Hats : a very UNnatural history / Malcolm Smith.
Other titles: A very unnatural history | Animal turn.
Description: First Edition. | East Lansing, Michigan : Michigan State University Press, 2020.
| Series: The animal turn | Includes bibliographical references and index.
Identifiers: LCCN 2019013217| ISBN 9781611863475 (Cloth) | ISBN 9781609176228 (PDF)
| ISBN 9781628953848 (ePub) | ISBN 9781628963854 (Kindle) Subjects: LCSH: Hats—History.
| Fur garments. | Featherwork. | Extinct animals. | Extinct birds.
Classification: LCC GT2110 .S65 2020 | DDC 391.4/309—dc23
LC record available at https://lccn.loc.gov/2019013217

Typesetting by Charlie Sharp, Sharp Des!gns, East Lansing, MI
Cover design by Erin Kirk New
Cover art: A velvet hat with a whole Lesser Bird of Paradise to decorate it
(Pacific Grove Museum of Natural History, California).

ℊ green Michigan State University Press is a member of the Green Press Initiative and is committed to
press developing and encouraging ecologically responsible publishing practices. For more information about
INITIATIVE
the Green Press Initiative and the use of recycled paper in book publishing, please visit www.greenpressinitiative.org.

Visit Michigan State University Press at www.msupress.org

For six indomitable Victorian ladies who made a difference

Catherine Hall
Minna Hall
Harriet Hemenway
Etta Lemon
Eliza Phillips
Emily Williamson

Contents

Acknowledgments

As a professional wildlife biologist, what I knew about hats before I started this project would not occupy even one page of this book. So I am particularly indebted to a range of people who have given me a remarkable insight into the manufacture, the use, and the decoration of one of the most fundamental human garments in many cultures and in different parts of the world. Others have helped on a wide range of other hat-related, mammal, and bird topics.

I am grateful to Sarah Aitken, visitor experience manager, RSPB Bempton Cliffs, the Yorkshire Seabird Centre, Bempton, East Yorkshire; Hadley Andersen, Molly Hagemann, and Kapaliku Maile, the Bernice Pauahi Bishop Museum, Honolulu, Hawaii; Professor Melissa Bateson for permission to use the photograph of Emily Williamson; Frances Berdan, emeritus professor of anthropology at California State University, San Bernardino; Tessa Boase, author of *Mrs Pankhurst's Purple Feather* (Aurum Press, 2018); Louis Chalmers, The Plumery, Whitehall Gardens, London; Ellen Colon-Lugo, president of the U.S. Milliners Guild and owner of Ellen Christine Couture, Inc., New York City; Robin Doughty, emeritus professor in human geography, University of Texas, Austin; Edwina Ehrman, senior exhibition curator, V&A Museum, London; Bernadette Driscoll Engelstad, independent Curator and Inuit art and cultural history research collaborator, Arctic Studies Center, Smithsonian Institution, Washington, DC; Claire Fowler, supporter engagement coordinator, and Jennifer White, media partnerships coordinator, People for the Ethical Treatment of Animals (PETA), London; Lesley Fox, executive director, The Fur-Bearers, North Vancouver, British Columbia, Canada; Anni Guttorm, curator at SIIDA, the Sámi Museum, Inari, Finland; the Hat Works Museum, Stockport Metropolitan Borough Council, Stockport, UK; Dr. Nancy Jacobs, professor, Department of History, Brown University, Providence, Rhode Island; Dr. Benjamin Jaffé, Jaffé et Fils Ltd., Axminster, Devon, UK; Yvette Jelfs, Noble Headwear Ltd., Melrose, Scotland; Miki Joelson, Assistant to the Chief Curator, Jack, Joseph, and Morton Mandel Wing for Jewish Art and Life, the Israel Museum, Jerusalem; Hanna Levy at Philip Treacy London; Amy Money of Amy Money Millinery, UK; Ester Muchawsky-Schnapper, senior curator emerita, the Israel Museum, Jerusalem, and independent curatorial consultant; Peter O'Donoghue, york herald, College of Arms, London; Dr. Merle Patchett, Department of Human Geography, University of Bristol; Petershams Millinery Supplies, London; Elen Phillips, principal curator of contemporary and community history, St Fagans National Museum of History, Cardiff, UK; Deborah Rooney, Chapter Office, College of St George, Windsor Castle, UK; Craig Sallis, production manager, and Daisy Ogle, wholesale sales account manager, Christys' Hats, Witney, Oxfordshire; Jayne Shrimpton, photo dating expert and dress historian; Dr. Olga Soffer, emeritus professor, Department of Anthropology, University of Illinois; Frieda Sorber, Mode Museum, Antwerp, Belgium; Phil Sykes, director, Parkin Fabrics Limited, Oldham, UK; Lindsay Whitehead, owner of Torb & Reiner, Melbourne, Australia.

I would also like to thank my editor, Gabriel Dotto, director of Michigan State University Press, for having faith in this project and for his patience answering my numerous queries and adjustments as the book progressed. And special thanks to Anastasia Wraight, project editor at the press, for her positive and constructive dialogue with me through the editing process. It made that job a pleasure.

My wife Viv has, as always, been nothing but encouraging in spite of the enormous amount of time I have spent in my study over the last year while this book developed from concept to reality. It has taken time away from our life together. I really am very grateful.

Introduction

An elegantly dressed lady and gentleman are taking an afternoon stroll along a city sidewalk, glancing at the impressive window displays in the adjacent department stores. They might be in a fashionable district of New York. It could equally be London, Paris perhaps, or Vienna. Fashion-conscious and stylish, both wear the à la mode hats of the day. It's 1886 and everyone, just everyone, well-to-do or otherwise, wears a hat of some sort every time they venture outdoors.

The gentleman wears a fashionable and characteristically elegant black top hat finished off with a delicately ribbed band of black silk. Made of hardened, polished beaver fur—North American beaver because Eurasian beavers have been virtually exterminated—it is the best quality top hat that money can buy.

His wife's hat is much more extravagant. Made from a softer beaver felt, it is dyed a distinguished pale green. Three tiny, iridescent-plumaged hummingbirds, resplendent in burnt carmine and cobalt blue, decorate the hat's top, each one stuffed and discreetly wired to pose as if they are about to take nectar from the artificial flowers that accompany them, a contrived habitat in miniature on the head. Her hat also sports a jaunty panache of black ostrich feathers wafting in the gentle afternoon breeze combined with a pair of gossamer-fine, snow-white egret plumes, known in the millinery trade the world over as "aigrettes."

Sometime that same year Frank Chapman, a leading American ornithologist, had taken a couple of afternoon strolls too. His were along the sidewalks of New York's uptown shopping district. Not the best place for spotting birds. But Chapman had an unusual purpose. He was counting birds on ladies' hats. And they proved to be especially productive walks. Chapman identified forty different species. In addition to flurries of feathers, three-quarters of the hats he counted were adorned with whole stuffed birds: warblers, woodpeckers, Baltimore orioles, snow buntings, even a whole green heron.

On that same day in 1886, and every day, hundreds of thousands of hunters around the world were laying traps for beavers, sables, and other fur-bearing animals in order to sell their pelts to local dealers; others were shooting tree-nesting egrets—in the few huge colonies that remained—to cut off and sell their elegant nuptial nape plumes, the "aigrettes," their bodies dumped and their calling offspring left to starve. In South American forests and on Caribbean islands, other hunters pointed long poles at nectar-laden flowers to wait for unsuspecting hummingbirds to adhere to their glue-smeared ends (see plate 1).

The trade in animal furs and for whole wild birds and feather adornments for hats had reached its zenith. It had been centuries in building to this crescendo of greed, a greed that exhibited no concern whatsoever for its impact on the huge range of animal species it exploited. One estimate is that up to two hundred million birds alone were being killed annually worldwide to adorn ladies' hats.[1] And that does not include those that were maimed but got away, probably to die a lingering death, nor the young birds left in nests to perish from starvation and attacks by predators when their adult parents were killed.

The quantities of feathers, and whole preserved bird skins, sold at the turn of the twentieth century at the regular feather auctions in London—the world epicenter of the trade—almost defies belief. One auction alone had twenty-five thousand tiny hummingbirds from the Caribbean, six thousand birds of paradise from New Guinea, and six thousand ounces of aigrettes from North America and southern Europe.

The fashion houses of Paris, New York, and London displayed hats with fabulous assemblies of birds and their plumes; they were marketed as elegant, colorful, and novel. They were what every lady desired. Mail-order firms that started in the United States and Canada made these latest fashions available outside the big cities; ladies in the smallest rural towns could walk out with an exotic and graceful bird of paradise and a panache of ostrich feathers above their heads.

Indigenous peoples living in the coldest extremes of the world had always killed fur-bearing mammals to provide the clothing, head coverings included, to keep them alive in the harshest conditions: caribou especially but sea otters, sables, Arctic foxes, and others too. It was against their interests to annihilate whole populations of fur bearers; depriving their children and grandchildren of such a precious resource was not an option. But when hunters from further south arrived in the mid-eighteenth century, all notion of sustainable harvesting dissipated; like the carnage of North American and Eurasian beavers to make the best-quality felts for the incredibly popular gentlemen's top hat, mammals such as the sea otter inhabiting the rocky coasts and islands of the North Pacific were all but exterminated. Their numbers are still recovering.

People have covered their heads since time immemorial. Headwear did the obvious: it offered protection from rain, cold weather, or strong sunlight. More robust designs protected against injury from falling rocks, weapons, or masonry. If historians are correct that hats were the first items of apparel worn by humans, then perhaps the first profession was not what is commonly purported, but hat making. The oldest physical hat in existence is over five thousand years old; it was made from the pelt of a brown bear and worn by a hunter who was killed in the European Alps, his body and the garments he wore preserved in ice. But there is indirect evidence in the form of figurines made of a variety of materials, and from primitive drawings, that hats woven from natural fibers might have been used very much earlier than that.

It was not long, though, before hats started to be used to convey rank and position in society. After all, in fashion terms, hats are the most noticeable item anyone can wear because an onlooker's attention is first drawn to the face. Little wonder that an old idiom claims: If you want to get ahead and get noticed, get a hat.

The shape and style of a hat has always helped indicate one's profession, wealth, social rank, and position; color, shape, and material all carried specific meaning. In ecclesiastical heraldry, for example, a red, wide-brimmed hat indicated that its wearer was a cardinal, and interactions required a specific social protocol. In seventeenth-century England, the shape and style of one's hat reflected political and religious affiliation. And because of the expense of a beaver fur hat, being able to purchase one made a very obvious visual statement about one's wealth and social standing. As hat fashion became far more important than function, the death warrants of vast numbers of fur-bearing mammals used to make them—and of birds and bird parts used to decorate them—were being signed around much of the world.

Soon, the hat industry, the milliners, the arbiters of purportedly sophisticated style—and the ladies who avidly sought out such fashion to wear—were responsible for the deaths of countless millions of birds and mammals around the world. Before the twentieth century dawned, many species had been extirpated from large parts of the regions they once inhabited. There were no ostriches left across the whole of North Africa or in the Middle East. If ostrich farming hadn't started up in South Africa in the 1880s, there can be little doubt that these huge flightless birds would today figure only in picture books. Farming them ensured that there was less incentive to hunt the wild birds by chasing them on horseback until they were exhausted so that they could then be shot or clubbed to death. Who would ever imagine today that one of our simplest garments—a mere hat—could ever have been the cause of such wanton cruelty and destruction.

The discovery of the felting process that used animal furs to manufacture an enormous range of top-quality hats for both men and women (cheaper hats used farmed rabbit fur or wool felt) resulted in the killing of vast numbers of both North American and Eurasian beavers, driving them to the very edge of extinction. Canada's economy was even founded on the pelts of the North American beaver; in the earliest days of Nouvelle-France, as it was known in the sixteenth century, the beaver skin trade was the cornerstone of the nation's economy.

Head coverings that became symbols of status or authority had progressed to become an art form. Doubtless, society Victorian ladies in New York, Vienna, or London sporting a flurry of ostrich and peacock feathers or whole birds of paradise on their bonnets would have dismissed any comparison with the headgear of what they would have described as very much more "primitive" societies (see plate 2). Yet the similarities with the incredibly colorful feathered headdresses of the elite of Aztec society in Central America in the fourteenth century or the stunning birds of paradise feathers and those of other exotic birds decorating the heads of Papuan New Guinea dancers are manifest.

The desire for colorful and showy feathers to decorate ladies' hats in Western societies began in twelfth-century Europe but only for the few who had the means to purchase them. For centuries such extravagance was limited to royalty, the ruling classes, and senior military officers. But in late eighteenth-century France, Marie Antoinette—the doomed wife of Louis XVI—set new standards of opulence and lavish spending, even by French royal court standards, with her extravagant dresses and enormous, feather-bedecked hats.

The style was emulated by anyone with sufficient money; it spread to the other fashion centers of Europe and to the United States. While in the years immediately following the French Revolution such affluence couldn't be displayed, feathers, birds' wings, birds' heads, and whole birds were to remain in vogue for ladies' hats across most of Europe and North America until at least the early years of the twentieth century. It might seem utterly absurd to us today that elegantly dressed ladies wore hats up to three feet across laden with displays of exotic birds, gull wings, even owl heads, but they were the apogee of Victorian fashion.

As material wealth increased for the rising Victorian middle classes, the pace of fashion and its adoption by a yet wider public accelerated. The desire for display and novelty became more pronounced. At the same time colonial expansion across the globe, and the exploration of distant lands, introduced new and ever more exotic commodities and natural specimens to European markets. Previously unknown species of birds such as impeyan pheasants from Southeast Asia, brilliantly colored little minivets from India, and equally exotic hummingbirds from the Caribbean and South American forests were just a few that were killed by the tens and hundreds of thousands and shipped out from their home continents.

Did the millions of fashion-conscious ladies in the late nineteenth century when highly feathered and whole bird–decorated hats were all the rage give even a passing thought to the demise of the species involved? Did they believe that all these birds had died naturally? Or that the feathers had somehow been plucked and the hapless birds flew off in a little pain but otherwise healthy?

Or could the answer lie instead with a very partial interpretation of biblical verses convincing the reader that man's dominion over the Earth was total, just as the early European pioneers had believed when they set out west to settle the vast American continent?

There were, though, a few brave souls who were determined to question this worldwide killing spree merely to decorate hats. They were determined to take on the influential millinery trade and change public attitudes. It was a battle begun in both the United States and the United Kingdom by some indomitable Victorian ladies who in the late 1800s vowed not to tolerate any longer this carnage of wild creatures, both in their home countries and around the world.

Coincidentally, in Boston, Massachusetts, and in Manchester, UK, they started campaigns to get the wild bird feather trade banned. Their efforts garnered increasing support and led eventually to the first effective bird protection legislation in both countries and to the creation of two of the most influential bird protection organizations in the world. Thanks to their persistence, public attitudes to the enormity of the destruction of birds merely for fashion started to change. It was a long and bitterly contested verbal battle between milliners and conservationists that lasted decades.

World Wars and austerity intervened too; showy hats were no longer appropriate as the abominable death and destruction wreaked by World War I shattered any notion of a quick and decisive victory. And with the coming of the motor car in the first decade of the twentieth century—a yet more attractive fashion statement and a harbinger of increased leisure time for the middle classes—a hat laden with stuffed birds and winnowing plumes of feathers was simply impractical and suddenly seemed utterly ridiculous.

In contrast, it was not until well into the twentieth century that any protection whatsoever was provided for most of the wild mammals that continued to be exploited for their fur. The anti-fur protests that began in the late 1970s and continued into the 1980s and beyond were targeted more at the farming of fur-bearing mammals such as foxes, chinchillas, and sables, rather than at wild mammal hunting and trapping. These campaigns reached their climax in the 1990s with models posing nude promoting the slogan, "I'd rather be naked than wear real fur." And while the fur industry has survived, and at times expanded since then, increasing numbers of influential clothing designers and retailers are today shunning animal furs and promoting the use of synthetic (or faux) fur instead.

Nevertheless, large numbers of wild, fur-bearing mammals from black bears to beavers are still being trapped and hunted, though almost always under license or other constraints imposed by state or regional authorities. Many inhabitants of northern latitudes continue to wear natural fur hats for warmth in bitterly cold climates, and many Arctic indigenous peoples still hunt and trap fur-bearing mammals such as caribou and foxes to provide insulating clothing. Away from such frigid parts of the world, Hasidic Jews wear *shtreimels*, large hats made traditionally from the tail tips of mammals such as sables and martens, while Britain's Guards' regiments continue to wear ceremonial bearskins that are just what the name indicates: the pelts of black bears. Should they, too, be converting their headwear to faux fur?

While feather-decorated hats have for the best part of the last century substituted domestic goose, cockerel, and ostrich feathers for those of wild egrets and birds of paradise, synthetic faux furs manufactured to mimic the appearance of most animal furs have certainly not eliminated substantial interest in the real thing. The debate, mostly highly polarized and often acrimonious, between the fur industry and those promoting animal welfare and animal rights, whether of wild trapped or farmed animals, is certainly not going to end soon.

This book tells the story through the ages of the prodigious impact of hats on the wild mammals whose fur is often used to make them and on the wild birds whose feathers, wings, heads, and even whole bodies were frequently used to decorate them. It is in part a story of breathtaking greed that showed a seemingly total disregard for the many species the trade exploited. But it is partly a story, too, of sustainable animal exploitation in some of the most challenging living environments on earth. It is a story about the devastating consequences for many of the exploited species, several driven to the very brink of extinction or extirpated from huge regions of the world they previously inhabited. And it is also a story that illustrates the remarkable resilience—and ultimate recovery—of many of the species formerly decimated by the hat trade and its seemingly untroubled fashionistas.

The Earliest Hats and Hat Decor

WITH THE WEATHER WORSENING AND MORE SNOW FORECAST, AVID MOUNTAIN HIKERS Erika and Helmut Simon decided to move to lower ground in the European Alps where they were on one of their frequent walking holidays. But noticing something dark protruding from the snow and ice, they stopped to investigate. What they discovered that day proved eventually to be one of the most important archaeological finds of recent years. The Simons—and other hikers and climbers that later joined the scene—assumed that the ice-preserved corpse in front of them, somewhat shriveled, stained dark brown in color, and with its head and shoulders poking out of the melting snow, was that of a mountaineer who had fallen to his death, maybe the previous century.

But it soon became obvious that Ötzi the Iceman, as he came to be known from his place of discovery high in the Ötztal Valley close to the Italian/Austrian border, was much older. Very much older. A hunter and perhaps a local tribal leader, Ötzi lived around 3300 B.C. in the late Neolithic, a time when the Stone Age was making way for the first copper tools of the Chalcolithic or Copper Age. He had been killed by a flint arrowhead that had severed an artery near one shoulder. Ötzi had bled to death.[1] His body had been preserved in deep snow and ice, at or near where he had been killed, for well over 5,000 years. It was September 1991, and the discovery set the archaeological world alight.

Europe's oldest known human mummy: brown-eyed, gap-toothed, and tattooed, Ötzi—on display since in the South Tyrol Museum of Archaeology in Bolzano, Italy—has provided not only an unprecedented insight into the life, clothing, and food of early Copper Age humans, he has provided us with the oldest hat ever to be found.

Ötzi's hat resembled a modern-day Russian *ushanka* fur hat without the flaps (see plate 3). It was made entirely of pieces of brown bear (*Ursus arctos*) skin, stitched together to form a hemispherical shape and worn with the fur on the outside. A bearskin chinstrap held it in place. Providing warmth and waterproofing—function not decoration—it would have been an excellent choice of material in regions with cooler and wetter climates.

None of the rest of Ötzi's clothing—his long coat and his leggings—were made of bear hide; instead, these were made of strips of domestic sheep and goat hide, stitched together with animal sinew. So why just his cap? Maybe because, for Copper Age man, hunting bears with spears, with bow and arrows, or by digging large pit traps would have been a hazardous undertaking fraught with risk of injury or worse. It was far easier to use domesticated animals as a supply of hides;

the hide from a brown bear kill (or maybe one found dead) would be used sparingly and perhaps reserved for wearing by those in the higher echelons of society.[2]

When he was discovered, Ötzi was carrying a yew bow and a deer-hide quiver of arrows with flint arrowheads. Experiments with a model of his bow have shown that the type of arrows he carried could kill an animal thirty to fifty meters distant, so it is quite possible for bears to be killed by a group of hunters working together.[3]

Brown bears would have been moderately common in the forested hills and valleys across most of northern Europe in the Copper Age. It's very unlikely that the low density of human population at that time would have threatened their numbers and distribution until the early Middle Ages when forest felling and agricultural development gathered pace, fracturing the habitats they relied upon. Indeed, Ötzi's fur hat was made from a genetic lineage of brown bear still seen in this area of the European Alps today.[4]

Ötzi is thought to have been a local tribal leader, and maybe his status allowed him to wear the best material available. Or brown bears might have been present in particularly high numbers in that part of the Alps at that time. There is certainly nothing to suggest that Bronze Age and Iron Age peoples commonly wore bearskin caps, even where brown bears were present and might have been relatively common. Most of that evidence comes from the discovery over the last couple of centuries of bodies buried in peat and preserved by it. These so-called bog bodies have mainly been found in Germany, Denmark, and Ireland, all countries with large peat deposits.

Emmer-Erfscheidenveen Man, a bog body discovered in Drenthe in the Netherlands in 1938 and dated to between 1310 B.C. and 1050 B.C. (mid- to late Bronze Age) is famous for the extent of his preserved clothing though almost all of his body was decomposed. He had a woolen cap made of sheepskin, deerskin shoes, a cowhide cape, and woolen undergarments, suggesting a mixed hunting and farming economy where he lived.[5] Unlike Ötzi's bearskin cap, this Bronze Age man wore his sheepskin cap with the fleece side against his head. Female Bronze Age bog bodies often had hairnets or woolen caps made using a primitive needlework technique to produce an elastic material similar to netting and made from wool or plant fibers. Tollund Man, dated to 400 B.C., an incredibly well-preserved bog body discovered in 1950 in Denmark, wore a well-crafted, pointed leather cap also made of sheepskin. It was secured with sheepskin leather straps.

Using protein analysis of eleven items of Iron Age bog body clothing found in Denmark (proteins remain better preserved than DNA in wet peat), Dr. Luise Brandt, then at the University of Copenhagen, found that two were from cattle, three from goats, and six from sheep. No wild animal skins were used to make any of the items of clothing.[6]

Brown bears are known to have become extinct in Denmark—maybe also in the Netherlands—around 3000 B.C. because of hunting and because much of their wooded habitat was already cleared for primitive farming.[7] So the Danish and Dutch bog bodies could not have had local bearskin for clothing. In Germany, where many other bog bodies have been found, bears didn't become extinct until the eighteenth or nineteenth centuries, yet no German bog bodies have been discovered bearing bearskin hats either.

The earliest human hunter-gatherer communities would have been reliant on whatever wild animals they could kill both to supplement their diet and to provide them with clothing. In wet and cold climates, headwear would surely have been essential and might have made use of deerskin or bearskin to provide warmth and waterproofing. By about 6000 B.C., the first European farmers had begun to breed sheep and cattle, and to grow crops. But because brown bears were highly dangerous animals to kill, maybe Iron Age farmers took the safer option, even where bears were still present, and used domesticated animal skins instead. Ötzi's hat might have been the exception rather than the rule.

Apart from Ötzi in the Copper Age and the few Bronze/Iron Age bog bodies found with hats, no other early hats have been discovered. As a result, we rely on depictions of hats in drawings and as part of sculpted figures to gather what understanding we can of the earliest hats and the degree to which they used wild animal parts in their construction.

The earliest are the so-called Venus figurines; small figures (between 1.5 and 9.8 inches high), mostly distinctly female in form, they are carved from soft stone, bone, or mammoth ivory or are made of clay and fired. Most have been found in Europe, though some are from further afield such as Siberian Russia. Of the more than two hundred found, most are dated to the Paleolithic between 24,000 B.C. and 19,000 B.C. though some date back to 33,000 B.C.[8]

Characterized by having small heads, wide hips, and legs tapering to a point, many exaggerate the abdomen, hips, breasts, and vulva. Arms and feet are usually absent, and the head in most is faceless. Expert opinion regarding the function and significance of these exquisite figurines is decidedly mixed: from fertility symbols, Stone Age dolls, depictions of women or of a mother goddess, as religious icons, or even the equivalent of pornographic imagery. Their true meaning might never be known.

Their heads often have a checkerboard-like pattern formed from a series of shallow channels cut at right angles to each other. Historically thought to be a representation of a hairstyle or a wig, many anthropologists now believe that these depict woven hats made from plant fibers, their exquisite detail reflecting the important role played by textiles in Upper Paleolithic (roughly 50,000 B.C. to 10,000 B.C.) cultures.[9] But it is impossible to know whether such depictions mean that hats like these were worn in real life by Paleolithic Age women. "There are a number of plants whose pollen has been recovered from Upper Paleolithic sites in both Moravia and Russia that could have been used to make cordage [fibers twisted or braided together], nettle being the most appealing," comments Dr. Olga Soffer, emeritus professor at the Department of Anthropology, University of Illinois, and a leading expert on perishable artifacts.[10]

A smaller number of ivory figurines, dated to around 18,000 B.C., has been found in Siberia. The Paleolithic people who carved them inhabited partially subterranean dwellings excavated into the ground; they positioned large animal bones to hold the walls with reindeer antlers used to construct a roof (probably covered with animal skins) for protection.[11]

They appear to depict a very different sort of head covering from that depicted on the figurines found in Europe. Here they seem to be wearing stylized hooded parkas and footed trousers or even overalls, a reflection, maybe, of the very much colder climate they had to endure. Recent detailed analysis by Dr. Lyudmila Lbova and Dr. Pavel Volkov at the Institute of Archaeology and Ethnography, part of the Siberian Branch of the Russian Academy of Sciences, has concluded that, far from representing idealized female forms, these figurines also include male forms and children.[12]

Their hooded clothing, often with fur helmets (hats covering the head and shoulders) seems to be made from animal skins and furs to help protect them against the harsh winter conditions. Herds of reindeer (*Rangifer tarandus*)—known as caribou in North America—would have been common on the Arctic Siberian tundra, and their southward migration every autumn, and its reverse in spring, would surely have been unmissable opportunities to kill both mature and young animals for their meat and hides. The figurines depict different hats, hairstyles, and other accessories, and their makers use different carving techniques to highlight a range of materials including fur and animal skins. The most popular outerwear depicted appears to be fur overalls with hoods, obtained presumably from killing deer, bears, seals, and other mammals. Native inhabitants of many parts of Siberia—such as the Itelmen of the Kamchatka Peninsula in the Russian far northeast—wore similar mammal-hide and fur clothing in recent centuries.

Initially migrating from northeast Siberia across the Bering Strait around 2000 B.C. to what is now Alaska—and on to Arctic Canada and Greenland—the Inuit made their clothing out of animal skins and furs. Parkas with hoods made from caribou or seal skin were the norm, and caribou were not difficult to hunt and kill.[13] But over the centuries, these northern deer have declined substantially and are today estimated to number about three million across their huge Arctic range from Alaska through Greenland to Arctic Russia.[14]

In warmer parts of the prehistoric world, animal skins and furs were rarely used for hat making. Their warmth was not required. Early hats depicted in drawings include an ancient Egyptian tomb painting of a man wearing a conical straw hat, dated to around 3200 B.C., presumably lightweight and made to protect against the sun. The ancient Greeks usually went bareheaded, but when men traveled they wore the *petasos*, a practical sunshade of wool felt or straw with a wide brim and held on by a chinstrap. Women wore a version made of fine straw with a tallish, conical crown. Other early Greek hats include the *pílos*, a simple, brimless skull cap, usually conical in shape and made from wool felt or leather, the latter almost certainly obtained from domestic livestock.

Both the petasos and the pílos became popular in ancient Rome too, the pílos particularly so with Roman soldiers and sailors. It was also worn at festivals and public games by athletes. The pílos is often confused with the Phrygian cap, made of leather or wool, a soft conical cap worn with its point pulled forward. Associated with the ancient Greeks since about 400 B.C., with several peoples in eastern Europe, and given to Roman slaves who had won their freedom, the Phrygian cap was worn as a symbol of liberty during the American Revolutionary War and the French Revolution.[15]

The helmet of the Roman warrior was a development of the beautifully designed Greek warrior's helmet; some worn by more senior ranks had a short crest, either of horse hair or of trimmed feathers, usually from ostrich. They were often dyed red; sometimes other colors too. Many ceremonial hats worn by ancient Egyptian nobility were highly decorated with jewels and elaborate braiding, though there is little evidence of animal parts used in their construction or decoration with the exception of an occasional single ostrich feather.

Only the depictions of gods the ancient Egyptians worshiped had any semblance of animal-derived decoration on their hats or headdresses: the Four Feathers Crown worn by the Egyptian god of war, Anhur; a feathered crown worn by the god of fertility and sexuality, Min; or the even taller feathers depicted on the crown of Anuket, the goddess of the Nile cataracts and the fields. All probably depict the feathers of the North African ostrich (a subspecies of the common ostrich, *Struthio camelus*), once a common flightless bird across much of Egypt but now reduced to a few remnant populations, a state of affairs that cannot be blamed on the ancient Egyptian gods.

Though very largely confined in ancient Egypt to the gods they worshipped, headdresses—ornamental head coverings—rather than hats, the more functional garment, have long made substantial use of animal parts, feathers in particular, in many other parts of the world. In the Aztec Empire of Central America, which flourished between about 1345 and 1521 (when it was overthrown by the Spanish), ordinary people didn't wear hats of any sort. In utter contrast, the upper echelons of Aztec society were notable for their extravagant dress, headdresses included. Made in the shape of a large disc representing the universe and the sky, their exquisite headdresses could be over forty inches high and sixty inches across.[16] There was no mistaking who was most important in hierarchical Aztec society.

Feathers were the most important components of their headdresses, and the species of bird from which the feathers were obtained determined the social standing of the wearer. The most precious were those of quetzals, birds slightly larger than mockingbirds, six species of which inhabit tropical forests in South and Central America. All of them are highly colored—including metallic greens, scarlet, and gold—and some sport elongated tail feathers that were of special importance for headdress decor. If you need impressively colored feathers, it is not easy to find any better suited than those of quetzals. To obtain them more easily, the Aztecs even bred these forest birds in captivity.[17]

At the height of the Aztec Empire, five of their provinces with cloud forest were compelled to furnish tributes annually in the form of as many as 2,500 "handfuls" of mostly tail-streamers from resplendent quetzals (*Pharomachrus mocinno*). Assuming that each "handful" contained ten to fifty such feathers, this would have meant a harvest of between six thousand and thirty-one thousand resplendent quetzals per year. Even if the lives of the birds were spared—and despite the edict of death on those who killed them, it seems inevitable that a large proportion might have been seriously injured in the capture and plucking process—the figure is still astonishing and indicates that the species must have been very much more abundant than it is today or that their captive breeding was very effective.[18]

The most impressive Aztec headdress still in existence is referred to, erroneously, as that of Motecuhzoma II who ruled the empire between 1502 and 1520 and was the emperor at the time of the Spanish invasion (see plate 4). Oddly, it is held in the Museum of Ethnology in Vienna, Austria, but how it got there is not at all clear.

"Several scientists have studied this object with great rigor, and I have also personally examined it. We agree that it is genuinely pre-Columbian [prior to European influence] There have been various repairs here and there on the headdress since its 'discovery' in 1596. The reason it is unlikely that it was worn by Motecuhzoma is that such a headdress was worn by high-ranking military officers, but not by a ruler. He wore a turquoise mosaic diadem as the sign of his exalted office," says Frances Berdan, emeritus professor of anthropology at California State University, San Bernardino, and the world's leading expert on Aztec culture.[19]

But this magnificent headdress does provide an insight into what birds' feathers the Aztecs used to decorate these, some of the most elaborate headdresses ever constructed in the world. Though deteriorated, the "Motecuhzoma" feathers have been identified as belonging to a number of different birds: the magnificent iridescent green feathers from the tails of the resplendent quetzal dominate the headdress, but there are also brilliant blue feathers from the lovely cotinga (*Cotinga amabalis*), a small, turquoise-blue and black forest bird; rose-pink feathers of the roseate spoonbill (*Platalea ajaja*), a large water bird; a layer of white-tipped, chestnut-brown feathers from the squirrel cuckoo (*Piaya cayana*), a large and long-tailed forest cuckoo; and some tiny hummingbird feathers.[20] Of these birds, only the resplendent quetzal is today under threat, though very largely because of more recent forest destruction.

Aztec warriors had feathers incorporated in their headdresses too; Eagle Warriors, a special class of infantry and the bravest soldiers of noble birth, dressed like eagles and had an eagle's head, complete with open beak, mounted on their heads. "The warriors wore headgear made of many different types of feathers; one of the most common was made of heron feathers. Other large, exceedingly colorful feathers, including those from quetzals and macaws were used for more elaborate headdresses," comments Professor Berdan.

But why the Aztec fascination with feathers? Maybe it was because they admired the fact that birds could do what no human could aspire to: they could fly. Birds could fly up to the sun god while Aztec citizens could not. After all, one of the most revered Aztec gods was Quetzalcoatl, known as "the Feathered Serpent"; only he was able to move freely on earth and in the sky, even in the underworld. And he supposedly wore a cape of hummingbird feathers and a headdress of flowers with hovering, feeding hummingbirds.

The earlier Mayan civilization that began in Central America before 2500 B.C. and continued until the sixteenth century also used the feathers of different birds, especially quetzals, to decorate headdresses worn by the elite of their society. While ordinary women in Mayan society seemingly did not incorporate any animal parts in their headwear, Mayan men often did; their turban-like headdresses were usually complicated structures and could include feathers, gems, and animal hides.[21]

The hierarchical Inca Empire that flourished along the west coast of South America from the thirteenth to the sixteenth centuries was renowned for the quality of its woolen cloth made mainly from domesticated llama, alpaca, and vicuña. Only high-ranking members of Inca society such as nobles and priests wore flamboyant headdresses; these were often adorned with highly colorful macaw and parrot feathers that could have been obtained from a wide range of species in their part of South America.

But no headdress was as flamboyant as that worn by the Sapa Inca, the Inca emperor. He wore the same clothes only once; then they were ceremoniously burned. Hummingbird feathers adorned the rim of his gold badge while his headdress was the only one to be decorated with two upright feathers of a supposedly "rare and curious bird" called a *coraquenque*.[22] No one is sure what bird this was; they were apparently obtained in desert country in the mountains where certain death awaited anyone who destroyed or took them because they were reserved for the Inca himself. His subjects were told that only two individuals of the species had ever existed, both solely for the Inca.

Could the coraquenque be the long-lived Andean condor (*Vultur gryphus*), one of the world's heaviest birds with a wingspan of over ten feet? Inhabiting the lower mountains of the Andes where, like most vultures, it feeds on carrion, its distribution includes the regions occupied by the Inca civilization. Even today the Andean condor plays a key role in Andean folklore and mythology; it has associations with the sun deity and was believed to be the ruler of the upper world. Another possibility is that the Inca's feathers were the two elongated tail feathers of the little, grey and white fork-tailed flycatcher (*Tyrannus savana*), a common bird in South America and in parts of Central America. But it is mainly a forest and parkland bird not found in arid mountains and it does not have any other established link with Inca culture.[23]

More than any other example of headdresses worn by indigenous peoples worldwide, it is those worn by some peoples in North America that have captured the public imagination. And it is the Western, that most popular Hollywood film genre at its peak from the early twentieth century to the 1960s, that brought the impressive Plains Indians headdresses of certain indigenous tribes to public attention. Usually referred to as war bonnets, these headdresses worn by the dozen or so tribes—such as the Sioux, Crow, and Blackfoot—that inhabited the vast open plains of central North America for many thousands of years are of great spiritual and political importance to their communities and can be worn only by those who have earned the right through formal recognition within their tribe. That included bravery in battle, selfless acts of courage and honor, but also political or diplomatic gains that benefited their people.

Each time a warrior earned a feather he would keep it until there were enough, usually thirty or so, to make a headdress, a task carried out solely by men of the tribe. A warrior would wear only one or two of his feathers in battle. Usually only a tribe's political and spiritual leaders could wear a full headdress in which the feathers were fixed together by a strap made of leather or deer sinew. They were always reserved for men.

The white, dark-tipped tail feathers of the golden eagle (*Aquila chrysaetos*) were usually used; sometimes those of the equally large bald eagle (*Haliaeetus leucocephalus*), the two main eagle species of North America. The traditional methods of acquiring these feathers included plucking the most mature tail feathers from full-grown young eagles still in the aerie. Apparently, this can be done up to three times with each bird; after that the feathers don't regrow. Another, more dangerous, method was to catch them by hand after lying in wait concealed under carrion-bated screens of foliage. Eagles were never killed to obtain their feathers; the indigenous tribes admired them too much as the greatest and most powerful of birds, the "a messenger and advisor." Some types of much simpler headdress incorporated other feathers, including those of owls and other birds of prey or wild turkey feathers, and used ermine skins (stoats, *Mustela erminea*, in their winter pelage) for their white fur trim.[24]

"Buffalo" (American bison, *Bison bison*)-horn headdresses were traditional regalia among some Plains Indian warriors including the Sioux, giving them a fearsome appearance. The Plains tribes hunted buffalo but held them in high esteem. Pre-1800 numbers were thought to be over sixty million, and killing by the tribes seems to have been sustainable. It was European settlers that shot them almost to extinction. Today there are around thirty-one thousand wild-living American bison left.[25] The headdresses were made of buffalo hide to which a pair of horns was attached. These were often adorned with shaggy buffalo fur and had the animal's tail trailing behind. Ermine skins and eagle feathers could be hung from them too or the whole thing combined with a more traditional feather war bonnet.

The tribal headband with one or a very few feathers tucked into it at the back of the head was another common image promoted by movies though it was, in reality, worn by only a few, woodland-inhabiting tribes of the northeast. Worn by men and women, it was made of a deerskin band (from deer common in the woods) tied around the head with a feather or two tucked in. The feathers might be from eagles or just as likely from other birds of prey, from wild turkeys (*Meleagris gallopavo*) that were abundant in the forests and killed for food, from egrets, and even from sandhill cranes (*Antigone canadensis*).

The vast bulk of the indigenous tribes (of which there were five hundred or more) wore roach headdresses not war bonnets, contrary to the false media image created by Westerns (see plate 5). Roach headdresses were made of stiff animal hair: North American porcupine (*Erethizon dorsatum*) guard hair, moose (*Alces alces*) hair, and deer's tail hair attached to a leather base so that it stood upright like a tuft or crest. These are all animals common today in much of North America. Often dyed in bright colors, other decorations were often attached to them. They were worn mainly by warriors and dancers.

Caps and turbans made of otter skin (from the North American river otter, *Lontra canadensis*) were worn on solemn occasions and as ceremonial headdresses by some Prairie and Southern Plains tribes including the Pawnee, Potawatomi, and Osage. Round hats with the otter's tail hanging down behind, they were elaborately decorated with paints and beads symbolizing the wearer's war honors. A tribal chief could attach eagle feathers to them. But they were never worn by warriors in battle; roach headdresses were substituted at such times.

There were other types of headdress used by a few tribes, some of them using animal parts, feathers in particular. One of the most spectacular was the "flicker headdress" worn in dances by the men of some northern California tribes such as the Hupa, Shasta, and Pomo. Rather more like a headband, they comprised wide leather strips decorated with the tail feathers of northern flickers (*Colaptes auratus*) and sometimes trimmed with ermine. This woodpecker species has three different tail color versions; yellow in regions east of the Rockies, red in the west, and gold-colored in the southwest.[26] In Northern California, the feathers of acorn woodpeckers (*Melanerpes formicivorus*) and pileated woodpeckers (*Dryocopus pileatus*) were used too along with the blue feathers of Steller's jay (*Cyanocitta stelleri*), all moderately common woodland birds, presumably then as well as now.

Shamans of the Klamath Indians of Oregon adorned themselves with tiaras made of the feathered skins of red-headed woodpeckers (*Melanerpes erythrocephalus*). And in Southern California, feathers of red-winged blackbird (*Agelaius phoeniceus*), hummingbirds, American crow (*Corvus brachyrhynchos*), and birds of prey including the now very rare California condor (*Gymnogyps californianus*) were incorporated in headdresses.[27] Presumably adult woodpeckers would be trapped in some way (not an easy task with such arboreal birds) or the young taken at fledging time from their tree nest holes.

On the other side of the world, highly elaborate and colorful headdresses have long been worn by many Pacific cultures, particularly in New Guinea, which was first inhabited maybe as long ago as 55,000 B.C. With many different types for different occasions and usually made out of vegetation, the designs often include bird of paradise feathers, often those from the highly sought-after King of Saxony bird of paradise (*Pteridophora alberti*)—known to local tribes as the "kisaba"—or even whole birds. From the brow of his head, a mature male King of Saxony, a thrush-sized bird, grows a pair of long (up to twenty inches), scalloped, enamel blue plumes that it uses to attract a decidedly dismally colored female. When these incredible plumes were first seen in England in the sixteenth century, they were thought to be fakes.

New Guinea headdresses could be huge. One might incorporate King of Saxony plumes plus some of the long, iridescent purple-black tail feathers of the male Princess Stephanie's astrapia (*Astrapia stephaniae*) and maybe a whole, twelve-inch-long, male lesser bird of paradise (*Paradisaea minor*) skewered into the construction, with its chestnut back and yellow and green head replete with its ornamental flank plumes that are yellow at their base fading outwards into a silky white mass. Male birds of paradise are nothing if not extravagantly showy.

Like all male birds of paradise, the King of Saxony loses its extravagant plumes each year after breeding, so it's possible that tribesmen could have collected them rather than obtaining them after trapping and killing the birds. But end-of-season plumes are usually worn and damaged, not the best for headdress displays, so it's much more likely that most feathers were obtained historically by killing the birds. Nevertheless, the incredibly showy King of Saxony bird of paradise is still reasonably common today and, according to the International Union for Conservation of Nature's status assessment classification, is not under immediate threat.[28] The collecting of the King of Saxony and other bird of paradise tail feathers—some of it for local trading as long ago as 3000 B.C.—by relatively small numbers of tribespeople over a large forested land area, combined with the fact that the showiest plumes are not developed in males until the birds are as much as seven years old, may have ameliorated its impact on their numbers.

Birds of paradise aren't the only species exploited historically in Papua New Guinea for headdresses; Pesquet's parrot (*Psittrichas fulgidus*), a crimson and black forest bird, has historically been killed to add its colors to the displays. Today, this gorgeous bird is declining and thought vulnerable to extinction.[29] Eagle, lorikeet, and cassowary feathers were also sometimes incorporated. So, too, was the striking yellow head of the forest-dwelling yellow-billed kingfisher (*Syma torotoro*); indigenous peoples of the Middle Sepik River would clean the heads of captured birds, mount them on sticks, and wear them in their hair.[30]

The indigenous Polynesian people of New Zealand, the Maori, who colonized these islands in about 1300, used to wear feathered headdresses to symbolize power. Feathers from a black bird with a white-tipped tail and a long, down-curved beak, the huia (*Heteralocha acutirostris*), were particularly highly prized, with chiefs wearing white-tipped huia feathers to symbolize power over chiefs wearing monotone feathers.

Huia feathers were revered as "taonga" or treasures by the Maori. They were often grouped in twos and were usually accompanied by a cloak made from the feathers of that better-known New Zealand bird, the rather dull brown and flightless kiwis (*Apteryx sp.*). The entire carcass of a huia was sometimes worn suspended from the ear, and its feathers were also used for decorating the dead. But, "taonga" or not, human greed helped kill off the huia. They became extinct around 1910, partly the result of too much collecting to decorate peoples' heads but also because of the impact of introduced predators like dogs and rats and the destruction of their forest habitat by the Maoris.

Both by the Maori and by the related Moriori, who originally inhabited the Chatham Islands about five hundred miles east of New Zealand, albatross feathers were also highly prized, especially for hair adornment. Ground nesters, several species of albatross bred on Chatham, on other outlying islands, and on the mainland of New Zealand itself. Trusting birds, all were potentially highly vulnerable. In recognition of the esteem with which these huge, ocean-going birds were held in society, the wearing of albatross feathers—from any one of the several species breeding in that part of the South Pacific—was reserved for those inhabitants of rank and status. The feathers they used were often those from the albatrosses' white underwings, or sometimes their tail feathers, white signifying light and brightness. They were worn as a small plume on their heads.[31]

The many islands at the southern tip of South America at Tierra del Fuego have historically been breeding sites for several species of albatross. The Yaghan people of the southernmost islands—the most southerly in the world—and the Kaweskar of the more western islands both used albatross feathers and down, the former favoring in particular the great albatrosses whose wingspans can be as much as eleven feet tip to tip. Both peoples used rolled strips of albatross skin with the thick down feathers attached as caps, and they sometimes also wore a whole albatross tail with the feathers upright as a kind of headdress.[32]

The more than five hundred Aboriginal nations that inhabited Australia developed a wide range of ceremonial headdresses in the perhaps sixty thousand years they have lived on that continent. At different times and in different parts of the continent, they made use of a wide range of feathers including the rather drab brown feathers of the flightless common emu (*Dromaius novaehollandiae*) and numerous much more colorful feathers of a number of species of cockatoos, lorikeets, and parrots, some of the most colorful birds that Australia boasts.[33]

There are many other examples the world over of the tribal use of feathers to adorn headdresses; the Zulus of South Africa used to use the feathers of turacos—large arboreal and very colorful forest birds—while in the Palas valley in northern Pakistan, people have long worn the spectacular plumes of the western tragopan (*Tragopan melanocephalus*), a ground bird related to pheasants with attractively mottled plumage, in their caps. Legend has it that the famous Zulu king Cetshwayo (ca. 1826–1884) would permit turaco feathers to be worn by no one but himself, but they were allowed to be worn by his eighteen thousand strong regiment of warriors at the Battle of Isandhlwana in 1879 when a British force was almost entirely wiped out. In eastern

Africa, the Masai incorporate the green feathers of Schalow's turaco (*Tauraco schalowi*) and the green and blue feathers of Hartlaub's turaco (*T. hartlaubi*) in ceremonial headdresses.[34]

In Borneo the tail feathers of the largest hornbills have long been used in ceremonial dances and rituals, and in New Caledonia, kagu (*Rhynochetos jubatus*) feathers were used in the war headdresses of chiefs and their calls mimicked in war dances.[35] Kagus are long-legged, crested ground birds that are virtually flightless and have blue-tinged white feathers. They would have been far easier to trap than the tree-living turacos of southern Africa.

Made from natural plant fiber netting, highly colorful, feather-covered helmets (*mahiole*) characterized by a crescent-shaped crest were worn with feather-covered cloaks by Hawaiian chiefs during important ceremonies or in battle. Each *mahiole* comprised tens of thousands of small feathers. One of seven such *mahiole* now in the collections of London's British Museum is composed of the fiery red feathers of the scarlet honeycreeper (*Drepanis coccinea*) contrasting with the yellow feathers of the Hawai'i 'amakihi (*Chlorodrepanis virens*), a honeyeater. Red and yellow are the most important colors to Hawaiians; they were *tapu*; they held a sacred quality. The mostly black and yellow feathers of the Hawaiian mohos (*Moho sp.*) were also used as well of those of other birds endemic to the islands.[36]

To early Hawaiian civilizations, feathers enhanced *mana*, a spiritual force that can fill individuals or objects with power. Ornamental featherwork was one of the most highly developed artistic skills in Hawaiian culture. Birds were regarded throughout Polynesia as spiritual messengers, and because of that, birds captured on the Hawaiian Islands were not usually killed; they were either caught in the air by experienced bird catchers using nets or by using decoy birds to lure them onto branches coated with a sticky substance.[37] A few feathers were plucked and the birds released. In spite of this, shock to the birds and maybe disease as a result of such stress induced by capture would have resulted in at least some mortality. Today, many of the species exploited for their feathers are extinct, partly the result of direct exploitation and partly due to wide-scale habitat destruction and the introduction of predators.

Across the world and in a huge variety of cultures, feathers have always been part of human self-adornment, frequently decorating some form of headdress and often making use of the most colorful feathers that could be obtained locally. Head decoration with feathers can indicate status, wealth, vitality, ardor, and defiance, sometimes all of these attributes at once. Whether their collection had any significant impact on the abundance of the bird populations that supplied the feathers is impossible to gauge for almost all species that have been exploited historically.

Almost all quetzals, exploited heavily by the Aztecs, remain abundant today. And Native Americans were particularly careful not to kill eagles to obtain their tail feathers. At the other extreme, we know that the huia was exploited for its feathers to such an extent in New Zealand that it was undoubtedly one of the main causes of its extinction. In general, much would have depended upon the density of the human population in relation to the abundance of the species exploited and the nature and veracity of that exploitation.

For head protection in cool and wet climates across the world, it seems logical that early civilizations, especially hunter-gatherer communities, would have worn animal-skin caps, similar to that worn by Ötzi for example. But there is no evidence showing that wild animals were commonly killed for this purpose; the limited evidence available suggests that domesticated animal skins might have been used more commonly, presumably because they were available when domestic livestock were killed for food and because killing wild animals would have been more time consuming and, in the case of bears in particular, exceedingly dangerous. Prior to the domestication of livestock there is no evidence to show whether or not hats were commonly made from wild animal skins. In very much colder climes, however, skins from wild animals such as caribou and seals have long been used for clothing, head coverings included. The species used historically remain abundant today.

As human populations expanded and hats became increasingly popular, not so much for protection from the elements but as a status symbol and a fashion statement, the exploitation of wild animals to satisfy such desires was about to change gear.

A Deadly Felt Revolution

IF YOU NEED A HEAVENLY ADVOCATE FOR YOUR PROFESSION, YOUR CRAFT, YOUR ACTIV-
ity, maybe even for your family, there's supposedly no one better than a patron saint. So it is that
travelers can rely on St. Christopher while animal lovers have adopted the image of St. Francis of
Assisi. But not many will be aware of the patron saint of felt makers and hatters. A particularly
noteworthy patron saint, St. Clement of Rome (35 A.D.-ca. 99) became the fourth pope of the
Catholic Church, holding that office from the year 88 to his death in 99.

But what has felt—and the patron saint of its makers—got to do with hats? The short answer
is almost everything. With the exception of knitted woolen head coverings, various types of
velvet, straw hats to keep out the sun, and military helmets, the basic structure of the majority of
every style and tradition of hat, both for men and for women, is made from felt.

Tradition has it that, as a wandering monk, Clement's feet got very sore. So he filled his san-
dals with wool he picked up on his meanderings in an attempt to provide a little more comfort.
What he discovered was that the wool fibers got compressed by the pressure and movement
of his feet into a primitive thin felt. It is a nice story. Unfortunately, though, St. Clement was
certainly not the first person to make felt. Believed to be one of the earliest textiles, felt has been
made, for example, by the nomadic peoples of Central Asia for over 2,500 years, and the craft still
thrives today as an integral part of their culture.[1]

Several different natural fibers can be used to make felt, but those most commonly used historically have been sheep or lamb's wool and furs from animals including rabbit, hare, beaver, and
coypu (often called nutria). The felt is formed when the fibers mat, condense, and link together,
making a flexible but sturdy material ideal for shaping into hats. Beaver fur makes a tighter felt
than the others and provides a finer, more durable finish to the hat. Nutria fur, from coypu
(*Myocastor coypus*), was an alternative that American hatmakers (the animal is native to southern
South America) started exploring around 1900. It produced a tight felt rather like beaver but not
as luxurious.

Felt is different from all other fabrics because the wool or fur fibers naturally twist together
and interlock when they are manipulated in hot water and steam. That gives felt a unique
strength. All other fabrics are made of fibers that are twisted into threads and then woven into
cloth by machine or by hand. So a woven fabric is fixed together in two lines at right angles to
each other (the warp and weft); felt consists of fibers interlocked in every direction. So felt is very
resilient, lightweight, more impervious to water, and if made using fine animal hair, it produces
what is probably the smoothest fabric known. That makes it ideal for hats.

In England, felt hat making on a significant scale began in London in the sixteenth century. By the seventeenth century it had developed in other parts of the country, especially in northwest England where it expanded considerably in the eighteenth and nineteenth centuries. *Baine's 1825 History, Directory and Gazetteer of Lancashire* lists fifty-eight hatmakers in Manchester, thirty-one in Stockport, twenty-five in Denton, nineteen in Oldham, and eleven in other nearby towns, all clustered in a small area of northwest England. Some used mainly sheep's wool; others used only rabbit fur, the pelts mostly imported from Belgium where large numbers were bred in captivity. Their peak in output occurred in the early twentieth century when just one manufacturer, Battersby & Co. of Stockport, produced around twelve thousand hats a week. From the 1930s on, the English hat industry declined; today there are virtually no hatmakers left in the northwest of England.

In the United States, the town of Danbury, Connecticut, became the center of felt hat making, reaching a peak in output in 1880 when the town's factories produced 4.5 million hats and thirty-one of the United States' sixty-three hatmakers were based there. In the late eighteenth century when hat making in Danbury got underway, the factories used North American beaver (*Castor canadensis*) fur for their best hats but mostly relied on captive-bred rabbits. The city's last hatmaker, Stetson, closed in Danbury in 1965.[2]

Producing a felt hat from animal fur is a lengthy process, made much quicker today by machinery but traditionally done by hand. Through the Middle Ages, and wherever felt hats were made, much of the process was appallingly unhealthy, unpleasant, and downright dangerous. Few hatmakers survived as old as fifty.[3]

Assuming that the hat was to be made from animal fur, rabbit or beaver maybe, the first task was to remove the coarse outer hairs of the fur pelt, the guard hairs on a mammal that shed rainwater to prevent the animal getting wet. This was because only the soft underfur fibers can be used to make felt. Then the soft underfur was shaved off the animal's skin using a semicircular knife. Fur of different qualities from the same mammal—or from different mammals, hare and rabbit perhaps—would be blended if necessary depending on the quality of the hat to be made.

Next, the correct amount of fur required for the particular style of hat to be made had to be measured out. For a derby (known as a "bowler" in the United Kingdom), three ounces of rabbit fur were needed. For a top hat, it would have been considerably more. Then came one of the most skilled operations. A bow—very much like an oversized violin bow, but with just one string made of catgut—was vibrated by twanging or plucking the string above the mix of fibers, causing them to distribute evenly and form a thick, loose mat. The process also shook out any dirt that fell through slits in the workbench being used. "Bowing," as it was called, resulted in fine pieces of fur being constantly suspended in the factory atmosphere and breathed in by workers. Most suffered all their lives from coughs.

This was followed by the unhealthiest stage. The fur was shaped into a flat triangle, a smaller piece of cloth or paper was placed between two such triangles, and the set was pressed using a wooden roller and periodically dipped into a hot vat of sulfuric acid and water to which other substances—urine, beer grounds, or wine sediment perhaps—were often added. While the acid caused permanent damage to the workers' hands, it was this pressure and wetting—the same process St. Clement had discovered courtesy of his weary feet—that caused the fur fibers to link and mat together in all directions. The two fur triangles matted together along their edges, but not in the middle where the paper or cloth prevented their contact. What resulted after much more rolling and dipping was a triangular felt hood in the shape of a "witches' cap."

In 1859 so-called forming cones, already in use in some countries, were introduced to British hat making; they replaced the dangerous drudgery of manually dipping and rolling the felts. The rotating metal cones were perforated, and air was sucked out from their inside when the fur was applied to the outside. That meant that the fur adhered to the cone. Sprayed with hot water, the felt started to form. The operator would carefully remove the soft, and still fragile, soft "witches' hat" felt.

These "hoods," as they were known, were then put through further cycles of dipping combined with rolling under pressure, gradually tightening up the fibers and shrinking the felt. They were also dyed in whatever color the hats were to be finished in. The hood still had the exaggerated conical appearance of a witches' hat, but the task of the hatmaker was then to transform it into a recognizable hat shape by wetting the felt and pulling it over a smooth wooden block in the shape of the hat to be made. Forcing the felt down over the block—a process known, not surprisingly, as "blocking"—left a brim at the base that would later be trimmed and shaped depending on the hat style being made (see plate 6). Hatters had to stock these hand-shaped wooden blocks for every style of hat they made, and in every likely size required. Making the blocks was a specialist task carried out by expert carpenters.

Once dried, the hat, now in its desired shape, would be stiffened by painting the inside with substances such as shellac in order to keep its shape when in use, the amount used depending on how hard the desired hat was intended to be. Ironing and brushing would complete the job, together with affixing whatever trimmings and lining were desired.

Mechanization, initially using steam power, gradually took over most of the manual jobs. Machines to cut the fur from animal skins were introduced in England by 1840, together with blowing machines to replace the hatter's bow. Machines to pressure roll and wet the felt came in from the United States where they were already in use in the late 1800s. And the wooden blocks that hats were manually formed on have long been replaced by fiberglass or metal except for the few hatmakers using traditional processes.

One early step in the lengthy manual hat-making process, introduced in the late seventeenth century and in use into the nineteenth century when fur felt-making for hats was at its peak, was a serious health hazard. Known as "carroting," it required the animal pelt (the skin with fur attached) to be brushed with a solution of mercury nitrate to help the fur fibers lock together. It got its name because it turned the fur an orange-red color. Done in a poorly ventilated room, as it often was, the mercury fumes were inhaled by the workers. It had an enormous impact on their central nervous system, a condition that became known as "Mad Hatters' Disease."[4]

Inhaling mercury vapor leads to its accumulation in the brain, which causes neurological symptoms including tremor, increased excitability, depression, behavioral and personality changes such as extreme shyness, loss of memory and hearing, sweating, and insomnia. Inhaled mercury can also affect other organs including the kidneys. Years of industrial exposure rendered the symptoms permanent, so retired workers were still affected.

Mad Hatters' Disease was made famous by Lewis Carroll's 1865 *Alice's Adventures in Wonderland* and its sequel, *Through the Looking-Glass*, published in 1871. Both stories are fantasies in which the iconic Mad Hatter is thought to have been inspired by the occupational hazards of hat making, although the common phrase "as mad as a hatter" predates both books. The Mad Hatter introduced in Carroll's first book wears a large top hat with a hatband reading "In this style 10/6." This is the hat's price tag, indicative of the Hatter's trade, and giving the price in predecimal British money as ten shillings and six pence. Hat making was the main trade in Stockport in northwest England where Carroll (real name, Charles Lutwidge Dodgson) was born in 1832, and he would have been familiar with hatworkers' frequently disturbed and confused appearance, although Carroll's Mad Hatter clearly doesn't exhibit their usual symptoms of shyness and timidity.

In 1898, legislation was passed in France to ban the use of mercury in the hat-making process; its use ceased in England a couple of years later, but in the United States it was not abandoned until the 1940s, mainly because influential employers professed ignorance of the problem and ascribed much of its impact to drunkenness among their workforce.

Until sometime in the fourteenth century or thereabouts, most hat felt was made from wool, hare fur, or rabbit fur, often dyed white, gray, or black. Wool felt was the cheapest, and Britain—especially lowland England and the English border counties of Wales—was the major producer of sheep's wool in Europe in the Middle Ages. Lamb's wool made a somewhat finer quality felt and was readily obtainable too. In the late thirteenth century, Britain was exporting around twenty-seven thousand woolsacks annually (a sack was 350 pounds' weight); by the mid-sixteenth century that had fallen to about five thousand sacks a year but only because the bulk was exported as finished cloth instead. As a consequence, wool from both sheep and lambs was readily available, cheap, and commonly used to make hat felt.[5]

Rabbit fur was readily available too. The European rabbit (*Oryctolagus cuniculus*) was originally a mammal confined to Spain, Portugal, and the very south of France, but introductions started by the Romans, combined with its natural spread and ability to reproduce rapidly, made it a common mammal across most of western Europe by or before the Middle Ages. From Roman times on, large numbers have been domesticated and kept as livestock. It was sought primarily for its meat; huge numbers of wild rabbits were trapped, shot, or hunted with falcons and ferrets. As a consequence, rabbit fur was cheap and plentiful for clothes and hat making. Because rabbits were so abundant, and often reared as livestock, hat making had no impact on their native populations in Spain and Portugal.

The closely related, but larger European hare (*Lepus europaeus*) is found across most of western Europe (excluding Iberia and large parts of Scandinavia), throughout large swathes of southeastern Europe and Southwest Asia. Five other hare species exist in Europe and several more worldwide, though some species are confined to geographically small regions. Historically hunted, shot, and trapped for food, European hares—which weigh roughly twice as much as rabbits—were always important game animals. In Britain they were an extremely common mammal through the Middle Ages (and presumably before that) and up until the Ground Game Act of 1880 that allowed their killing year-round to protect crops. From then on, large numbers were shot as farmland pests.

From some time in the later Middle Ages, the town of Dumfries held the largest annual fur fair in Scotland; by the early nineteenth century it was the most important fur market in Britain. There were many other minor fairs in other Scottish towns too, but none as large or well attended as that at Dumfries. Held in winter when the pelage of trapped mammals was at its thickest, the furs of many mammals common in Scotland—European hares, pine martens (*Martes martes*), stoats, Eurasian beavers (*Castor fiber*), and red foxes (*Vulpes vulpes*)—were renowned throughout Europe for their quality and quantity. The majority of skins sold there were of hares, peaking at seventy thousand in 1860, followed by rabbits. Most were exported to various European countries, but increasing numbers were retained for the British hat industry.

Before the end of the nineteenth century, the market was in decline, at least partly due to depleting numbers of the mammals concerned but also because pelts of some North American mammals, the North American beaver in particular, were flooding the market and because silk was taking over from beaver fur as the primary material for making top hats and similar hat styles. Otters and polecats, in particular, had become too rare for commerce, although European hares might still have been reasonably well distributed in the Scottish lowlands.[6]

In North America, in addition to using domesticated rabbits for their fur, the two most widespread and abundant wild hare species, the black-tailed (*Lepus californicus*) and white-tailed jackrabbit (*L. townsendii*)—both hares in spite of their name—were trapped for their fur, the whitetails providing a generally better yield of cut fur for felt making. Species of cottontail rabbit and similar species native to North America (closely related to the European rabbit) were safe from the milliners desires; their skin was considered to be too small, thin, and papery and too easily torn.[7]

The fur of coypu, otherwise known as nutria, a large, semiaquatic and herbivorous rodent native to parts of South America, has also been used frequently for felt making. Coypu have been introduced to many parts of the world, primarily for their fur that resembles that of beaver, and it was sometimes used mixed with rabbit or hare fur to make hat felt. Nutria became more commonplace for hats from about 1900 on; most of the fur was used for other clothing, and increasing amounts were obtained from farmed coypu. The first successful coypu farms were set up in South America in the 1920s largely because of local extinction of the wild mammal's populations due to trapping.[8]

In 1323, Paris hatmakers were allowed to use beaver fur for the first time rather than their usual lamb's wool, thereby making a lustrous, malleable, waterproof felt that was also much lighter in weight than wool felt hats. Many of the Eurasian beavers were seemingly trapped on the Bièvre, a tributary of the River Seine near Paris that was named after the aquatic mammal. Pelts were also imported from Russia and northern Europe where the hapless mammals were almost certainly more abundant. The Low Countries, Flanders especially, had become the hub of beaver hat production at this time, and it is a beaver hat from Flanders that Geoffrey Chaucer's rich merchant wears (in his immortal *Canterbury Tales*) for his pilgrimage to Canterbury, England, in 1386.[9]

Beaver felt hats were worn by both ladies and gentlemen, but their price at this time restricted them to the moneyed classes in European society. Strict controls even determined what furs the different echelons of society could wear; ordinary folk went hatless or wore a simple petasos-style hat made of wool felt, leather, or straw. At the other extreme, Philippa of England (1394–1430), queen of Denmark, Sweden, and Norway, had a beaver cap lined with fifty ermine (stoats in their white winter pelage) skins made especially for her. It seems rather odd today, but such hats were often included in lists of personal "jewelry" in the Middle Ages. So it was that in the inventory of Sir John Fastolf (1380–1459)—a knight-administrator who is said to have been the inspiration for Shakespeare's Falstaff—a single beaver hat, lined with damask and with a gilt hatband, is specifically listed as such because of its high value.[10]

Historically, the Eurasian beaver was a common mammal in rivers, lakes, marshes, and a range of other freshwater habitats across Europe. From Wales in the west to northern Russia and Asia, and from the northernmost point of Scandinavia south to the Black Sea, beavers had originally gnawed waterside trees and built their breeding lodges with relative impunity. Between thirty and forty inches in length, and ranging in color from light brown to almost black, Eurasian beavers are enthralling to watch as they swim quietly, their paddle-like tails used as rudders, only their heads showing above water and sometimes disappearing into an underwater tunnel that exits unseen higher up the riverbank where they have built their breeding lodge.

But since at least the early Middle Ages, maybe earlier still, Eurasian beavers had been trapped and killed for castoreum, a secretion they use in combination with urine to mark their territories.

Traditionally used in perfumes to impart a leather-like odor, castoreum has been claimed to have a range of medicinal properties including as a painkiller, for reducing fever and hysteria, and even helping to cure epilepsy. Beavers were also eaten; with an adult weighing up to sixty pounds, sometimes more, a beaver could feed a family for days. Mainly because of hunting—but also because of increasing drainage of marshes for farmland—Eurasian beavers were extinct in England by the twelfth century, in Wales by the fifteenth century, and in Scotland and Italy a century later.[11]

By the thirteenth century, London had become a prosperous European center of the international fur trade with the pelts of a multitude of mammals (though seemingly not yet beaver) including vast numbers of squirrels, pine martens, beech martens (*Martes foina*), European hares, and many more being imported by ship. Incoming pelts were shipped up the River Thames to the docks in the East End of the city where the skinners who treated and traded in furs based themselves. The finished clothes and hats for export were shipped out the same way.

Eurasian beavers were in steep decline in Britain by this time and extinct in England. Beavers from Wales were sufficiently rare that their price was fixed, at some time in or even before the thirteenth century, at 120 times the price of sheepskin.[12] From Scotland, beaver pelts were seemingly easier to obtain; Inverness was for a time the center of the trade, followed later by Dumfries, and their high quality was said to attract German and other merchants. By the fourteenth century, though, beaver skins were being imported into London from Continental Europe. The finest furs, beaver included, were from northern Europe, Scandinavia, the Baltic countries, and northern Russia, simply because the colder climate ensured that mammals there developed a thicker winter coat. So winter-trapped beaver from the north was more valuable. Cities such as Novgorod, today in western Russia, became major fur-dealing centers; furs had been traded there since the tenth century, and by the Middle Ages, many beaver skins destined for top-quality hat felt from the extensive rivers and wetlands of northern Russia arrived in Western Europe via Novgorod. During the sixteenth and seventeenth centuries, furs would become Russia's richest source of wealth.

In the woodcuts that illustrate the pages of the *Historia de Gentibus Septentrionalibus*, written by Olavus Magnus, archbishop of Uppsala, and published in 1555, we see trappers at work, some of whom are setting nets to catch beavers. Not all of the beaver pelts would have been used for hat making; beaver fur was used for trimming clothing too. But as furs became less popular for clothing into the sixteenth and seventeenth centuries—because of changing fashions and their increasing scarcity due to overhunting—most beaver pelts were used for hat felt making.

With Eurasian beavers being extirpated across most of Europe, Russia became a major supplier until there, too, human greed with no concept of the sustainable harvesting of a species—both to safeguard its populations and to provide its products into the future—guaranteed that most beavers were gone by the nineteenth century.

No one knows how many Eurasian beavers inhabited that continent historically; they certainly numbered well in excess of a million because reintroductions, combined with natural recolonization, over the last century have resulted in over a million recolonizing the remaining European aquatic habitats, and they are still absent from several river systems formerly inhabited. What we do know is that by the start of the twentieth century, Eurasian beavers had been reduced to just eight surviving populations totaling just 1,200 animals.[13] The scale of their destruction had been enormous; the small surviving populations were on parts of the Rivers Rhone and Elbe, in southern Norway, the Neman River in Lithuania, the Dnepr Basin in Belarus, and the Voronezh River in Russia.

Most Eurasian beavers had become hats. The conical-shaped hat of the puritans, made usually of beaver fur, became particularly popular in the sixteenth and seventeenth centuries. It is emblematic of almost every image of the early puritan settlers on the east coast of America in the seventeenth century. It was not much different from the type of hat—wide-brimmed with a sugarloaf crown—worn by the Gunpowder plotters of 1605 in their failed attempt to blow up the House of Lords in the English Parliament and kill King James I (1566–1625) of England.

By 1638 the first flat-brimmed and flat-crowned hats made of beaver fur appeared, often trimmed with an ostrich feather; these so-called cavalier hats became very popular both in Britain and across Europe and were worn by supporters of King Charles I (1600–1649) in the English Civil War. "The wearing of beaver hats," proclaimed the king in that year, "has of late times become much in use, especially by those of sort and quality." And early in the seventeenth century, ladies in England, too, began to wear large beaver-felt hats rather like those worn by their spouses.[14]

The massive decline of the Eurasian beaver cannot be blamed entirely on hat making. Killing for their castoreum, for meat, and to use their thick fur for other items of clothing were also factors; so, too, was the increasing scale of marshland drainage as Europe's farmers strove for more land to cultivate and raise livestock. But with the Eurasian beaver in steep decline, and extirpated from the bulk of its former range, how was it possible to find enough beavers to satisfy demand for the vast numbers of hats made of beaver fur from the late sixteenth century on? Enter the North American beaver, which was about to suffer a very similar catastrophe to its European cousin.

Before European colonization of the North American continent, it is likely that the North American beaver was widespread in almost any freshwater habitat from the Arctic tundra to the edge of the Mexican deserts and from the west to the east coasts. Some indigenous peoples trapped and killed them for food, but it is not likely that this had a significant impact on their numbers or their distribution. But that changed sometime soon after 1497 when the Venetian explorer Giovanni Caboto (ca. 1450–ca. 1500), better known as John Cabot, discovered the coast of Newfoundland and what became known as the highly productive fishing grounds of the Grand Banks.

Attracting French, Portuguese, Spanish, and (later on) English fishing boats for netting cod, the onshore outposts the fishermen set up attracted local indigenous peoples who came to trade the pelts of mammals such as American mink (*Neovison vison*) and North American river otter (*Lontra canadensis*) for knives or other metal-based products and textiles. At some point beaver fur must have been offered. When broad-brimmed felt hats became exceedingly popular by the late sixteenth and early seventeenth century across Europe, there was no better fur to make those of the highest quality but with the dense belly fur of North American beavers. A trade started to develop that would eventually decimate the "new" continent's beaver population. High-quality pelts with their thicker fur that kept beavers warm in the severe northern American winters were particularly prized and were used back in Britain and elsewhere in Europe to make the most expensive hats.[15]

The first fur dealers to participate were French; their trade spread along the St Lawrence and Ottawa Rivers and south down the Mississippi. In the seventeenth century the Dutch and British built up a trade too. In 1670, a charter was granted by King Charles II (1630–1685) of England to the Hudson's Bay Company, which functioned as the de facto government in parts of North America before other European states and, later, the United States, claimed those territories. It illustrated very clearly the seriousness with which a rising mercantile nation considered the fur trade, itself very largely dependent on one mammal, the North American beaver (see plate 7).

With a large network of trading posts, for centuries the company controlled the fur trade throughout British-controlled North America. Working inland from small sea ports and scouring the main rivers and marshes, they killed hundreds of thousands of beavers, floating their precious furs downriver to the trading posts and shipping them over to Britain. For roughly the next hundred years, the French, Dutch, and English competed for the lucrative fur trade, much of it for the highly valuable hat-making beaver fur but also for the pelts of many other mammals including muskrat (*Ondatra zibethicus*), raccoon (*Procyon lotor*), fox, and deer.

Beavers were trapped initially by indigenous tribes such as the Cree and the Iroquois and exchanged for goods locally with the Dutch, French, and English traders with whom they formed trading alliances. Much later, mainly through the nineteenth century, so-called mountain men—white settlers who helped establish settlement trails west across the continent (especially routes through the Rocky Mountains)—were attracted to the rewards of beaver trapping too. Mostly employed by the fur-trading companies, they operated mainly in the lakes and rivers in the Rockies and what was then called "Oregon country," mostly British Columbia today.

The pelts were shipped to Europe for processing and final sale. Many of these were *castor sec*—dry beaver—fresh skins stretched and dried, then sold and shipped. But someone, whether a fur trader or, more likely, some local indigenous tribes, created a more sought-after beaver fur. Known as *castor gras*—greasy beaver—these were skins that had been stitched together to make a rough coat which was then worn for a year or more, fur side inwards, by local people. During this process, the beaver guard hairs were worn away, leaving the valuable underfur that had become more pliable. *Castor gras* fetched higher prices and was used for the best quality hats; the inevitable rank smell for the wearer, and those in his or her vicinity, never seemingly gets mentioned.[16]

Top-quality hats were made entirely using *castor gras*; the next quality level down contained a mix of *castor gras* and *castor sec* followed by those made entirely of *castor sec* and, lower quality still, those using a mix of *castor sec* with other felted fibers such as rabbit, hare, or even lamb's wool.

From the accounts of the Hudson's Bay Company, between 1713 and 1726, *castor gras* pelts averaged 6.6 shillings each and *castor sec* pelts 5.5 shillings (although prices for both doubled toward the end of the eighteenth century). But the differential was reversed by the introduction in about 1720 of the carroting process; it made *castor sec* more pliable and the fibers link together better to produce the desired top-quality felt.[17]

The trappers killed beavers in a number of ways, and most were killed in winter or early spring when their coats were thickest. Some were shot from canoes at dusk (when the mammals came out to feed in the waterways); others were dug out of their hibernating lodges in winter, enticed into traps using castoreum to attract them, or sometimes even grabbed by hand if the trappers could get close enough. Alexander Henry (1739–1824) was a partner in the North West Company, a fur trapping and trading company chartered in London and operating in North America. Although steel traps were available and widely used after about 1750, Henry's men often dug out their lodges before grabbing the animals by hand or probably using guns or clubs to kill them. It was dangerous work: beaver have sharp teeth and are aggressive if cornered, and while canoeing in cold waters, trappers risked drowning and hypothermia. An account he wrote in 1809 described his men's practices:

> To kill beaver, we used to go several miles up the rivers, before the approach of night, and after the dusk came on, suffer the canoe to drift gently down the current, without noise. The beaver, in this part of the evening, come abroad to procure food, or materials for repairing their habitations; and as they

are not alarmed by the canoe, they often pass it within gun-shot. The most common way of taking the beaver is that of breaking up its house, which is done with trenching-tools, during the winter, when the ice is strong enough to allow of approaching them; and when, also, the fur is in its most valuable state. Breaking up the house, however, is only a preparatory step. During the operation, the family make their escape to one or more of their washes. These are to be discovered, by striking the ice along the bank, and where the holes are, a hollow sound is returned. I was taught occasionally to distinguish a full wash from an empty one, by the motion of the water above its entrance, occasioned by the breathing of the animals concealed in it. From the washes, they must be taken out with the hands; and in doing this, the hunter sometimes receives severe wounds from their teeth.[18]

The beaver felt hat trend in England was spurred on by King James I when he ordered twenty beaver hats at the time of his ascent to the throne in 1603. Seventeen of them were to be black, lined with taffeta, trimmed with black bands and feathers, perhaps for a period of court mourning (see plate 8).[19] Quite quickly the demand for beaver hats broadened across all the social classes of the day as prices fell because of the surfeit of pelts being imported from North America.

The best hats—those made entirely of beaver fur—were treated very carefully by their owners. They were kept in hat boxes to protect them, only to be brought out when worn. These top-quality hats were, of course, a temptation for thieves. One such was John Averye, a London thief. He was convicted on 31 August 1688 of stealing two such beaver hats, and one partly made of beaver fur, and was sentenced to be transported, in all probability to the then American colonies. His brief hearing before judges at the Old Bailey in London is recorded as follows:

> John Averye of the Parish of St. Andrew's Holbourn, was Tryed for stealing two Beaver Hats, value 40 s. one Demy Castor [part beaver, part hare] Hat, value 8 s. the Goods of Thomas Coller, on the 28th. day of July last: The Evidence against him was very plain, how that he came into the Shop of the Prosecutor and took away the Hats, and being pursued, he had the Hats in his Custody: The Prisoner not much denying it, and having no Witness on his side, he was found guilty of the Felony.[20]

Men's felt hats of varying styles—the more expensive ones made solely of beaver—retained their popularity from the late fifteenth century through to the nineteenth century in a variety of manifestations. Bonnets and berets, sometimes adorned with feathers and other decorations; birettas, the square cap with, usually, three peaks worn by the clergy; and toques, the tall and often brimless hat now metamorphosed into today's chef's hat, were just some of the earlier styles.

Late in the second half of the sixteenth century, the crown of a man's hat had become more important than the brim; fashion was emphasizing height rather than the width typified by the cavalier-type hat originally worn by followers of King Charles I. Eventually this would lead to the distinctly tall "stove-pipe," "chimney pot," and "top hat" designs for men prevalent from the late eighteenth century and through much of the nineteenth century. Well-to-do gentlemen could afford top hats made of beaver fur; those worn by the less well-off were usually made of cheaper furs or wool felt. Some ladies' hats, too, also had a structure made of beaver felt, sometimes with considerable adornment: feathers, flowers, velvet ribbons, and much else.

There is little information on the numbers of hats being worn at this time, but Gregory King (1648–1712), reputedly the first great economic statistician, calculated in 1688 that the consumption of all hats in England was about 3.3 million or nearly one hat per person. Caps (usually soft, flat hats without a brim) he estimated at another 1.6 million. Over the next century, increasing numbers of hats were made of beaver fur rather than other furs or wool, and there was a move away from caps to hats as prices fell. No longer was a beaver fur hat the sole domain of the upper echelons of society. The cheaper "demi-castor" versions using a mix of hare and beaver furs became widely available too. The market for beaver fur—most of it from North America—seemed insatiable. The continent was supplying England with about 70 percent of its total fur imports in the early years of the eighteenth century. Beaver fur made up half of the total, followed by hare, rabbit, and muskrat fur for cheaper felts.[21]

France was thought to have imported even more beaver fur, probably a quarter to a half more at different times, simply because it had a much larger area of North America from which to harvest the animals. Because of competition from French importers who could buy pelts more cheaply and obtain larger numbers, England's felt makers and hatters complained that they were disadvantaged; in response, in 1722 the United Kingdom Parliament reduced the import duty on beaver pelts coming into Britain.

In the seventy years to1770, the number of beaver felt hats made in Britain using North American beaver pelts and shipped abroad (some of them back to North America) totaled twenty-one million. That does not, of course, include the number of hats made for the British market. Trade statistics for France are not available, but French exports of made hats were also thought to have been considerable at this time. In addition, both countries were re-exporting beaver pelts to many other parts of Europe, pelts that had been imported originally from North America.

So what do these huge numbers tell us about the impact on the North American beaver? It took, on average, perhaps three beavers to provide enough underbelly fur to make one high-quality top hat. So twenty-one million hats exported from Britain, assuming all were of high quality, would have consumed at least sixty million beavers over the seventy-year period. France might have been exporting as many again. The difficulty is that there was, of course, no monitoring of beaver numbers. What we do know is that to find beavers, trappers had to move to rivers and wetlands further and further west from the North American northeast where beaver trapping had begun. The well-documented returns recorded at the two main Hudson's Bay Company trading posts—Fort Albany and York Factory—illustrate how rapid a decline it was.[22]

At Fort Albany the number of beaver pelts traded over the period 1700 to 1720 averaged roughly 19,000 a year though with wide year-to-year fluctuations; the range was about 15,000 to 30,000. After 1720 and until the late 1740s average returns declined by about 5,000 pelts a year and remained within the range of roughly 10,000 to 20,000 pelts with a few years bringing in more. But by 1756 fewer than 6,000 beaver pelts were received annually. There was a brief recovery in the early 1760s, presumably as trappers exploited new waterways, but by the end of that decade trade had fallen below even the mid-1750s levels. In 1770, Fort Albany took in just 3,600 beaver pelts. This pattern suggests strongly that beavers traded there and obtained from a very large land area were being seriously depleted.

The beaver returns at York Factory from 1716 to 1770 follow a similar pattern. After some low returns early on (from 1716 to 1720), the number of beaver pelts increased to an average of 35,000 annually. There were extraordinary returns in 1730 and 1731, when the average was 55,600 pelts, but beaver receipts then stabilized at about 31,000 over the remainder of the decade. The first break in the pattern came in the early 1740s shortly after the French established competing trading posts in the area. After 1745 the trade in beaver pelts began a decline that continued through to 1770. Average returns over the rest of the decade were 25,000 pelts and just 15,500 in the 1760s. So the pattern of beaver returns at York Factory—high returns in the early 1740s followed by a large decline—strongly suggests that, as in the Fort Albany hinterland, the beaver population had been substantially depleted.

It was not only beavers that were being killed and their pelts exported to a great many countries in Europe, as well as to Turkey and even to China, though beaver pelts were the largest and most valuable export. In 1787, 139,509 beaver pelts were exported from what is now Canada together with the pelts of 68,142 martens, 26,330 otters, 16,951 mink, 8,913 foxes, 17,109 bears, 102,656 deer, 140,346 raccoons, 9,816 elks, 9,687 wolves, and 125 seals. It was animal carnage on a massive scale.[23]

Predictably, the price of a beaver pelt rose steadily through the eighteenth century, from around five shillings at the start to twenty-one shillings (about £110 today) by the end, reflecting the increasing scarcity of the mammal. John Jacob Astor (1763–1848) controlled the largest fur trading company, the American Fur Company and its subsidiaries, and the beaver pelt was the first great American commodity. Astor became the continent's first multimillionaire, at the expense of the North American beaver (and other mammals killed in huge numbers for other fur clothing). Astor was nothing if not astute. By 1834, he realized that all fur-bearing animals in North America were becoming scarce and moved into New York City real estate instead.

In the eighteenth and nineteenth centuries demand for beaver hats increased. But because the Eurasian beaver was so scarce, and because of more competition from the French in North America for beaver pelts, the trappers supplying the British could demand higher prices. That put even more pressure on the remaining North American beaver populations. Although many indigenous tribes were known for hunting sustainably so that the resources at their disposal were safeguarded for future generations, such a principle did not seem to apply when it came to hunting beaver to sell their pelts. There is evidence, for instance, that the trappers increased their efforts to obtain more beaver pelts as prices for the pelts rose in the 1730s because of rising demand in Europe.[24]

Some of the goods the indigenous trappers acquired in exchange for beaver pelts, such as knives, awls and twine, kettles, blankets, handkerchiefs, buttons, combs, and cloth of various sorts, were highly practical and popular. They would have helped in raising the standard of living of their families. But they were also acquiring guns, shot, and powder handed out irresponsibly by the colonists as well as a good amount of tobacco and alcohol.[25]

With beaver pelts becoming more and more expensive as the mammal was hunted to extinction, and top hats having become de rigueur since the early nineteenth century for a well-dressed gentleman, French hatmakers were the first to make such hats from "demi-castor." Some ingenious hatters also started "plating" hats: using beaver fur for the surface and much cheaper hair such as rabbit for the rest, thereby not breaking strict regulations on fur mixing. Some even used wool mixed with the rabbit fur. The resulting hat looked like beaver and cost much less. Customers were happy. But in 1654 the French government, alive to the compromise in standards, imposed a substantial fine for a first offense and, incredibly, death for a second offense. Nevertheless, the demi-castor trade flourished, it spread to hatmakers in England and Germany, and in 1734 the regulation was rescinded.[26]

The value of a beaver skin even became the "gold standard" for trade. The Hudson's Bay Company used the "made beaver" as the unit of currency for everything such pelts were traded for. A "made beaver" was defined as a prime beaver skin, flesh removed, stretched, and dried. One "made beaver" could be exchanged for one brass kettle or two shirts or eight knives but it needed four "made beavers" to obtain a pistol and eleven to get a musket. The beaver was so valuable that all other mammal furs were valued against it. Eventually the fur companies issued tokens; even then the token value was based on the value of a beaver pelt.

With such a heady mix of available traded commodities, competition between the trappers to get more beaver pelts, and tensions between the occupying European forces and their fur traders, it is hardly surprising that serious problems soon broke out. Beavers became extinct throughout much of the land of the tribes of the Iroquois Confederacy (the Mohawk, Oneida, Onodaga, Cayuga, and Seneca, joined later by the Tuscarora) in what is today upstate New York. The tribes moved west into the territory of the Huron and into other tribes' territories, killing their members in acts that can only be described as genocide. It was the start of the little-known "Beaver Wars" that were to last for nearly half a century from 1638.

Brutally destructive, decimating whole native indigenous tribes, they created patterns of indigenous–European relations that would influence the course of the French and Indian War (1754–1763) that followed and even the later American Revolution.[27] The fur trade, beaver furs especially, came to have profound social, demographic, and environmental impacts on the various inhabitants of seventeenth- and eighteenth-century North America.

With different tribes forming alliances with the British or with the French in particular, conflict had been predictable. Ambushes and murders characterized the first decade of the Beaver Wars and became commonplace, fueled by firearms supplied at some of the trading posts. Competition for beaver pelts between the main European occupying representatives had resulted effectively in a vicious proxy war fought between competing indigenous tribes where unspeakable terror, burning of villages, extreme torture, and genocide were all commonplace. Eventually the Huron nation ceased to exist as an organized entity.

In 1653, four of the five Iroquois tribes reached a peace settlement, breaking with the Mohawks (the most easterly of the Iroquois) who had often dominated the beaver pelt trade, trading mainly with the Dutch though sometimes with the French. But the fighting restarted, and parts of the Iroquois Confederacy eliminated the Erie, Tabaccos, and Neutral tribes who were largely allied with the French. Further violent campaigns by the Iroquois to attempt domination of the beaver trade eventually resulted in their defeat, in 1684, by the Shawnee and Miami tribes. The Beaver Wars had proved catastrophic.[28]

Before the trade began there were thought to be between sixty and four hundred million North American beavers across the whole of North America; around five million of them in Canada.[29] They were absent only from Florida, parts of southern California, and southern Nevada. By 1900, they had been extirpated in eastern North America and the Pacific Northwest of the continent and substantially reduced in numbers almost everywhere else. Maybe there were about one hundred thousand left.

In 1780, just four years after American independence, Zadoc Benedict established the first felt hat factory in North America at Danbury, Connecticut. The industry blossomed, and by 1800 when Philadelphia had become the main center of production, the American hat-making industry was at its peak. But its use of beaver fur declined rapidly as the mammals became increasingly rare. Instead the industry used mainly rabbit, hare, and nutria (coypu) fur. These furs were used to make many of the most popular men's hat styles, for both the U.S. and British markets: the fedora (popular with ladies too) with its soft brim and indented crown; the similar trilby; the more formal homburg with its stiff brim, raffish yet respectable; and the derby—known as the bowler in Britain—a hard felt hat with a rounded crown that was the most popular headwear in the American West.

By the mid-nineteenth century, the beaver trade was in serious decline; many of the mountain men gave up their trapping and settled into jobs as army scouts, wagon train guides, and settlers in the lands in the west of the continent that they had helped open up, initially as overland routes to get beaver pelts to the American east coast and shipped to Europe.

While wetland drainage, mostly for farming, had played some role in their enormous decline, it was the unfettered greed and commerce of the beaver pelt trade, with no concept of sustainably managing a valuable resource, that brought this once abundant and magnificent mammal close to extinction. No one ever seemed to consider that perfectly good quality hats could have been made entirely of rabbit fur without depleting either the Eurasian or the North American beaver. It would be pleasing to think that the traders, dealers, and trappers—and the felt- and hat-making trades themselves—had realized that their boom-and-bust attitude had been counterproductive. But no. The vicissitudes of fashion were dictating a move away from beaver fur for the very best top hats; silk would be the material that everyone wanted their top hat made of now.

Silk top hats, finished to a more attractive sheen than beaver, replaced beaver fur, and when silk became cheap and ubiquitous by the 1840s—medium-quality silk toppers cost around eighteen shillings; fine beaver toppers, thirty-two shillings—dress-conscious men and women in Europe wanted the latest fashion. On almost a whim, beaver was out; silk was in. Another factor in the abandonment of beaver was the increasing urbanization of populations. Better-off people traveled more frequently in covered coaches in the burgeoning towns and cities, so the durability and hardness of beaver felt hats became less necessary. Their price plummeted as silk took center stage. At almost the last minute, centuries of greedy commercial pressure on both the Eurasian and the North American beaver ceased. But there was plenty of other wildlife that hatmakers could, and did, destroy.

When the Fur Flies

IN YAKUTSK ON THE BANKS OF THE LENA RIVER IN SIBERIAN RUSSIA, REPUTED TO BE the coldest city in the world, winter lasts at least seven months. With daytime temperatures—and there is no "daytime" in midwinter—around minus forty degrees Fahrenheit and occasional plunges as low as minus seventy Fahrenheit, no sane individual would venture outdoors without being specially dressed for the conditions. And that means fur: lots of it. Caribou skin boots, fox fur coats, and muskrat fur hats. Known as an *ushanka*, the Russian fur cap—much copied in cold climes the world over—has ear flaps that can be tied up to the crown or fastened down under the chin to protect the ears, jaw, and chin in very cold weather. It is worn by both men and women.

Ushanka-style hats have been worn for centuries across Siberia and much of northern Europe, though they could not have been made from muskrat (*Ondatra zibethicus*) fur until more recent times. Until early in the twentieth century, these furry, semiaquatic rodents could be found only in North America where they are native and abundant. The first recorded introductions in Europe were made in Czechoslovakia in 1905 for breeding in fur farms. Ultimately, some of them escaped and began to colonize aquatic habitats in their new locations.

Other introductions in many other European countries followed, either as direct releases into waterways or for fur farms. The worldwide economic crisis that began in 1929 caused several of the farms to close, their owners releasing their muskrats into the countryside. In the then USSR, the first intentional releases were made between 1928 and 1932 using animals from European countries; the numbers involved were massive, and releases were made countrywide. By 1955, there were around 160,000 muskrats in the USSR; today there are far more.[1]

The muskrat has become an economic pest, burrowing into riverbanks, flood protection bunds, and other structures, digging up agricultural crops, cutting open fishing nets, and much else. It is an environmental pest too, altering aquatic habitats and depleting some of their plant and animal species. As a result, this large rodent is listed by the Bern Convention on the Preservation of European Wild Plants and Animals as an invasive species recommended for extermination in those countries that are outside its natural North American range.[2] Consequently, hunting them is widespread and a year-round activity. In some ways, their pelts are a by-product.

Although ushankas made with muskrat fur have been more common since the mid-1900s in Russia, many of the more expensive versions are made entirely of sheepskin, deerskin, beaver, or rabbit fur. Cheaper versions are made of artificial fur, wool pile, or with the partial use of leather and cloth. Before the 1900s, fur ushankas were probably often made from fox. Of the three species of fox found in Russia, only the red fox (*Vulpes vulpes*) is abundant and widespread. Shot and trapped as an agricultural pest, red fox fur is widely used and much sought after for fur coats, jackets, muffs, and scarves. It is one of the most important fur-bearing animals exploited by the international fur trade, and some red fox pelts are still used to make ushankas.[3]

Oddly, and in spite of the ushanka's warmth in very cold conditions, the Red Army of the USSR did not at first adopt it, perhaps because it was associated with pre-revolutionary Russian Army dress. The Red Army soldiers initially wore the *budenovka*, a soft woolen hat with a peak and flaps that cover the ears and neck. Only after the USSR/Finland war in 1939/40 (part of World War II) in which many Russian soldiers died of hypothermia did the Red Army get issued with ushankas as standard head gear. German soldiers in World War II at the Battle of Moscow even replaced their hats with ushankas because of the extreme Russian winter weather.[4]

The ushanka dates back to the seventeenth century when fur or woolen hats with earflaps called "treukh" were worn in central and northern Russia. But many other types of warm hats had been worn historically at different times by different people across this vast land area. One ancient version was a *klobuk*; high and pointed, it had a fur trim, while a *murmolka* was also high but had a flat crown. Murmolkas were made of velvet or brocade with fur cuffs; they were sometimes decorated with feathers and pearls because these hats were made for only the privileged classes to wear. In general, Russian hats for the higher echelons in society were trimmed with the most expensive furs, usually from sables (*Martes zibellina*), foxes, or beavers.

Up to twenty inches high and almost cylindrical in shape, Russian hats called *gorlatayas* were also made partly of velvet or brocade (richly decorated fabrics usually of silk) covered in fox, weasel, marten, or sable fur. Made for the boyars, the Russian aristocracy, mainly between the fifteenth and seventeenth centuries, they used only the fur from the throat ("gorlo" means throat in Russian) of such mammals—their softest fur—hence their great expense. The taller the hat, the more important the wearer. Ordinary people were strictly forbidden to wear a gorlataya, even wealthy ordinary people.[5]

The ushanka has become a standard winter hat in many other colder parts of the world including Canada and the United States. It is standard issue in most eastern European armies. In China it was part of the People's Liberation Army's winter uniform; there it is still referred to as the "Lei Feng hat" after Lei Feng (1940–1962), a soldier in the army who became a communist legend and cultural icon in China, though even his short existence remains controversial. He was always pictured wearing an ushanka.[6]

Throughout northern latitudes and in mountainous countries with particularly cold winters, fur hats have traditionally been essential wear rather than a fashion accessory. To a large extent they still are, though synthetic materials have cornered at least a part of the market. The range of wild mammals killed to make fur hats has historically been very wide and includes muskrats, sables, martens, foxes, raccoons (*Procyon lotor*), seals, and bears. Beaver was rarely used to make whole fur hats, though it was sometimes used as a trim, simply because almost all beaver fur was used to make the best hatting felt; as a result it attracted higher prices.

In Tibet, winter wear has always included hats made of fox pelts with a generous amount of fur around the rim to protect the face. Three species of fox occur on the Tibetan plateau: red fox, corsac fox (*Vulpes corsac*), and the Tibetan sand fox (*V. ferrilata*). But it is the corsac foxes that are hunted most because they are slow runners and are more easily caught. Corsac foxes are a little smaller than red foxes, and their fur is gray to yellowish over much of the body, though paler underneath; in winter their coat is much thicker, silkier, and straw-gray in color. Occurring across the arid steppes of northern and central Asia, corsacs are widely hunted for their pelts. Up to fifty thousand of them were killed in Russia in some years during the twentieth century, sometimes even more. And in Mongolia, an estimated 1.1 million pelts were sold to the then USSR in the forty years up to 1972. Most pelts would have been used for a range of warm clothing and accessories rather than solely for hat making.[7]

To live in such a challenging environment, historically the peoples of the circumpolar Arctic have had to rely on fur for warm clothing and bedding. The Inuit, a grouping of culturally similar indigenous peoples that inhabit Arctic Russia, the very north of the United States, Canada, and Greenland, have traditionally made parkas with built-in hoods mostly using caribou (*Rangifer tarandus*) or seal skin: an inner layer with the fur against the wearer's skin and an outer layer with the fur facing out. Caribou fur is particularly warm because, as in all deer species, the individual hairs that comprise it are hollow. In consequence, insulating air is not only trapped between the hairs, but inside them too.

Caribou—known as reindeer outside the United States and Canada—have a circumpolar distribution. They are native to Arctic, subarctic, tundra, boreal, and mountainous regions in the very north of Europe, Siberia, and North America. There are several subspecies, and they include both migratory and sedentary populations. Northern peoples have depended upon them for meat and clothing for millennia, and many herds have been semi-domesticated. Extensive comparative testing under controlled environmental conditions has found that traditionally made caribou-fur parkas are significantly more insulating than any synthetic or wool-based clothing available today including clothing selected for military use in extreme cold weather environments.[8]

Although Inuit men and women traditionally wore similar clothing, the hoods on women's parkas—called *amautis*—were larger with a built-in baby pouch to accommodate carrying a baby or young child up to the age of about two years old. And children's parkas were always made of softer fur using the skins of younger animals. The fur ruff around the edge of a parka hood is very much more vital than it might seem in protecting the only part of the body exposed to the perishingly cold outside air, the face. For Arctic-living people, preventing damaging facial frostbite or the buildup of facial frost is vital. It also ensures that they can see properly to hunt and travel.

The fur of wolverine (*Gulo gulo*), a stocky, muscular carnivorous mammal with a reputation for ferocity, has long been considered the best fur for making the ruff. Wolverine fur is long and uneven; when breath condenses on it, the resulting hoar frost is easily shaken free with a quick brushing. And the uneven hair length reduces the chilling effect of wind by creating eddies that reduce wind speed. It is an example of small advantages providing extra comfort and safety.[9] Other furs were sometimes used for these trims too—Arctic fox (*Vulpes lagopus*), Arctic wolf (*Canis lupus arctos*), or even dog hair—but the advantages of wolverine fur have been tried and tested to perfection over millennia.[10]

The Inuit hunted traditionally mainly using bows and arrows though they also used spears and often laid snares made of caribou or moose (*Alces alces*) hide. They made baited deadfall traps to catch small fur-bearing animals by using a propped heavy stone that would fall when the prop was triggered, and they also built hidden pitfall traps for animals to fall into. In winter they mostly killed seals using hand-thrown harpoons, both for food and to use their skins for clothing. Ringed seals (*Phoca hispida*) were their most common prey because of their very wide distribution and presumed abundance, but they also hunted some hooded (*Cystophora cristata*), bearded (*Erignathus barbatus*), and harp seals (*Pagophilus groenlandicus*), all of which spend time out on the ice at that coldest time of year. In summer they would hunt caribou inland and seals along the coast, but in autumn Inuit hunters would not want to miss the enormous southward migration to better winter feeding areas of often huge numbers of caribou.[11]

Historically the Sámi, the native peoples of the very north of Scandinavia and the northwestern tip of Russia, have herded caribou/reindeer, using their skins covered in its dense, very insulating fur to make clothing including hats. Less often the fur of young domesticated goats was used, and for some parts of a hat, or as decoration, the Sámi have used other furs including red fox, Eurasian beaver, and mountain hare (*Lepus timidus*). Winter hats were sometimes also stuffed with dry grass for additional warmth.[12]

Because they lived gregariously, because they were not dangerous animals to hunt, very rarely attacking a hunter even when injured, and because they mostly used predictable routes of movement, huge numbers of caribou must have been killed by Arctic peoples over many centuries. Even though these indigenous peoples had a sound sense of the need for sustainable harvesting, historically there is no way of knowing whether this annual culling might have reduced caribou populations, but their numbers are known to have declined substantially, almost certainly for several reasons. There is no evidence that Arctic seal species have been depleted by indigenous hunters; most populations today are large, and they are not currently endangered though the future impact of climate warming causing a reduction in ice cover is a significant concern.

Social events, including communal gatherings to celebrate a successful hunt, required the Inuit to wear their best clothes. These included dancing caps, the most notable being those worn by the Kilusiktormiut, formerly known as the Copper Inuit, who live north of the tree line in Canada's Northwest Territories. Their caps are often made of the skins of caribou, seal, and ermine sewn together with sinew but featuring a section of the skin of a loon—water birds known as "divers" in Europe—complete with their beak. The five species of loon worldwide can all be found in Arctic waters, and the birds have a mystical and symbolic significance for the Inuit. They have haunting, rather desolate calls audible over surprisingly long distances.

To cope with sea spray and sleet, Inuit men and women often wore an outer hooded parka made of tough seal intestines over their everyday parkas in order to keep their insulating clothing dry, an essential requirement in subzero temperatures. The intestines for making such outer parkas had to go through a great deal of scraping, cleaning, and washing before pieces of the material could be stitched together by hand with animal sinew, a time-consuming process. The finished garment was translucent and totally waterproof; decoration often consisted of the horny, orange-colored sheaths from the beak of the crested auklet (*Aethia cristatella*), a small, predominantly black seabird common in northern seas, to which were attached dark feathers from the bird's head crest.[13]

The Yupik peoples of western Alaska and the Russian Far East are related to the Inuit and, like them, historically also made copious use of animal skins. Like the Inuit, Yupik women are skilled at sewing such skins, making particular use of caribou (both wild and domesticated) and sealskin to manufacture hooded parkas. But they also traditionally used the skins and fur of Arctic ground squirrels (*Urocitellus parryii*), muskrat, birds, and fish. Yupik men wore knee length, or longer, hooded parkas with straight hemlines; Yupik women wore slightly shorter parkas.[14]

Yupik people also wore outer rainproof parkas made of sections of seal intestine—sometimes bear intestine—stitched together. Only the larger seals such as the bearded seal and the closely related walrus (*Odobenus rosmarus*) had suitably large intestines to use. A whole waterproof parka could be made from the intestines of a single bearded seal. They were ideal in wet weather and for sea travel by kayak when protection against near freezing seawater spray was essential, but they were also worn for celebrations and dance. They were decorated with fur from wolverines, bears, or musk ox (*Ovibos moschatus*); human or dog hair; cormorant and murre feathers; eagle down; and auklet feathers and beaks.[15]

Inupiat family in Alaska, 1929, wearing fur-trimmed, hooded caribou-skin parkas for insulation (photo by Edward S. Curtis, restored).

As with the Inuit, the Yupik also made waterproof hooded parkas from fish or bird skin, some with an Arctic fox fur ruff on the edge of the hood. The fish skins were stretched, smoke-dried, and descaled before sections were sewn together. The species exploited varied from place to place and according to which Yupik peoples or communities made them; they might include chum salmon (*Oncorhynchus keta*), silver salmon (*O. kisutch*), and brown trout (*Salmo trutta*), all of which were caught for food.

Yupik hooded parkas made of bird skin provided waterproofing and warmth. They were lightweight and comfortable, but they tore easily, requiring frequent repair. They were reversible, worn with the feathers next to the body in winter, and they could be used as blankets at night with the feathers on the outside. Arctic peoples have always relied on killing a variety of birds for food and for their eggs; many were relatively easily obtained because they nested in huge colonies on sea cliffs. Medium-sized birds such as murres (known as "auks" in Europe), crested auklets, a variety of sea ducks, loons, and gulls were all available at different times of year from which bird skin parkas could be made.

The central Alaskan Yupik who live on Nunivak Island, the second largest island in the Bering Sea, have traditionally made bird skin and feather parkas with hoods from a combination of different species. Most commonly used were the pelagic cormorant (*Phalacrocorax pelagicus*); ducks including common eider (*Somateria mollissima*), king eider (*S. mollissima*), and Steller's eider (*Polysticta stelleri*); common murre (*Uria aalge*); and horned puffin (*Fratercula corniculata*) though a number of other birds at different times too. Depending on where these birds nested, communities often had to trade in order to obtain sufficient skins. Cormorant skins were considered the most valuable and conveyed prestige on the owner; they were usually worn only by women. Thirty-four horned puffin skins were needed to make a man's hooded parka, twenty-eight for a woman's, and a few more if the smaller Atlantic puffin (*Fratercula arctica*) was used.[16]

The Aleut people who inhabit the Aleutian Islands in the Bering Sea (part of the U.S. state of Alaska) traditionally wore highly insulating clothing similar to that worn by the Inuit and Yupik, including hooded parkas and waterproof outer parkas. Aleut women usually had parkas made of seal or sea otter (*Enhydra lutris*) skin, while Aleut men wore parkas of bird skin, mainly the same bird species exploited by the Inuit and Yupik. Sea otters were known for their incredibly dense fur, a necessity in the cold North Pacific Ocean waters they inhabit. Aleut waterproof outer parkas were made of seal or Steller's sea lion (*Eumetopias jubatus*) intestines, sometimes those of bear, walrus, or even whales.[17]

Historically, sea otters ranged across the North Pacific Rim, from Hokkaido, Japan, through the Kuril Islands, the Kamchatka Peninsula, the Commander Islands, the Aleutian Islands, coastal Alaska, and south as far as Baja California, Mexico.[18] They had been hunted by Arctic peoples for their highly insulating fur and their meat for millennia. Most were killed using spears thrown from kayaks or similar boats. Whether these peoples hunted sustainably—it was obviously in their long-term interest to do so—is debatable. Although sea otter populations were certainly not depleted overall by the eighteenth century, there is some evidence that the Aleut, for instance, did overexploit sea otter populations locally.[19]

Indigenous hunting alone was not to last. Killing on an industrial scale began in the mid-eighteenth century in the inshore waters off numerous islands in the Bering Sea between eastern Siberia and Alaska and along the mainland coast when hunters and traders arrived from many parts of the world, Russians in particular but the Spanish too. There was growing demand for their pelts. What happened next was all too predictable; it was the maritime equivalent of the North American beaver trade. Trading posts were established from the Aleutian Islands to Baja California. Sea otter pelts were worth many times the value of sable pelts and were used to make expensive fur coats and fur hats. It proved to be an extremely lucrative trade that stimulated yet more sea otter hunting. Along with the otters, many thousands of Aleuts, many forced to hunt for otters, were murdered or died of disease brought by the incoming hunters.

Sea otter fur is dense and dark but silver-tipped. Many pelts ended up being sold through the London fur market although they were also in high demand in Russia and China as trimming for robes, for making caps for the top echelons of Chinese society, and for bed covers by those who could afford such warm luxury. In China, sea otter furs were exchanged at a good profit for prized Oriental goods. In European countries, where the fur was also popular, it was used mainly for fur collars on coats and to make fur hats.[20]

The Aleutian Islands and Kamchatka in the Russian Far East were the first, by 1790, to have their sea otters decimated. The hunting moved further south, down the Pacific Northwest coast of America to coastal California and Mexico, where they were also decimated by American and Russian hunters. That move south allowed the Alaskan/Bering sea otter population to recover through the early nineteenth century only for hunters to decimate them yet again.[21]

Before 1900, the trade had dwindled almost to nothing, not because demand had slumped but simply because, within a century or so, almost all the sea otters had been killed. An estimated 150,000 to 300,000 otters had been reduced to 2,000 or less. It had, as with both Eurasian and North American beavers, been a completely predictable boom-and-bust trade.[22]

A similarly destructive but highly lucrative industry also developed in several parts of the world to exploit fur seals, eight of the nine species occurring in Antarctic and other southern oceans with one, the northern fur seal (*Callorhinus ursinus*), occurring in the North Pacific, the Bering Sea, and the Sea of Okhotsk. Breeding in often huge coastal colonies, vast numbers of several species were shot and clubbed to death beginning late in the eighteenth century and through much of the nineteenth century, with the peak of the trade lasting only from 1780 to 1830. Their fur was used mainly for coats though sometimes for hats. Albany, New York, became a center of seal fur cap production, at its height producing two thousand caps a day, many for export. But overexploitation of fur seals soon curtailed the business.

Guadalupe fur seals (*Arctocephalus townsendi*), breeding on islands west of Baja California, Mexico, were massacred; they were believed to be extinct, but a few survived to form the nucleus of a recovering population. The then huge breeding colonies of the Antarctic fur seal (*Arctocephalus gazella*) in the southern oceans were exploited by British and American sealers in the eighteenth and nineteenth centuries and their numbers also reduced to the brink of extinction.[23]

In July 1911, the North Pacific Fur Seal Convention was signed by the United States, the United Kingdom, Japan, and Russia and was the first international treaty to start addressing wildlife conservation concerns. It applied only to the northern fur seal and to the sea otter, the latter added in almost as an afterthought. While it banned killing at sea, it merely restricted the killing of seals in their breeding colonies on the basis of minimum quotas set for each country and provided exemptions to indigenous Arctic peoples.[24] But it set a precedent that eventually led to increasingly onerous restrictions on seal kills, presaging the more severe U.S. Fur Seal Act, 1966 (which applied only to the same pair of mammals), and the U.S. Marine Mammal Protection Act, 1972, which applied to all marine mammals.

Oddly perhaps, it is not only in cold climates that people wear fur hats. On a hot summer's day outside Buckingham Palace in London, and on every day of the year, thousands of tourists gather to watch the changing of the guard as the Old Guard forms up in the palace forecourt to be replaced by the New Guard marching in from nearby Wellington Barracks. Accompanied by guards' bands, dressed in their bright red tunics and their enormous black bearskin hats, it is a classic part of British tradition and pageantry (see plate 9). Most people viewing the spectacle probably do not realize that each bearskin really is what its name says: the skin and fur of a whole American black bear (*Ursus americanus*). The bearskins have not been replaced—yet anyway—with a synthetic lookalike. The reason why? Military tradition, of course.

Where did this tradition begin? It was certainly well underway in Davy Crockett's days in Tennessee in the early 1800s. "Newly married with two small boys, hunting was the only way in which Crockett could feed them adequately. Shooting a deer or turkey would be good eating for days but killing a Black Bear provided abundant meat and fat for lighting oil. Bear pelts were made into a variety of goods such as rugs, bed robes, coats and the fur hats worn by various British army regiments, the bearskins. In the mid-1700s colonial America exported thousands of bear pelts," writes Michael Wallis in his biography of the frontiersman.[25]

Grenadiers—originally specialized infantry armed with grenades and usually the front line in any attack—originally wore caps trimmed with fur; that changed in the later eighteenth century when British, French, and Spanish armies introduced bearskins. Originally the tall hats had cloth tops, and some were fitted with ornamental front metal plates. As with well-to-do ladies decorating their hats with all manner of feathers and whole birds, the grenadiers were kitted out in bearskins to give them added height and to make them more impressive when seen on parade grounds and on the battlefield. As they remain, bearskins were decorative, not practical.

By the nineteenth century, the almost impossibility of maintaining the bearskins in decent condition on active service, and their expense, led to them being confined in use to guardsmen, army musicians, and other units with a ceremonial rather than a fighting role in the armies of many countries including Britain, Belgium, Denmark, the Netherlands, Germany, Russia, and Sweden.[26]

They were also worn by some militia companies in the United States prior to the Civil War. "It is a custom which is rather old, it is true, but which is practically a useless one save for the purpose of military display; for, as was shown in Egypt a few years ago, the time will never come again when the Guards will wear their bearskins on active service, unless indeed they chance to be ordered to the North Pole or Nova Zembla," commented the *New York Times* on 3 August 1888.[27]

Nevertheless, the British Foot Guards (senior infantry regiments) and the Royal Scots Greys (a British horse-mounted cavalry regiment) wore bearskins in battle during the Crimean War between 1853 and 1856. But it proved to be the last time that any part of the British Army would do so.[28]

The bearskin worn today by British Foot Guards is 18 inches tall and weighs 1.5 pounds. Still referred to as a "cap" in typical British understatement, each is made entirely from the fur of an American black bear shot in Canada under license. By tradition—and tradition features heavily in military dress—an officer's bearskin is made from the fur of a brown bear, also shot under license in Canada, that is dyed black. Brown bears reputedly have thicker, fuller fur, a case of better-quality wear for officers. The British army bearskins are made specially by hatmakers who purchase between fifty and a hundred bear skins a year at international auctions and sell the finished product to the UK government's Ministry of Defence.

Heavily persecuted since European settlers spread across North America, and compounded by the rapid felling of forest cover as they did so, American black bear populations declined rapidly, probably reaching their nadir in the early 1900s. Only a very small part of this decline can be attributed to military bearskin requirements; most bears were shot for food, for other items of clothing and bedding, and because of human safety fears. It is impossible to know how many black bears inhabited the forests of the North American continent prior to human colonization. Today, the International Union for Conservation of Nature estimates the total at between 850,000 and 950,000 animals.[29] Given that a considerable area of their forest habitat has been cleared between then and now, it's perhaps safe to assume that the original population might have been as much as two million.

Not all military hats that look like bearskins are what they seem. The Royal Guards of Thailand (dedicated to the protection of that country's royal family) have long worn what appear to be rather luridly colored bearskins—often pink or blue—with their ceremonial uniforms, depending on their military unit. In fact what they are wearing are pith helmets—lightweight, cloth-covered helmets made of plant material—covered densely in ostrich feathers.[30]

The busby, the English name for a Hungarian shako military hat worn originally by Hungarian hussars—cavalry regiment soldiers—is much shorter in height (about eight inches tall) and more cylindrical in shape. It was traditionally made of fur, sometimes sealskin, raccoon skin, or fox fur, occasionally from black bear skins. The hat is not likely to have been responsible for any significant depletion in any of these common mammals. Some types of busby were made of astrakhan, the dark curly fleece of young karakul lambs from central Asia. The origin of the unusual name is rather lost in the mists of time. One neat suggestion is that it was named after the hatter who supplied the officer's version, a Mr. W. Busby of the Strand, London.[31]

A busby was usually worn with a bag made of colored cloth hanging from the top, the other end of which was attached to the wearer's right shoulder as a defense against saber cuts. As with bearskins, the busby often had a uniquely colored feather or fur hackle attached to it to identify the regiment of the wearer.[32] Busbys were in use by infantry units of several countries, reaching their height of popularity before World War I especially in Britain, Germany, Russia, and some other European countries.

The Royal Canadian Mounted Police—the "Mounties," Canada's national police force—have a much stronger case for insisting on fur hats in winter than London's guardsmen outside Buckingham Palace. A wedge-shaped cap covered in either seal skin fur or lamb's wool was first used in 1876 by parts of the Canadian military and by the forerunners of the Mounties. They were worn only in winter; the Mounties are much better known for the Stetson type hat they wear during the rest of the year.[33] In 1901 they adopted the Klondike-style fur hat, somewhat similar to an ushanka, made of the fur of muskrat; each one, complete with earflaps, requires two or three muskrat pelts of the highest quality.[34]

Apart from a guardsman's bearskin, another fur hat worn to impress by its stature is a shtreimel. Worn by married Haredi Jewish men—Orthodox Jews who reject secular culture—on Shabbat (Judaism's day of rest from Friday night to Saturday night) and certain other Jewish holidays and festivals, the prevailing custom is for a bridegroom to receive his shtreimel as a wedding gift from his future father-in-law. It will be the most expensive item of clothing he ever owns.[35]

Shtreimels are made of cotton velvet surrounded by large quantities of animal fur. Traditionally that fur has come from the tails of sables, beech martens (*Martes foina*), and European pine martens (*M. martes*) for shtreimels made in Europe or from gray fox (*Urocyon cinereoargenteus*), American marten (*Martes americana*), and fishers (*Pekania pennanti*) for those made in the United States, their fur wrapped in a ring clockwise around the structure. It takes perhaps thirty tails to make one shtreimel. The hat enhances and beautifies Shabbat and has considerable spiritual significance for Haredi Jews, but it is not of any religious significance.[36]

Similar hats, also made of mammal fur, usually sable, are the spodik and the kolpik that are also worn by some Haredi Jews of particular sects, although they are not as common as the shtreimel. Spodiks are slightly taller and less bulky than shtreimels and are the traditional Shabbat headwear of Polish Hasidic Jews. The kolpik is worn almost only by rabbis of certain Hasidic Jewish sects on special occasions.

The mammals used to make these hats were usually trapped for their body pelts that were in demand for making fur coats. But it is unlikely that the unwanted mammals' tails were used to make shtreimels and similar hats simply because they were surplus to requirements. The answer might instead be related to the early origins of these rather unusual and impressive hats.

In the late Middle Ages, well before they became characteristic of Hasidic costume, somewhat similar fur hats were worn by non-Jews in Russia and other parts of Eastern Europe. And in the sixteenth century, wealthy Polish peasants wore not dissimilar but taller fur hats called kolpaks. Appearing in Polish costume in the sixteenth and seventeenth centuries, a hat similar to the shtreimel was probably introduced into Poland by Cossacks or by Tatars from the Black Sea region and adopted by Jews there. So maybe Jews merely copied what was worn around them.

The Hasidim themselves, though, often prefer a different explanation: a government decree in eighteenth-century Poland attempted to humiliate the Jews by forcing them to wear the animal tails of unkosher mammals as a public display of shame. But the Jews turned this degradation into something positive, embracing the decree but turning it around by making a regal headgear out of the animal tails that Jews then wore with great pride.[37] Historically, though, few Hasidic Jews in Eastern Europe wore shtreimels; poverty simply precluded it. And the hat was never popular among all orthodox Jews either.[38]

Sables, small, mainly forest mammals no more than twenty inches in body length, were the first fur-bearing animals in Siberia to interest Russians (see plate 10). With shades of beige, brown, gold, silver, and black, their almost weightless, silky, and lustrous thick fur, very insulating and durable, quickly became the most sought-after fur in the world. A wealthy seventeenth-century Russian diplomat described sable as "a beast full marvelous and prolific . . . a beast that the Ancient Greeks and Romans called the Golden Fleece."[39] It was known to be the favorite fur of King Henry VIII of England, especially after he received five sets of it from Emperor Charles V (1500–1558), the then ruler of the Holy Roman and the Spanish Empires. He later decreed that sable fur was to be worn only by nobles exceeding the rank of viscount, a rather futile effort because the vast majority of his subjects could not possibly have afforded such luxury anyway.

Traditionally, Siberians hunted for survival, using the fur from small animals like these to make gloves and hats and the meat to enhance a very poor diet. The small mammals they hunted were caught in traps and usually met with a painful death. Sable fur, along with the somewhat less valuable furs of many other mammals, became the primary reason for the bloody conquest of Siberia by Russians that began in 1580 and continued into the seventeenth century.[40] The incoming Russians forced local hunters to use more effective steel traps to kill a range of mammals in much greater numbers for a more international fur trade.

The trade peaked in the seventeenth century taking large numbers of sables, red foxes, ermines, Eurasian beavers, red squirrels (*Sciurus vulgaris*), Eurasian lynx (*Lynx lynx*), gray wolves, wolverines, mountain hares, European pine martens, walruses, and sea otters, with most of their fur sold via international markets for very expensive clothing and household rugs. In 1910, the pelts of seventy thousand sables, ten times that many ermine, and fifteen million squirrels from Siberia accounted for almost half of the world's furs traded.[41] This intensified level of hunting was not sustainable; by the nineteenth and twentieth centuries sables were in severe decline across their northern Russian range. A five-year hunting ban was put in place in 1935 followed by annual, winter-only hunting licenses that allowed a limited cull. The decline continued until the 1940s, but numbers have recovered since.

In North America, many shtreimels were made historically from the tails of fishers, small martens common in forests across much of the continent. They have been trapped for their fur since the eighteenth century, most of it used for clothing, especially for scarves and neck pieces.[42] As with sables in Russia, overtrapping of fishers—in their case between 1900 and 1940—combined with forest clearance and the conversion of native forest to commercial plantations, threatened them with near extinction in the southern part of their range and led to their extirpation in other areas. They were not protected in law until 1934.[43]

The tails of the wild-caught mammals used to make shtreimels were of less value than the highly valuable body pelts, whether from sables in Siberia or from fishers in North America. In that sense, shtreimels supplied a ready market for a much less valuable by-product of this large-scale mammal trapping.

Furs remain a valuable, internationally traded commodity today, and many fur-bearing mammals are still trapped or shot for their pelts, albeit now under far stricter controls on the numbers killed and the methods used to trap them. In the coldest regions of the world, many indigenous peoples still hunt and trap fur-bearing wild mammals to make head coverings and other insulating clothing, although synthetic, insulating, and waterproof clothing alternatives are also valued. There are other changes too. Several fur-bearing species are today farmed rather than wild-caught, and faux fur, often indistinguishable from the real thing, is today available at much cheaper prices. Faux fur is also increasingly being adopted by leading couturiers worldwide who are shunning the real thing whether it is farmed or wild trapped.

While most head coverings made of mammal fur, though certainly not all, are worn for the very practical reason of warmth, hats have always been fashion statements too.

European Flamboyance

MAKE YOUR WAY THROUGH THE CROWDS THAT THRONG THE FOURTEENTH-CENTURY Charles Bridge crossing the Vltava River in Prague to the Malá Strana, the elegant baroque sector of this fabulous city, and you will walk past the pale yellow-washed Hotel U trí pštrosu—the curiously named Hotel at the Three Ostriches. Built in the sixteenth century for Jan Fux, a wealthy supplier of ostrich feathers, he had his house decorated with three ostriches to advertise his business, a seemingly common practice in the city at the time. They have been the symbol of the house—in more recent years a hotel and restaurant—ever since. In medieval Prague the huge, fast-running but flightless ostrich, and its sought-after feathers, must have seemed incredibly exotic, associated as it was with the far-off lands of North Africa and the Middle East hardly any Praguers would ever experience.

Fux specialized in decorating ladies' hats with ostrich feathers, in making feather fans and other decorations for those who could afford his services, and in decorating horse harnesses and carriages for special occasions such as weddings. Ostrich feathers were in demand, too, by courtiers and military officers at Prague Castle; along with Paris and Vienna, Prague in the sixteenth century was one of the cultural and fashion cities of Europe.[1] Fux had a good business; hence his splendid home.

Jan Fux was most certainly not a one-off. Before the sixteenth century, feather working had become big business across the main cultural centers of Europe. Exotic bird feathers were being imported, and an industry had developed to treat the plumes and to dye them. By the sixteenth century, the most affluent ladies in European cities and the officer class in many European armies were using large numbers of feathers to adorn their headwear.

Ostrich feathers had been used for human adornment for at least five thousand years, and, though they were not hats, by the twelfth century or earlier feathers were used to embellish some of the Venetian masks worn at the city's colorful annual carnival. By the end of that century the flourishing cities of Florence and Venice were beginning to set the dress tone for the rest of Europe; oriental luxuries including ostrich feathers, and maybe others, had reached the continent during the early Crusades (from the eleventh century on) and were shipped into Italian ports.

In the thirteenth century the clothing trades of Paris included the *chapeliers de paon*, who manufactured headdresses decorated with peacock feathers, the *aumussiers* who made hoods incorporating animal furs, the *fourreurs de chapeaux* who made fur-trimmed hats, and the *chapeliers de feûtre* who made felt hats, presumably using Eurasian beaver pelts as well as other furs.[2]

Ordinary people, though, wore plain hats and clothes, a restriction imposed by affordability but also by class distinction. Sumptuary legislation was commonplace in most European countries (including much later in early colonial North America) and in other parts of the world to regulate and enforce social hierarchies and morals by restricting expenditure according to a person's social rank. Such legislation was introduced in England in the early fourteenth century. In general it was the nobility, the "upper classes" who alone had the right to ostentation—including feathers and furs—although the protocol seems to have been broken regularly by those not of noble birth who had gathered enough wealth or had sufficient chutzpah.[3]

Early in the fourteenth century, the feather had appeared commonly for the first time as decoration on European hats. At first it was a single, long, upright (usually) ostrich feather. By the end of the fifteenth century, feathers on hats had become something of a fashion craze, though restricted to society's upper echelons. Feathers of other birds started to adorn hats too, peacock and pheasant feathers in particular. By the second half of the fifteenth century, feathers were used in profusion on fashionable gentlemen's hats, each one often dyed a different color and its shaft ornamented with pearls or other gems. Hat styles varied at different times: tall steeple hats made of beaver fur embellished with streaming ostrich plumes; satin turbans with a fan of feathers; felt bonnets topped with a flurry of peacock feathers.[4]

Although ostrich plumes were worn by soldiers in ancient Egypt to decorate their helmets, it was the development of chivalry in the twelfth and thirteenth centuries that led to the ostrich plume becoming an important heraldic symbol in Europe, especially among the newly created knights. By the early fifteenth century, military helmets in Europe began to get more ostentatious. Out went the former very practical styles using boiled leather and metal designed solely to protect the head in battle, and in came ostrich feathers. They streamed, often in profusion, from the top of the helmet, which was manufactured with a tube or socket built-in to hold such adornments in place. The matchlock musket, which first appeared on the battlefield in the mid-fifteenth century in Europe and which soon came to dominate warfare, rendered useless the heavy armor and helmets worn by infantry until then. Musket balls could penetrate the metal, so there was no point in wearing a heavy metal helmet. Felt hats of various designs became the norm for most infantrymen and for cavalry too.

A few feathers on the apex of a hat were known as a "panache"; several worn at the side or back was a "plume." A famous panache, worn by the ever flamboyant King Henry VIII of England (1491–1547), comprised no fewer than eight feathers, each one being over four feet long and seemingly obtained from an unknown Indian bird. He wore this incredible adornment when he majestically rode into Boulogne, his forces having seized it from the French in September 1544.

There are very few birds from which such long feathers could possibly be obtained. If they were from India as recorded, they are most likely to be the highly colorful tail feathers of either the more widespread Indian peafowl (*Pavo cristatus*), long since introduced in many countries to adorn stately gardens, or the now much rarer green peafowl (*P. muticus*) found in parts of Southeast Asia and formerly found in the very east of India. The males of both species have characteristically long, colorful, and flamboyant tail feathers. An alternative might be Reeves's pheasant (*Syrmaticus reevesii*), males of which have incredibly attractive, long (up to seven feet) silvery white tail feathers barred with chestnut brown. The disadvantage is that this pheasant, restricted to parts of China, has never occurred naturally in India. Whichever bird was used for Henry's panache, it would have been a guarantee that heads would have turned to admire him. Just what he wanted.

But a plume or a panache of colorful feathers, usually naturally white or black ostrich feathers (or dyed in other colors), atop an officer's hat did have a useful function and was not simply some rather effete adornment. It made the wearer much more visually obvious to his soldiers. Before the Battle of Ivry in Normandy in 1590, King Henry IV of France (1553–1610), who led Huguenot and English forces in battle against the Catholic League and Spanish forces, commanded his leaders, "not to lose sight of his white panache, that it would lead them to victory and honor." His forces won the battle, thanks to his panache or otherwise.[5]

Within the armies of Europe what had hitherto been a feminine fashion choice had become an essential part of military costume. With few standing armies, drafting soldiers when conflict arose might not have proved easy. Making their uniforms more graceful and highly decorated, hats included, might have helped in recruitment, emphasizing its noble calling.

Wide-brimmed, beaver felt "cavalier" hats became popular in civilian life in the seventeenth century, and most were trimmed with a single ostrich plume though some carried a more flamboyant panache of downward curving plumes. They got their name from the supporters of King Charles I of England who fought on the side of the king and were known as "cavaliers." It was a common hat style Europe-wide for non-soldiers and soldiers alike until it was replaced by the tricorn in the eighteenth century, hats with three sides of their brim turned upward (see plate 11). The more expensive "cavaliers" were made of beaver fur, the cheaper versions from wool or rabbit felt, and only the more extravagant versions were decorated with feathers, usually of ostrich.

First adopted by the Spanish, then the French for their infantrymen and cavalry, the tricorn also became popular for both civilians and soldiers Europe-wide and in the United States. It survives today in some militarized units such as Spain's Guardia Civil. Tricorns metamorphosed into the bicorne hat with two rather than three turned-up corners that was worn as an item of uniform by both European and American military officers. It was the classic hat of Napoleon Bonaparte (1769–1821) and was widely in use at least until World War I. It, too, could be made of beaver fur with cheaper versions of rabbit or hare.[6]

Lock & Co., established in 1676 in London (and which claims to be the world's oldest hat shop), made the bicorne hats from beaver fur worn by Vice Admiral Horatio Nelson (1758–1805). It was presumably made using imported North American beaver fur. In September 1805 Nelson visited Lock & Co. in St. James's Street, London, to pay his bill; the following month he was killed by a marksman firing from the French gunship *Redoubtable* at the Battle of Trafalgar.

Hussars, mounted light cavalry regiments that originated in central and eastern Europe during the fifteenth and sixteenth centuries, and adopted Europe-wide by the seventeenth and eighteenth centuries, had a reputation as the dashing adventurers of any army. For headgear they usually wore a shako (a cylindrical military cap) or a busby (a fur hat usually made of bearskin or raccoon skin) almost always adorned with a short spray of egret feathers (dyed or left white), sometimes with vulture feathers at its base. The British Eighth and Eleventh Hussars in their full uniform under the command of the 7th Earl of Cardigan were a feature of the fateful Light Brigade charge against Russian artillery in the Crimean War in 1854.

The Bersaglieri, an elite light infantry unit of the Italian Army created in 1836, wore a large, drooping panache of western capercaillie (*Tetrao urogallus*, a large grouse) or black grouse (*T. tetrix*) feathers on their dress uniform's wide-brimmed hats and a smaller panache attached to their fighting uniform's helmets. The feathers supposedly acted as camouflage or as a sunshade when firing a gun; the Bersaglieri were trained to be marksmen. But the feathers were probably as much to do with regimental pride and building an esprit de corps. According to the Museo Bersaglieri in Rome, no less than four hundred capercaillie feathers were attached to each ceremonial hat, but more like half that number to combat helmets. The Bersaglieri have seen considerable action since they were created, including in World War I—when Benito Mussolini (1883–1945) served in the regiment—and in World War II.[7]

Military plumes had perhaps reached their apogee at one notorious and cataclysmic event in world history that signed the death warrant of millions of soldiers across Europe and beyond: the assassination of Archduke Franz Ferdinand and his wife on 28 June 1914 in Sarajevo. Look back at the pictures taken that day, and what dominates the archduke's head is a huge panache of green-dyed ostrich plumes sprouting from his rather unobtrusive helmet. When the fatal bullets were fired and the archduke slumped, his hat fell to the floor of the car, scattering its feather display.

Two species of ostrich are recognized today: the common ostrich (*Struthio camelus*) and the very similar Somali ostrich (*S. molybdophanes*), the latter confined to northeast Africa.[8] The largest and heaviest of living birds standing up to eight feet high, ostriches are flightless but are capable of running particularly fast in short bursts, often out-pacing a nonhuman predator.

Common ostriches historically occupied virtually all of North Africa, much of the extensive East African savanna, southern Africa south of the tropical belt, the Arabian peninsula, and much of modern-day Turkey and southern Asia. There are claims that their total population was in the millions, but there is no data to either support or dispute this assertion.[9] They were seemingly abundant in the Sahara before climate change caused its conversion from savanna to desert around 3000 to 5000 B.C. Fragments of ostrich eggshells are common in the sands of the Sahara today, and drawings of the huge birds—sometimes being caught in traps—are a common component of ancient rock drawings in parts of that huge desert.

For thousands of years, ostriches have been trapped and killed for their meat and for their skins to be made into leather; their large, thick-shelled eggs were also prized, not only to eat but to be used as receptacles and in rituals. Hunting scenes in the remains of Roman villas include ostriches as game animals being captured and killed. Roman dignitaries sometimes wore ostrich feathers as head ornamentation; the birds were used to pull chariots and featured as public entertainment in circuses. Some North African peoples bred small numbers of them in captivity, but hunting or trying to domesticate ostriches could be dangerous; their vestigial wings can cause serious injury, and a kick from their clawed feet can easily kill a person.

Hunting was often done on horseback to stand any chance of keeping pace with a running ostrich. Arabs trained their fastest horses for the job, exhausted the poor birds, and then cut their throats when they collapsed. Some African peoples such as the San, nomadic hunter-gatherers of southern Africa, would dress in the full skin of an ostrich and approach their prey slowly until close enough to kill the fleeing birds with a bow and arrow hidden under their costume. Other methods involved driving them into prelaid nets or hunting them with dogs.[10] A more sustainable approach was tried: plucking the white wing plumes from live birds. But catching them was fraught with problems, plucking was presumably very painful for the birds (not that anyone was concerned), and this often resulted in stunted feathers regrowing instead of marketable plumes. That made no business sense.

Once a market developed in Europe for ostrich feathers in the fourteenth and fifteenth centuries, the killing was stepped up. It stepped up several gears more in subsequent centuries as feathers became increasingly popular for hat decoration across a widening spectrum of society. Skins from wild ostriches complete with feathers were taken north by camel caravan through the immense sands of the Sahara to North African ports, and from there they were shipped to southern European ports such as Livorno, Venice, Trieste, and Marseille. These cities became

Europe's early feather hubs from where the best feathers were transported to the couture cities of Europe. Sarah Abrevaya Stein in her authoritative study of the ostrich feather trade has mapped the five principal camel trade routes from Africa south of the Sahara to the North African ports and has described the requirement for safe passage having to be negotiated to get the goods safely to their destinations over hugely challenging distances and arid terrain.[11]

The killing of common (and probably Somali) ostriches accelerated through the following few centuries, steadily depleting their populations over vast areas of Africa. By the end of the sixteenth century they were found only in isolated pockets in Egypt, having been recorded as abundant up to the previous century. Nevertheless, in 1807 an estimated 509 kilos of ostrich feathers were imported into France, all from wild birds. By 1850 they were extinct in Egypt,[12] and they had been reduced to near extinction across the Arabian Peninsula and the rest of North Africa before the nineteenth century was out.

The killing of wild birds only slowed when the first ostrich farms were set up in the Southern Cape of South Africa in the 1860s. After that, feathers from farmed ostriches dominated the trade. They were clipped rather than plucked, thereby allowing the undamaged skin follicles to regrow quality plumes. A new set could be clipped every eight months, and well-fed ostriches in captivity are long-lived birds. By the late nineteenth century, the Cape had been transformed into the world's principal ostrich feather supplier.[13]

But why were ostrich feathers so incredibly popular? It's largely because they are different from those of most birds. Instead of having rigid barbed veins on either side of their feather shafts (necessary for flight but a requirement irrelevant for ostriches), they tend to be more soft and downy wherever the feathers are located on the bird's body. Ostrich feathers can be grouped into three broad types: downy ones found under the wings, often known as floss; plumes such as those on the edge of their wings; and hard feathers such as those found on the remainder of the wing. The white plumes—the most sought-after feathers for hat decoration—have a rather loose or evaporated look, a gossamer light and airy appearance; they give the impression of luxury, their fronds lightly curled, their tips plump and casually drooping.

The finest white plumes come from the edges of the ostrich's rudimentary wings. These are its primary feathers, essential for flight in all other birds. The wing coverts that protect the primary feathers are black in the ostrich and are shorter. They were still important in the hat trade. The bird's white tail feathers were also used but were never as valuable.

Ostrich feathers as hat decoration reached their apogee between the mid-1800s and World War I when farmed ostriches supplied increasing numbers. They adorned hats for both the young and older wearer in Europe and in the United States. With countless grades of feather available, and their prices much reduced because of their availability, the ostrich feather's appeal crossed class lines.

Peafowl are some of the most easily recognized birds the world over, the iridescent green tail feathers of the male a particular attraction. That is mainly because the most abundant of the three species of peafowl, the Indian peafowl, native to India and adjacent countries, has for millennia been introduced to parks and gardens in many parts of the world. The Romans brought them to Western Europe, and they were in Britain by the fourth century. They were often kept for the table until the meaty wild turkey (*Meleagris gallopavo*) was introduced to Europe from North America after Spanish conquistadors took them back home in the fifteenth century. As a consequence, peacock feathers used to adorn European hats in the Middle Ages are likely to have been taken from domesticated birds kept locally either for their meat or to decorate large parks and the gardens of stately homes. Like the peacock, pheasants—of which there are a number of

1700 to 1795

blue taffeta hat-white ostrich tipped with rose-pearls-powdered hair-cadogan-French-1780's

silk riding hat with ostrich-button and loop-powdered hair-French-1785

headdress of tulle, spotted net-pearls-blue taffeta fillet-white satin loops poised on lappets-rose and white ostrich-powdered hair-cadogan-English-1780's

taffeta hat-satin bowknot-ostrich feather-powdered hair-French-1780's

black velvet hat-satin ribbon-ostrich-worn over white lawn mobcap with taffeta ribbon-English-1780's

leghorn hat with light brown facing and ostrich-blue and white striped satin ribbon-sheer white frilled lawn cap-French-1787

RTW

ABOVE AND OPPOSITE: Ladies' hats adorned with feathers and whole birds at the zenith of their popularity: 1880–1890 (R. Turner Wilcox, *The Mode in Hats and Headdress* [Mineola, NY: Dover Publications, 2008], 260–261).

1900 to 1910

"burnt orange" straw—emerald green velvet band— green wings— amber ball pin— English— 1907

the marcel wave with puffs— French— 1907

black velvet— weeping ostrich plumes shaded blue and cerise— French— 1908

black straw— Venice lace round crown— white ostrich— black veil— French—1909

white straw— white tulle and white paradise— French— 1909

black velvet— black paradise— hair wrapped close to head— French— 1909

hair brushed to top of head—ends held by shell comb with knobs— French— 1909

RTW

species—were other birds that were transported to many parts of the world to be reared as game birds from their natural home in parts of Asia. The males of all species sport impressively long and colorful tail feathers, though they are not as flamboyant as those of peacocks. It isn't just the tail feathers that were used to decorate ladies' hats; the body plumage of all male pheasant species is especially attractive.[14] And because pheasants were easy to rear for the table, there was no shortage of their feathers to decorate hats rather cheaply.

Through the Middle Ages, swans were highly regarded as good eating at many a royal banquet in several European capitals; trade in their feathers was often reserved to royalty. Hunters and fishermen were obliged to take live swans to royal courts annually where they were plucked live and then released.[15] While their down feathers were used for making boas and powder puffs, their skins used for bedroom mats and "fur" coats, and their feather quills used as pens, there is no evidence that swan feathers were much used to decorate ladies' hats. Maybe they couldn't compete with more exotic and more impressive, equally white ostrich plumes. There were other commonly hunted European birds whose feathers never figure as hat decoration. Wild species of geese and duck, several of which are attractively marked, were frequently shot or caught in nets for food; they were especially good eating, and their feathers were used for bedding. But as with swans, there is no evidence that feathers from wild geese were used to decorate hats either[16]

One popular feather frequently listed for hat making was "marabou," which is almost always recorded as having been obtained from the huge marabou stork (*Leptoptilos crumenifer*) found only in central and southern Africa. Typical is the definition given in the *Oxford English Dictionary*: "the down from the wing or tail of the marabou stork." It seems a perfectly reasonable assumption, but it is actually a case of mistaken identity.

The first clue is that it seems to be impossible to find any mention of imports to Europe of marabou from any part of Africa. In India, however, two closely related stork species, both also large, are very similar in appearance to Africa's marabou; they are the greater and lesser adjutant storks (*Leptoptilos dubius* and *L. javanicus*), apparently named as such because of their propensity to appear on military parade grounds.[17] In the nineteenth century at the height of Britain's colonial powers, both were common birds across India.

Mainly dark colored, both species usually look surprisingly drab, dusty, and dirty because they often delight in feeding at open refuse sites and in urban squalor. Nevertheless, their very fine, downy and fluffy under-tail feathers became popular in the millinery trade across Europe from the fifteenth century on. They were often dyed rather than being left naturally white (perhaps because the feathers were frequently dirty) and were used for soft trimmings on hats and not as individual plumes.

A commentary on daily Anglo-Indian life on the subcontinent in the early nineteenth century includes references to these storks, seemingly often then known as "butcher birds" because of their habit of eating up food scraps:

> It is not generally known that the marabout feathers . . . are in fact furnished by this disgusting looking animal whose coarse ragged attire gives no promise of the delicate beauty of the plumes so much in esteem in France and England. They grow in a tuft under the tail and are not visible except on close inspection. The tuft is easily extracted. . . . It is only necessary to catch him by the feathers under the tail; the first struggle to be free, leaves them in the hand of the marauder. Excepting the heron's [presumably egrets] there are no other Indian plumes so highly prized, and, as an article of commerce, the marabouts' are the most important.[18]

Whether this practice ever resulted in their death from injury during handling is not recorded.

Another contemporary report refers to "the Adjutant of India from which marabou feathers are obtained and a kindred species, the marabou of Africa,"[19] whereas the reports by juries on the thirty different classes of exhibit at the 1851 Great Exhibition held in London includes "awards for furs, skins, feathers, artificial hair" and refers to India only:

> the feathers . . . of the marabout stork which are of two kinds, white and grey. These are imported into this country from Calcutta in great quantities. They are very much admired for their beautiful texture and extreme lightness, and are used for headdresses, muffs and boas. The white kind have at times been so scarce as to be worth their weight in gold.[20]

More exotic feathers still—even whole stuffed birds—had started to make an appearance in the couture centers of Europe in the sixteenth century, adding substantial variety to those commonly used such as peacock, ostrich, and pheasant and extending the exotic variety available at a price for those with the means to purchase them and of sufficient standing in society to be allowed to do so legally.[21] The exoticism of ostrich feathers would soon be challenged.

Ferdinand Magellan (ca. 1480–1521), the Portuguese explorer who led the first expedition that successfully circumnavigated the globe, is generally attributed with bringing to Europe the first birds of paradise skins. It was to be the starting point for one of the most destructive episodes of wild animal exploitation carried out for no deeper purpose than the decoration of ladies' hats. It is likely, though, that skins of these incredibly decorous birds had been traded across much of Southeast Asia from New Guinea for maybe five thousand years; they were certainly valued in Asia more than two thousand years ago.[22]

On one of the smaller Indonesian islands, his expedition had been presented with two very beautiful birds, gifts for the king of Spain. They were later named as Wallace's standardwing (*Semioptera wallacii*), an extraordinarily mundane name for a particularly gorgeous bird. The size of a kingbird, the male has a glossy violet- and lilac-colored crown and an emerald green breast. But those are not his most striking features. In the breeding season he grows two pairs of long white plumes from the bend of the wing that can be raised or lowered like pendants. Males gather and perform a spectacular aerial display, "parachuting" with their wings, their vivid green breast shield spread and the wing "standards" fluttering above their backs.[23]

By 1600, skins of both the greater and lesser birds of paradise (*Paradisaea apoda* and *P. minor*) were regularly imported for sale in European cities.[24] In the 1770s, Georges-Louis Leclerc (1707–1788), a French naturalist and polymath, described six separate species of birds of paradise, their plumage admired for their extraordinary colors, extravagant display plumes, and airy lightness. Maybe not all of these were used for millinery decoration, but we do know that four species in particular became widely used in Europe in the nineteenth century to ornament ladies' hats: sometimes a few selected feathers, sometimes a whole wing, and sometimes even the whole bird stuffed to give the impression that it happened to land where it was pinned.

Based on several years of travel through numerous locations in Southeast Asia, the famous British naturalist Alfred Russel Wallace (1823–1913) wrote:

> When the earliest European voyagers reached the Moluccas in search of cloves and nutmegs, which were then rare and precious spices, they were presented with the dried skins of birds so strange and beautiful as to excite the admiration even of those wealth-seeking rovers. The Malay traders gave them the name of "Manuk dewata," or God's birds . . . while the learned Dutchmen, who wrote in

Latin, called them "Avis paradiseus," or Paradise Bird. John van Linschoten gives these names in 1598, and tells us that no one has seen these birds alive, for they live in the air, always turning towards the sun, and never lighting on the earth till they die . . . but being very costly they were then rarely seen in Europe.[25]

From 1905 to 1920, between thirty thousand and eighty thousand skins of birds of paradise were exported to the feather auctions of London, Paris, and Amsterdam.[26] The huge demand for their feathers encouraged Malay, Chinese, and Australian hunters to seek their fortunes in New Guinea's rain forest, usually employing local guides to help them. The usual hunting strategy was to wait at the appropriate time of year for male birds of paradise to congregate in the trees they selected regularly for displaying. As in North America with beavers, local indigenous peoples obtained steel axes, knives, and tobacco in exchange for dead birds.

Wallace also commented on the methods of capture:

the males assemble early in the morning to exhibit themselves in the singular manner already described. . . . This habit enables the natives to obtain specimens with comparative ease. As soon as they find that the birds have fled upon a tree on which to assemble, they build a little shelter of palm leaves in a convenient place among the branches, and the hunter ensconces himself in it before daylight, armed with his bow and a number of arrows terminating in a round knob. A boy waits at the foot of the tree, and when the birds come at sunrise, and a sufficient number have assembled, and have begun to dance, the hunter shoots with his blunt arrow so strongly as to stun the bird, which drops down, and is secured and killed by the boy without its plumage being injured by a drop of blood. The rest take no notice, and fall one after another till some of them take the alarm. The indigenous mode of preserving them is to cut off the wings and feet, and then skin the body up to the beak, taking out the skull. A stout stick is then run up through the specimen coming out at the mouth.[27]

It was not until 1908 that hunting of birds of paradise—except for local use by indigenous tribes—was banned by the British who then administered much of New Guinea. The Dutch followed suit there in 1931, a good example of an age-old phrase: closing the stable door after the horse has bolted.

Almost no information exists about the quantities of many birds' feathers imported and used to decorate hats in the couture centers of Europe. The *Chambers's Journal* of 1863 does, though, give an insight into the variety of feathers most used, though whether they were all used for hats or some for other clothing adornment is never very clear. It lists ostrich feathers, pheasant, peacock, birds of paradise, and marabou but also emu (*Dromaius novaehollandiae*), vulture, eagle, swan, turkey, and heron feathers.[28]

Parrot wings and tails are known to have been used, though there is no record from what species; their vibrant blues and greens were in complete contrast to whole owl heads (again, species unknown) that, incredulously, were also popular. More exotic still—for those with sufficient means to purchase them—was the elegant but fragile, white-tipped, lacy blue crest of the large Victoria crowned pigeon (*Goura victoria*), an inhabitant of some of the Indonesian islands. An elegant blue-gray pigeon with a fabulous lacy blue crest, it has historically been shot for eating and to sell its feather crest; the pigeon today is regarded as "near threatened" by IUCN though in more recent times because of habitat loss more than continued illegal hunting.[29]

But why did the wearers of the hats decorated with the remains of these birds have such an interest in exotic feathers from distant parts of the world? After all, the vast majority of people in

Europe in the late Middle Ages and into the eighteenth century would certainly never see these birds in the wild nor see the places they inhabited. One factor was exploration: the discovery of new lands far away. Compared with many of the other species that early European colonists encountered on their distant travels, exotic birds could be captured, killed, transported, and kept with relative ease. Europe experienced a sudden bird-craze as stuffed birds of paradise from New Guinea and parrots from the Americas and Africa became a relatively common sight in the continent's largest markets.

Ruling European elites wore feathers partly to express their power and their foreign conquest of territories. At its peak, the Dutch Empire, for instance, included Indonesia, half of New Guinea, and several Caribbean islands. The French Empire included almost all of northwest Africa, Madagascar, and much else, while the British Empire enveloped Australia, India, much of East Africa, and many other countries. Little wonder, then, that exotic bird feathers were easy to obtain in the cultural centers of fifteenth- to twentieth-century Europe.

In England, a royal lead in hat decoration was taken by Queen Elizabeth I (1533–1603); she is reputed to have dressed the part as monarch of a thrusting, nouveau-riche state very conscious of its growing role in world politics. Many of her hats were dyed black; they would have been made of beaver felt. The hatbands, though, were often jeweled and sported ostrich or egret feathers, sometimes in combination.[30] Ladies at court followed her lead in fashion, and other ladies of privilege would doubtless have followed them in turn, at least as well as they could afford to, and other European monarchs and their entourages often copied such a lead.

Across Europe, egrets had for centuries been *aves non grata*. Like their less showy plumaged cousins, the herons, they were disliked because they took fish from ponds, lakes, and rivers, depriving people of a protein-rich food. In the breeding season, male little egrets (*Egretta garzetta*) and great white egrets (*E. alba*), common birds of wetlands and waterways across southern Europe, develop elongated, white, lacy plumes on the back of the head, breast, and mantle.

Known as "aigrettes" in the millinery trade (from the French for egret), for hat decoration such gossamer fine feathers as soft as silk were seemingly impossible to resist. They seemed to convey on the wearer an illusion of balletic grace and height. Dyed black they were lustrous, sophisticated, and scintillating. Those of the great white egret can reach lengths of twenty inches. Large numbers of egrets were shot or caught in snares, particularly in the nineteenth and twentieth centuries when fashionable European ladies frequently wore hats decorated with aigrettes, though the killing had begun as early as the seventeenth century.[31]

The egret feather trade was a source of considerable wealth for many dealers. In 1914 in India (where both egrets occur) one ounce of little egret plumes was trading at between ten and twenty-eight times the equivalent weight of silver. Distributed in Europe illegally (such exports had been banned) they were fetching £15 an ounce, around £1600 today. The booming trade encouraged entrepreneurs to develop egret farms in India, Pakistan, and a few other parts of Southeast Asia where the birds were held in pens unable to fly.

There are no accurate records of the numbers of wild egrets killed; estimates vary between five and two hundred million little egrets alone being supplied annually for millinery,[32] a level of persecution that massively depleted their numbers across southern Europe and Asia. Only in recent decades have their numbers recovered.

Because the male egrets grow their plumes in spring for displaying to females prior to breeding, the birds had to be shot before early summer or these fine feathers became worn and valueless. As a consequence, many were shot on their nests; because egrets nest communally in trees and woods, their locations were well known. Some were picked up after poisoned fish or shrimp were introduced into egret feeding pools. Deprived of adults, the young egrets left in the nests often starved to death or were killed by predators. The valuable plumes were torn off the dead birds, and their carcasses were left to rot.[33]

The breeding plumes of both snowy egrets (*Egretta thula*) and great white egrets were imported into Europe from much of South and Central America where both species were widely distributed. A total of about 110 pounds' weight of egret plumes was exported from Argentina between 1895 and 1898, increasing to a staggering 3,300 pounds between 1899 and 1907, most of it to France and Germany (and some to the United States). To try to assuage the growing number of critics of the feather trade in the late nineteenth century, the millinery trade claimed that some or many of these plumes were picked up from the ground after the birds molted or that large numbers of egrets were raised and treated humanely in egret farms. Objective evidence from observers and the fact that molted plumes are naturally worn and damaged made these arguments spurious.[34]

The Chinese egret (*Egretta eulophotes*), formerly common in much of eastern Russia, China, and Korea, was killed for its nape plumes along with feathers from other water birds including spot-billed pelicans (*Pelecanus philippensis*). Shanghai shipped feathers from all parts of China to Hong Kong and on to the European centers of the millinery trade such as London and Paris.

Although Queen Elizabeth I had her own "capper and hatter" who might have advised her on style and décor, it seems highly unlikely that they developed the same intimate relationship enjoyed by Marie Antoinette and her milliner nearly two centuries later. Austrian by birth, Marie Antoinette (1755–1793), the last queen of France before the Revolution, was married to Louis XVI, renamed as Citizen Louis Capet during the final weeks of his life before he was beheaded. Paris had long ruled European fashion, regularly sending elegant fashion dolls as models to foreign capitals including Vienna where Marie was born, the daughter of Francis I, the Holy Roman Emperor.

Once she became queen, she rebelled against the traditional heavy dress style demanded by the French court, ordering instead the latest, much more provocative styles from Rose Bertin (1747–1813) who, largely as a result of this lucrative and increasingly close royal connection, became a leading French milliner and dressmaker.[35] Bosom-enhancing bodices, ankle-baring skirts, and a mountain of powdered hair piled high and decked with a large panache of ostrich and other plumes—mostly dyed in a variety of colors—set a fashion and projected extreme extravagance in precisely the wrong political times when the majority of the French people endured unbearable taxes and shortages (see plate 14).

As a commoner, Bertin wasn't welcome in royal circles and started to acquire the derisive "title" Minister of Fashion. In more recent times she has been credited with bringing haute couture to the forefront of popular culture, and in the last quarter of the eighteenth century—partly, at least, due to Bertin—Paris fashion became the envy of women of means Europe- and America-wide. Soon the names of the crowned heads and nobility of Europe were to be found in her account book. Not that the new flamboyance was welcomed by everyone.

At first, the English aristocracy claimed to be shocked. To Lady Charlotte Bury (1775–1861), a novelist, noted beauty, and delight of the highest circles of London Society, "the ugliest part of the habillements [attire] is the high chimneys on their heads, which chimneys are covered with feathers and flowers." Nevertheless, English society, and Lady Charlotte, was soon persuaded. Feathers, mainly ostrich for plumes and marabou for trimmings, adorned wide-brimmed hats set atop hair piled high; it was fashion in the extreme, caricatured mercilessly in cartoons of the day.[36]

Marie Antoinette had grotesquely overspent on hats designed by Bertin, and the plain, ugly mobcap in Jacques-Louis David's caricature of her on the way to her execution in 1793 mocks her excesses. Bertin's millinery business in Paris suffered a distinct downturn with the loss of Marie Antoinette and the reduction in business overall because there were fewer and fewer noble heads needing hats as the Revolution and its guillotine took its course. So the ever resourceful Bertin moved herself and her business to London for a few years, survived the Revolution, returned to France, and died twenty years after her most famous client.

The French Revolution ushered in an era of simplicity in dress, hats included. So feather decoration was out of fashion, in France especially, and what Paris couture did, others followed. But it was a temporary blip. When the French monarchy was restored in the early nineteenth century, hats started growing again in size and extravagant decoration, feathers included. As in the United States, from the mid-nineteenth century it was the catalogs of the large department stores that brought a huge variety of hats—many of them feather and bird decorated—to a much wider clientele. In France it was Bon Marché and Galeries Lafayette; in London, Whiteleys followed by Peter Robinson, Liberty, and Harrods.

Ladies' hats rose even higher in the late nineteenth century and into the first decade of the twentieth. An extreme example was known as "four stories and a basement." They included not only ostrich feathers, plumes from herons and egrets, owl heads, whole birds of paradise, and sometimes canaries (presumably caged in origin) but also insects, foliage, even lobsters, lizards, toads, and a whole stuffed ermine.[37] It was as if a macabre obsession with dead wildlife had hijacked the millinery trade and high fashion just to spite the momentum starting to be generated to bring about protection for birds.

But it was a look that would not last. World War I brought austerity and a strong sense that showiness in fashion was wholly inappropriate. Public opinion was turning against animal slaughter, and increasing bird protection legislation was one result. More prosaically, automobiles were the latest desire of those in society who could afford them, and "four stories and a basement" on a lady's head was highly impractical automobile wear whether the vehicle had a roof or was open-topped. Closer fitting, snugger hats without much decoration were in fashion: turbans, toques, berets, and pillbox styles for ladies.

As the twentieth century progressed, more ornately decorated hats gained some popularity at times, not least as a result of ostrich fans and headdresses becoming components of big box office Hollywood movies in the United States starring Fred Astaire and Ginger Rogers. Many of the plumassiers assembling these on-set creations were recruited from former feather factories following the 1930s economic crash. What feather revival there was could not any longer exploit wild birds; instead the feathers of rather more mundane domesticated species—ostrich, pheasant, peafowl, even chickens and geese—dyed in a cornucopia of colors were to decorate hats.

A Feather in London's Cap

IN FEBRUARY 1911 IN A DUSTY AND COLD AUCTION HOUSE IN MINCING LANE IN THE EAST End of London, close to the Victoria and Albert Docks on the River Thames into which a plethora of foreign imports arrived daily, buyers gathered for a well-advertised sale of exotic goods. Not on this day spices, silks, oriental carpets, perfumes, porcelain, or tobacco from distant parts of the world. This was a very different auction.

The pungent smell of naphthalene—mothballs—permeated the whole place. The mothballs had been packed in with enormous quantities of loose feathers and the feather-covered skins of whole birds to prevent insect attacks on this precious booty over their often lengthy journeys by ship in wooden crates. Many had arrived from the most far-flung parts of the world, from the Caribbean, New Guinea, South America, even Australia. They were laid out in neat sections, each lot of feathers or dead birds separated by chalked wooden boards according to their source and quality.

Over many years, London had gradually cornered the international feather market, and buyers came from across Europe and from the United States to view and buy the stock. No one from outside the feather trade was allowed inside the auction house's many floors; identities were always checked. Prying eyes were not encouraged, maybe because the quantity of bird parts on show might have alarmed the public.

At its peak at the end of the nineteenth century it was a trade worth £20 million a year to Britain, around £2.5 billion today. That month, four dealers—Figgis & Co., Lewis & Peat, Hale & Sons, and Dalton & Young—were selling feathers. International interest in what was on offer was intense. Buyers had been given two days in which they could inspect the stock on offer prior to the sale.[1]

Here were nearly 25,000 tiny, delicate hummingbird skins, the skins of well over 6,000 flamboyantly colored birds of paradise, 2,600 eagle skins, and over 6,000 ounces of egret head plumes (aigrettes). There were other bird skins or parceled up lots of individual feathers too: herons, condors (birds of prey related to vultures and found in the western United States and the west of South America), bustards (large ground birds probably killed in Africa or India), and highly colorful trogons from South America shimmering in bright green, yellow, and scarlet.

Not that this February sale was at all unusual. A sale in May of the same year provided buyers with another 7,000 birds of paradise and 6,000 hummingbird skins imported from New Guinea and the Americas respectively. The May auction included some birds not offered in February: skins of scarlet ibis (*Eudocimus ruber*); junglefowl, the wild forebears of domestic chickens; 1,700 parrot skins; 1,500 skins of falcons and hawks; 1,000 skins of golden pheasants from Southeast Asia; and numerous heads of crowned pigeons, four species of which from New Guinea have elaborate feather head crests. The quantities arriving by ship were huge; in 1811, for example, no less than six hundred tons of bird skins and feathers had been detained in a single shipload during a workers' strike at the London ports.[2]

By the early 1900s, auctions were held increasingly regularly: quarterly had given way to bimonthly and then monthly; sometimes they could even be held every fortnight such was the demand by milliners for whole birds, their wings, and their feathers to decorate ladies' hats. Much of what was sold was re-exported to New York, Berlin, Vienna, and Paris where it would be processed under sweatshop conditions into the hat decorations that increasing numbers of ladies desired and could afford.[3]

W. H. Hudson (1841–1922), the author, naturalist, and leading British ornithologist of his day who became involved in early attempts to secure bird protection legislation, recoiled with horror as he witnessed the sale of 80,000 parrot and 1,700 bird of paradise skins late in 1897. "Spread out in Trafalgar Square they would have covered a large proportion of that space with a grass-green carpet, flecked with vivid purple, rose and scarlet," he commented.[4]

One London dealer warned New Zealand ornithologist Walter Buller in 1880 that he would accept no more New Zealand birds because he already had 385 kakapos (*Strigops habroptilus*), (a ground-dwelling parrot today critically endangered) and 90 little spotted kiwis (*Apteryx owenii*) in stock. In records of London auctions in 1908, the list included 180 lyrebird tails taken from the superb lyrebird (*Menura novaehollandiae*) of southeastern Australia.[5] So it was that whole lyrebird tails were shipped in numbers (though there are no records of how many) to the London auctions. They were incredibly popular; fashionable ladies found them irresistible.[6]

William Hornaday (1854–1937), the American zoologist, conservationist, taxidermist, and author, made a list of the species of birds being killed around the world and shipped to London feather sales. It includes nine birds of paradise, five species of pheasant including impeyan pheasants (*Lophophorus impejanus*) whose iridescent blue and green crest feather was used on men's hats, "all" species of terns and gulls, albatrosses, kingfishers, even common starlings (*Sturnus vulgaris*) and many more;[7] several cannot be identified because of the unusual names being used by the feather trade. White-throated kingfishers (*Halcyon smyrnensis*), large, cobalt-blue, chestnut, and white kingfishers found across the Indian subcontinent and much of Southeast Asia, were particularly popular. Tens of thousands were netted, killed, and their skins exported, mostly through London auctions. There are reports by a British ornithologist, Mr. H. A. Macpherson, of "Indian fowlers clearing five or six miles of kingfisher river in a single morning."[8]

Particularly valuable and sought after were the immensely attractive, lacy white breeding nape plumes from egrets, no species of which inhabited Britain in the nineteenth and twentieth centuries. It gave them an even more exotic appeal. In an analogous killing spree to that of snowy egrets in wetlands and coastal regions across the United States and spurred on by ladies' demand for the most impressive feathers to decorate their hats, little egrets and great white egrets were decimated across much of southern Europe and southern Asia.

As early as the seventeenth century, Francis Willughby (1635–1672), the well-traveled and eminent English ornithologist and ichthyologist, had written of egret plumes used "in caps and head pieces for ornament, and which are sold very dear in the cities subject to the Turk." Killed in India (then ruled by the English Crown) and exported to London, in 1914 one ounce of egret feathers was trading at up to twenty-eight times the value of an ounce of silver. Once in Britain, they were worth around £15 an ounce, over £1,700 at today's prices (see plate 13).[9]

One response to the lucrative trade was the creation in India—mainly in Sind Province though more widely across parts of Southeast Asia later—of egret farms with pens holding between 80 and 120 birds each. The day-to-day management of these farms was carried out by the Mirbahars, the peoples of the inland waters of the area who lived mainly by fishing and catching wildfowl. The Mirbahars already had relevant experience: they kept herons in captivity as decoys to attract wildfowl into their nets.[10]

Observers recorded that the egrets were kept in good conditions and were well fed. By removing laid eggs and hand rearing the hatched youngsters, the birds would re-lay, and the farmers could get four or five broods of egrets per season. Each adult had its springtime nuptial feathers plucked without being killed, and each yielded less than half an ounce of the long, gossamer white plumes. It was easy money; by the end of the nineteenth century, egret farming had largely replaced the slaughter of wild birds. Some of these egret farms operated until 1930 or even later.[11]

But milliners required the best plumes for their most affluent clientele, and farm-raised plumes seemingly were not good enough to attract the highest prices. Wild egrets produced the most pristine feather plumes, not birds crammed in pens. So snaring the birds in the wild, or shooting them in their communal tree breeding colonies—just like the horrendous killing sprees of snowy egrets in the United States—was preferable. It was particularly prevalent in Burma (Myanmar today), Malaysia, and Indonesia. Killing also started up in parts of China and ravaged egret colonies there in spite of these stately birds enjoying local respect for centuries. Money was to be made, and greed outweighed tradition. In Australia and the West Pacific, Japanese hunters exploited egret colonies mercilessly too.[12]

In the first quarter of 1885 alone, a total of 750,000 egret skins were sold at London auctions, and in 1887 a single London dealer handled two million of them.[13] A commodity for sale just like oriental spices or rugs, presumably no one much cared whether they were the plumes of the great white or little egret; they weren't differentiated at feather auctions. Profit was all that mattered, and quality was the guarantor of that.

There was concern in some parts of India about the numbers of wild birds being killed and shipped to Britain (India was under British colonial rule until 1947), especially small, insect-eating species such as flycatchers and minivets that were thought to be useful for devouring agricultural insect pests. Sir Herbert Maxwell (1845–1937), a Conservative MP, novelist, antiquarian, and much else, writing in 1896, was of the opinion that

> rather than wear the wings and heads, it would be more flattering if, assuming it to be necessary for ladies to display the spoils of animated nature in their attire, they should adopt the fashion of wearing the carcasses of rats, mice and other furred marauders on their heads.[14]

A series of Wild Birds Protection Acts that became law in the United Kingdom between 1872 and 1896 empowered local governments in India to regulate the possession and sale of plumage from wild birds. It led to a total prohibition of the trade in 1902. Nevertheless, the legislation was enforced piecemeal, and an illicit plumage trade flourished because of considerable corruption by local officials. Plumage from egrets and small Indian birds was sold openly in the London auctions in considerable quantities.[15] No less than thirty-two different Indian bird species were traded. Charles Downham, appearing before a House of Lords Select Committee in the British Parliament on 24 June 1908, pointed out that over fifteen thousand parrot skins from India had been sold at the London auctions in June the previous year despite the prohibition.

George Reid, a British ornithologist living in India, wrote in 1887:

The Crested Grebe (wintering in India) is another bird that has become exceeding rare in localities where formerly it was very abundant. Slaughtered wholesale and systematically for the sake of its beautiful skin, we now seldom see its silvery-white breast glistening in the sun. Slowly, but surely, too, our beautiful White Herons and Egrets are sharing a similar fate. A price has been put upon their feathery snow-white plumes, and man must needs debase his manhood by pandering to the insatiable vagaries or depravities of fashion.

If I have written strongly it is because I feel strongly on a subject that requires immediate attention. The destruction not only of Grebe, Herons, Egrets, Pheasants, &c, but of beautiful small birds of every description, is going on apace, and while the depredators are reaping a rich harvest by pilfering the nation's property—its game birds and the beautiful songsters of its woods and fields—those who ought to protect them by holding aloof are simply participating in their destruction. This state of affairs can only lead to extermination.[16]

There was even more shocking commentary, this by a Mr. P. T. L. Dodsworth, another British ornithologist living in India, who wrote in 1910:

From all parts of the country came the same cries of destruction and diminution, which amounted to virtual extermination. Of Impeyan and Argus pheasants throughout the Himalaya, of Peacocks and Black Partridges from Bombay, of Egrets from Sind and Burma and of a host of others including Jungle-cocks, Paddy-birds, Kingfishers, Jays and Orioles throughout India generally. So lucrative was the trade that single districts such as Lucknow in the United Provinces, and Amritsar in the Punjab contributed between them nearly 16,000 Lbs. of plumage annually. Taking as an average 30 skins to the pound, the figures indicated the destruction of nearly five hundred thousand birds in a single year from two districts alone! From Bombay it was reported that a single Railway Station to the north of Sind had exported within a few months 30,000 skins of Black Partridges, and that over many square miles in the Rohri Division these birds had, within two seasons, been absolutely exterminated by a single party of professional trappers. Various other reports showed that birds were netted and trapped, not by thousands, but by millions, without any regard to season or sex.[17]

Dodsworth goes on to state:

As this prohibition [the 1902 ban on exports] was issued without notice or warning, a large number of representations were received, notably from a trader in Simla, who had in stock skins of Impeyans and black Argus to the value of Kb. 6,000, and from two firms in Calcutta who had in hand 6,000 skins of Impeyan and Argus pheasants, and six cases of Kingfishers' feathers, and to enable them to dispose of their stocks, and to wind up their businesses, the operation of the orders was suspended until the 1st January 1903.

James Buckland, a British writer, ornithologist, and activist who played a central role in promoting bird protection, added a critique of feather dealers encouraged by the trade. In 1914 he wrote:

As an object lesson on the respect which the feather-dealer pays to the wishes of India—or of any other country, for the matter of that—that she may be allowed to keep her own birds for the benefit of her agriculture and of her people, it may serve a useful purpose to let you know that the plumage of all that

COLOR PLATE 1. A ruby topaz hummingbird, one of the millions of hummingbirds from South America that ended their lives perched on hats (Charles J. Sharp).

COLOR PLATE 2. The height of Edwardian fashion: a velvet hat with a whole lesser bird of paradise to decorate it (Pacific Grove Museum of Natural History, California).

COLOR PLATE 3. Ötzi's bearskin hat, over five thousand years old and made from pieces of brown bear pelt, is the oldest physical hat in existence (South Tyrol Museum of Archaeology; photo by Harald Wisthaler).

COLOR PLATE 4. Said to be the headdress of Motecuhzoma II, but probably worn by a high-ranking military officer, it contains feathers from an array of exotic birds including the green and scarlet resplendent quetzal (Thomas Ledl).

COLOR PLATE 5. Roach headdress worn by Sharitarish (Wicked Chief), Pawnee tribe, painted by Charles Bird King about 1822. More common than the better-known war bonnets of the Plains tribes, these headdresses were made of stiff animal hair from porcupine, moose, and deer attached to a leather base (The White House Collection, Washington, DC).

COLOR PLATE 6. Traditional felt hat making; marking the extent of the brim (Carles Marti).

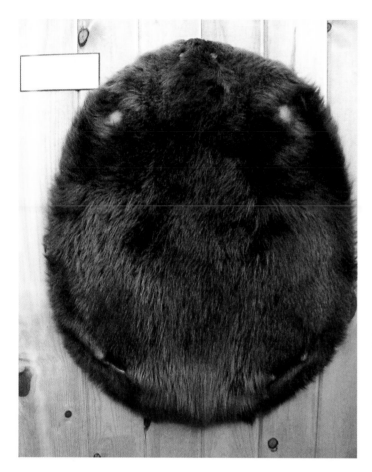

COLOR PLATE 7. North American beaver pelt at the Museum of the Fur Trade, Chadron, Nebraska. Millions were trapped and killed for hat felt making (courtesy of Napa).

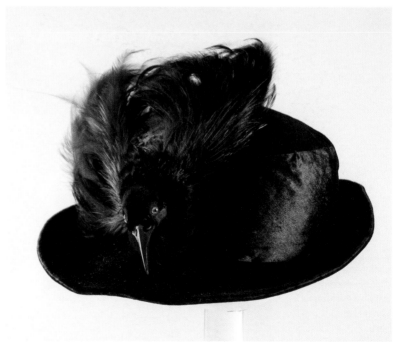

COLOR PLATE 8. A velvet mourning hat with a whole bird of paradise dyed black, dated ca. 1914–1920 (© Amgueddfa Cymru–National Museum Wales).

COLOR PLATE 9. Welsh Guards wearing their traditional bearskins made from black bears hunted in North America and identifiable to regiment by their white and green feather hackle (Ronnie Macdonald).

COLOR PLATE 10. An array of sable pelts for sale in Milan. Forest-dwelling mustelids related to stoats, they are abundant across much of northern Russia where huge numbers are trapped (Kuerschner).

COLOR PLATE 11. Tricorn hat made of beaver fur, ca. 1780. Popular through the eighteenth century, they were usually referred to as "cocked hats" (Los Angeles County Museum of Art; LACMA Image Library).

COLOR PLATE 12. The use of the ear frill feathers of breeding great crested grebe, called "tippit" by milliners, led to their near extinction in Britain (Bengt Nyman).

COLOR PLATE 13. Last survivor of London's massive international feather trade: Plumage House, the former premises of feather merchants H. Bestimt & Co. Ltd., 2018.

COLOR PLATE 14. Marie Antoinette and her children at the Palace of Versailles by Élisabeth Vigée Lebrun, 1787. Her hat is embellished with white and red-dyed ostrich plumes and other cut feathers (photographer unknown).

COLOR PLATE 15. Black-legged kittiwake with chicks at a typical sea-cliff breeding site, Farne Islands, UK. Young birds' black W-marking on near-white wings were popular hat decorations (Darrel Birkett).

COLOR PLATE 16. A female northern flicker, Seedskadee National Wildlife Refuge, Wyoming, one of hundreds of small bird species exploited for hat decor (Tom Koerner/ USFWS).

COLOR PLATE 17. Snowy egret showing their extravagant nuptial plumes with young birds in the nest, St. Augustine, Florida. Almost all U.S. breeding colonies were extirpated to obtain the impressive plumes of the breeding adults. The young were left to perish (Ke Wu).

COLOR PLATE 18. Northern raccoon showing its formidable tree-climbing skills, Lower Klamath National Wildlife Refuge, California/Oregon (David Menke).

COLOR PLATE 19. The "Davy Crockett" hat, made entirely of a northern raccoon pelt and its tail, worn by Fess Parker in the 1950s five-part TV series (Division of Culture and the Arts, National Museum of American History, Smithsonian Institution).

COLOR PLATE 20. Made in the mid-1930s by Lucienne Rabaté for the House of Reboux, Paris, this hat is constructed entirely of Himalayan monal pheasant feathers on a silk base (V&A Galleries).

COLOR PLATE 21. North African ostrich, Chay Bar Yotvata, Israel, showing the especially popular white plumes on its vestigial wings. The species was extirpated across much of its range by hat decoration (Math Knight).

COLOR PLATE 22. Corsac fox showing its pale, sandy-colored pelage much sought after by hunters for the quality and light color of its fur (Wim Stam).

COLOR PLATE 23. Sea otter in Morro Bay, California, a mammal brought to the edge of extinction across its northern range by voracious hunting for its particularly dense fur (Marshal Hedin).

COLOR PLATE 24. "Snow White": a hat of guinea fowl, goose, and ostrich feathers designed and made by Ellen Christine Couture, New York (photo by Tom Bloom).

COLOR PLATE 25. A hat decorated entirely with dyed cockerel/rooster feathers designed by Philip Treacy, London, Autumn/ Winter 2017, one of the millinery industry's proponents of the continued use of feathers and a leading British hat designer (photo by Kurtiss Lloyd).

COLOR PLATE 26. Highland piper wearing a traditional feather bonnet made of black ostrich feathers and a red-dyed feather hackle, all mounted on a hidden wire frame (USAF Staff Sergeant Stephanie Mancha).

COLOR PLATE 27. A *shtreimel* worn by Hasidic Jews is made entirely of numerous tails of martens, fishers, sables, or other similar small mammals (Adobe Stock Images).

is held most sacred in Hindu mythology, all that is most prized for beauty or utility, in the wild-bird life of India, is, to this hour, smuggled out of that country and sold in the London feather mart.[18]

The trade in bird of paradise skins, which had begun commercially in the 1880s, continued until 1924. Of the many species inhabiting the extensive New Guinea Forests, four were the most commonly killed: the greater bird of paradise, lesser bird of paradise, red bird of paradise (*P. rubra*), and Raggiana bird of paradise (*P. raggiana*). But several other species were killed too. Their skins were shipped back to London and fetched high prices in the auction rooms. During the first decade of the twentieth century, hundreds of thousands of birds of paradise skins were exported from New Guinea, as many as eighty thousand a year reaching Europe; most went through the London auctions. Individual buyers would purchase five or six thousand skins at a time.[19]

Conservationists began to express growing concern about the impact on these exquisite species, but others such as Ernst Mayr (1904–2005), one of the twentieth century's leading biologists, discounted claims of permanent harm because of the vast extent of New Guinea's rainforest and because it was only the older, well-plumaged males that were being shot for their feathers. That left young males and all females unharmed.[20]

Between 1872 and 1920 the major source countries or regions for feathers coming into the London feather markets were scattered worldwide. They included India, the British East Indies (Southeast Asia excluding India), much of South and Central America, Egypt, the United States, plus France and Holland, the last two presumably mainly trans-shipments from some of their colonies in Africa and Southeast Asia including, perhaps, birds of paradise skins via Holland.[21]

Paris was an important source of ornamental plumage imported into London for auction; some of it came from across France itself where a multitude of birds were trapped and shot, but more exotic skins and plumes came via Paris to London from other parts of southern Europe and from the French colonies including parts of modern-day Brazil, the Caribbean, extensive areas of Africa, Southeast Asia, and the Pacific. Hundreds of thousands of small, colorful tropical birds' skins came onto the market: tanagers, honeycreepers, and cotingas from South America including the closely related Andean (*Rupicola peruvianus*) and Guianan cock of the rock (*R. rupicola*) with their vibrant orange plumage and half-moon head crests. Killed by native hunters to supply local dealers, they were shipped to the London auctions by the crate load.[22]

Tiny hummingbirds were particularly sought after; these little gems were skinned, stuffed, and reassembled whole, then fixed—sometimes singly but more often in small groups—onto ladies' hats. Others were used for making feather decorations and for taxidermy displays. With around 330 species, all confined to the Americas, there was enormous choice potentially available, and the European and North American fashion houses became obsessed with them.

The usual way of capturing tiny hummingbirds—still in use today in parts of South America—is to use a long, flexible rod several yards in length with a blob of sticky lime at the end. It is carefully lowered onto the back of a hummingbird as it hovers at a flower, and the bird gets stuck to the rod and is hauled in to be killed. An alternative method employed by local hunters was to kill or stun them using tiny clay pellets shot from a blowpipe.[23] The Caribbean island of Trinidad exported fifteen thousand stuffed hummingbirds of a variety of species every week at the height of the trade in the late nineteenth century. Most would have come through London.[24] At one London sale in 1888, nearly thirty-eight thousand of them were auctioned, and a single delivery from Brazil contained three thousand ruby topaz hummingbird (*Chrysolampis mosquitus*) skins.

Many of the species collected probably suffered near extinction in the regions where collections were most concentrated.[25]

Between 1881 and 1890, over 5.5 million pounds' weight of feathers from all wild bird species—excluding ostrich, which by that time were almost all from farmed birds—were imported into London. The quantities increased up until the 1901–1910 decade by which time the total weight had doubled to 10 million pounds. According to these figures, which Professor Robin Doughty extracted from UK Board of Trade and UK Customs Office statistics, nearly 40 million pounds' weight (over eighteen thousand tonnes) of ornamental plumage and whole bird skins, excluding ostrich feathers, was imported into the United Kingdom between 1870 and 1920. It represents what Doughty referred to as "scores of millions of birds killed all over the world."[26]

Ostrich plumes remained an important component of the sales. By about 1750, they had become de rigueur for English ladies attending the British royal court. The flamboyant use of ostrich plumes as a fashionable millinery adornment was popularized in Britain by Georgiana Cavendish, Duchess of Devonshire (1757–1806), a well-known socialite, style icon, and activist in her day.[27] The duchess started the craze by attaching an arc of ostrich feathers to her hair, but that soon escalated into increasingly elaborate displays. Widely adopted by well-to-do ladies, the creations worn by the duchess were padded with horsehair piled up to three feet high culminating in an arrangement of stuffed exotic birds and ostrich feathers. She was the English equivalent of Marie Antoinette.

There was, though, much public criticism of such flamboyant ostentation. Queen Charlotte (1744–1818), wife of George III, banned such hats at court, but the demand for ostrich feathers still continued until at least the early years of the twentieth century. Nor did the court ban survive. The lord chamberlain, the official in charge of the British royal household, intervened in 1878 to declare that colored feathers were prohibited at court; white plumes were acceptable, and black feathers were permitted for mourning. The lord chamberlain's "Dress and Insignia Worn at Court," produced in 1937 and still in use today, allows ostrich feathers to be worn as part of formal court dress.

For centuries, attendance at formal ceremonies and gatherings of the royal court had been essential for politicians and anyone seeking social advancement. Surprisingly perhaps, displaying ostrich plumes did run risks: "Charge the dear girls not to have their feathers too long or too forward as to brush the royal cheek as they rise," commented Fanny Burney (1752–1840), the English satirical novelist, diarist, and playwright.[28]

The amounts of feathers imported from ostriches farmed in the Cape and auctioned in London were prodigious. In 1893, Britain imported nearly £475,000 worth of ostrich feathers; by 1912 that had risen to £2.2 million (£249 million today). That was nearly three times the amount imported by France and nearly five times that imported into Germany. A good proportion of the ostrich feathers auctioned in London were re-exported to the United States, though many were bought up by milliners in Britain.[29]

The ostrich feather had proved to be an enduring and potent mark of social distinction in elite British circles for at least two centuries. Maybe it was because the wearer was elevated into a world of conspicuous consumption and leisure, or because of its sheer impracticality and hint of outrageousness. The rigid dress code of the English royal court determined who was, and who was not, part of "good" English society and thereby eligible for presentation. For ladies, it was apparently signaled by a pom-pom of ostrich feathers.

Fashions changed, and World War I intervened; the use of ostrich feathers for hat decoration was largely abandoned by the 1920s, though there were exceptions for royal court attendance and for attending Royal Ascot horse racing. A number of feather dealers in South Africa went into liquidation, but the Union of South Africa, formed in 1910, was, after all, a British dominion, so buying their ostrich feathers was seen as a patriotic duty. Nevertheless, the market had slumped, and most of the feathers had to be sold off cheaply to make far less glamorous feather dusters.

The tradition in the British Army—and in the armies of several Commonwealth countries—of wearing a hackle, a small clipped plume of feathers attached to a military headdress, has a long history. It has its origins in a much longer plume, usually of ostrich, and originally referred to by its Scottish name, the *heckle*. The heckle was attached to the feather bonnet worn by Scottish Highland regiments between the mid-eighteenth century and World War I. The feather bonnet (worn today only by pipers, bandsmen, and drummers), which itself was derived from an original woolen bonnet, was initially decorated with a few ostrich plumes, dyed black, before becoming a full feather covering supported by a lightweight internal wire cage to provide its structure and to give some head protection against sword cuts in battle. The heckle or hackle of clipped feathers, dyed in a different color, was then attached to the side of the bonnet.

Surprisingly, it seems probable that this feathered version of the Highland bonnet developed because of the influence of indigenous Americans when regiments were stationed on the North American continent between 1760 and 1790. Highland regiments remaining in Scotland at this time did not have their bonnets modified to provide the full feather covering.[30]

With ostrich farming not starting until at least the mid-1800s, ostrich feathers for the bonnets, both for their structure and for the heckle, must have been derived originally from wild-caught birds, almost certainly contributing significantly to their demise across North Africa and the Middle East. Presumably, the feathers were purchased through the London auction houses by the specialist milliners who made regimental bonnets.

"Historically, the feathers used to make hackles depended on the rank of the soldier, his regiment and the period of time," says Louis Chalmers of the Plumery who manufacture horsehair, feather, and military plumes today. "Officers' hackles were usually of ostrich, swan or egret; other ranks were usually of chicken feathers."[31] Most are dyed in particular colors depending on the regiment. In today's British Army, for instance, the Royal Regiment of Fusiliers has a red and white hackle; the Royal Welsh wear a white hackle; while the Argyll and Sutherland Highlanders wear a green hackle.

But the majority of feathers would have ended up atop vast numbers of ladies' heads. Some would have been used to make a delicate panache or a flurry of plumes; other hats would have been decorated with a whole wing or a pair of wings, of parrots or seabirds maybe. Some would have been endowed with a whole bird, a bird of paradise perhaps. Inexplicably, whole owl heads with staring glass eyes were popular in the late 1880s. And others would have had a group of miniscule hummingbirds together with some artificial flowers, a pathetic, wired reconstruction of some unlikely family gathering of these tiny, delicate creatures poised in death yet seemingly about to hover at a flower.

Delicate feather decorations swayed tantalizingly with every movement the wearer made and were the perfect fashion accessory to achieve the desired look of dignified pride, delicate vulnerability, and, of course, purchasing power. The hat itself had become a comparatively minor part of the fashionable head covering. It was "simply an excuse for a feather, a pretext for a spray of flowers, the support for an aigrette, the fastening for a plume … of feathers," wrote Charles Blanc (1813–1882), the French art critic.[32]

Bird plumage could be made into eight basic forms for an average lady's hat. The larger plumes of ostrich, herons, egrets, and others could be made into flamboyant sprays used to give hats some height. Padding inside hats to provide "body" usually came from cheaper feathers such as those of chickens and pheasants. Wings, breasts, pompons, and quills came from a range of birds, particularly brightly colored ones. And many birds were dismembered and reassembled in striking, not always very natural, poses.[33]

One particularly colorful bird is strangely missing from the list of those whose feathers were desired to decorate ladies' hats: the flamingo. All five species in the world have varying amounts of pink and near crimson plumage with black flight feathers, ideal, you might assume, for a well-dressed lady's hat. But their pink coloration is rather transitory; it derives from carotenoid pigments synthesized by algae and other minute organisms that flamingoes consume in vast numbers, either directly or indirectly via the invertebrates that feed on them. But once shed, flamingo feathers quickly lose their pigment-acquired color.[34] Early plume hunters must have found this out much to their chagrin; it was the luckiest break ever for flamingoes.

The desire to be fashionable led millions of women to milliners to purchase something elegant, eye-catching, even coquettish. Feathers were costly, whole exotic birds much more so, but living standards were improving and were gradually proving less and less of a barrier to decorated hat purchases by nearly all strands of society. The more costly looking the plumes, wings, or whole birds, the more that elegant ladies demanded them by the crate load, stimulating the killing spree across much of the globe with no consideration whatsoever for the fate of the sources of their head décor. In the last decade of the nineteenth century almost every lady's hat could boast a pair of wings of doves, blackbirds, swallows, birds of paradise, or seabirds.

The information from the London feather auctions does not include any details about the species of birds shipped, but from what we know of the wide range of countries and regions from which they were obtained, it almost certainly included a very wide selection. Not all of these feathers would have been used to decorate hats; some would have been used to embellish other items of clothing including gowns, capes, boas, and muffs or for decorating fans and parasols.

Some families of birds, though very rarely individual species, are mentioned by name.[35] They include thirty-nine sales between 1897 and 1911 that offered in total well over a million herons and egrets; three sales in 1908 that included a total of 51,200 sooty terns (*Chlidonias niger*), a tropical seabird; two sales in 1907 selling the tails of 180 lyrebirds; three other sales with 50,000 kingfishers and eight with 152,000 hummingbirds.

A note in *The Auk* of 1888 summarized the content of one auction held by Hale & Son, a dealer in Mincing Lane, London, on 21 March of that year:[36]

> Birds' skins, wings, plumes and feathers representing in the aggregate more birds than are contained in all the ornithological collections of this country . . . in other words hundreds of thousands in this single auction sale! Under the heading of various bird skins we figure up between 7,000 and 8,000 parrots shipped mainly from Bombay and Calcutta, but including some from South America, about 1,000 Impeyan and 500 Argus Pheasants; about 1,000 woodpeckers; 1,450 penguins, maybe auks and grebes; some 14,000 grouse, quails and partridges; about 4,000 snipes and plovers; about 7,000 starlings, jays and magpies; over 12,000 hummingbirds; about 5,000 tanagers; 4,000 Blue Creepers and 1,500 other creepers [perhaps honeycreepers] several hundred each of hawks, owls, gulls, terns, ducks, ibises, finches, orioles, larks, toucans, birds of paradise etc.[37]

The passage concluded:

last year the trade in birds for womens' hats was so enormous that a single London dealer admitted that he had sold 2,000,000 small birds of every kind and color. In one auction . . . were sold 6,000 birds of paradise, 5,000 impeyan pheasants, 400,000 hummingbirds and other birds from North and South America, and 360,000 feathered skins from India.

Auction houses and dealers probably only had a limited knowledge of what birds' skins and feathers they were dealing in. While ostrich plumes, aigrettes (the nape plumes of egrets), pheasants, and several other birds would have been very familiar to them—and easily identified—many others, especially small birds, would only have been identified, perhaps at best, by family such as hummingbirds or birds of paradise. The dealers probably cared even less what the birds were; provided the skins and their feathers were colorful and got sold, would they be bothered to find out what particular species they were dealing in, how they were obtained, or what implications their trade had for the survival of the species concerned?

Hummingbirds, that "flash of harmless lightning, a mist of rainbow dyes, the burnished sunbeams brightening from flower to flower," as the American poet and priest John Tabb (1845–1909) described them, were far too beautiful to be disregarded by the millinery trade. So it was that 605,000 skins of these tiny sunbeams passed through the London auction houses between about 1887 and 1911. Large quantities probably passed through auctions in other centers, too, New York in particular.[38] Some estimates put the total kill in the millions; some species were doubtless hunted to extinction by the trade, first described from collected skins and never seen again.[39] Fashion, as ever, was fickle. Hummingbirds on a lady's hat were the height of chic in the late nineteenth century. Within a couple of decades they were not wanted. The fashion craze was over, and these tiny jewels that assault existence with improbability could hardly find buyers at a farthing apiece in London auctions in 1912.[40]

At the opposite end of the size spectrum, feathers and whole wings of albatrosses—some of the largest birds in the world—had become a hat fashion accessory too. Historically harvested for food and feathers by indigenous peoples on islands across the southern oceans where they breed on open ground, by the late nineteenth century they had become yet another valuable commodity to kill and trade. Rather trusting of humans when they are breeding, and particularly clumsy birds on land, most albatrosses could all too easily be clubbed to death where they stood. A century after Tristan da Cunha, the most isolated island in the world located in the South Atlantic, was settled by the British in 1817, its large colony of Tristan albatrosses (*Diomedea dabbenena*) had been killed off. They have never returned. Other species were exploited too. Killed for food, their eggs were eaten, and their down feathers often used to stuff mattresses. Their wings and other feathers were traded for millinery use, most ending up in the auction houses of Paris and London.

The Japanese also began to recognize the business potential of albatrosses. Supervised and funded by the Tokyo-based South Seas Trading Company, hunters landed in 1887 on the island of Torishima, one of the southern Izu Islands south of Japan. It was the main breeding island for the short-tailed albatross (*Phoebastria albatrus*). Between then and 1903, they killed an estimated five million of the birds. Ten other islands were used for breeding by this huge seabird; it was exterminated from them all.[41] Most of the plumage was exported to the west, probably mainly through London and other European centers; while the down, marketed as "swansdown," was used for stuffing pillows and quilts, the wing and tail feathers were sold as "eagle" feathers for hats and other clothing ornamentation.

The same wanton destruction took place on other ocean islands, wiping out whole breeding colonies of Laysan (*Phoebastria immutabilis*) and black-footed albatrosses (*P. nigripes*) for the same markets. A party of twenty-three Japanese feather hunters wiped out around three hundred thousand albatrosses on Laysan Island and Lisianski Island west of Hawaii in nine months between 1909 and 1910. Their methods were particularly brutal. The wings and feathers were shipped to Europe and the United States via Japan. Contemporary reports refer to huge heaps of dead, rotting birds.[42]

By no means all of the feathers traded in the London auction houses were obtained from exotic birds killed in faraway countries. Many were obtained from British birds such as the great crested grebe, an elegant, medium-sized bird commonly to be seen on lakes and other water bodies (see plate 12).[43] Unfortunately for the grebe, it has a particularly elaborate courtship display when both sexes develop a corolla of elongated black and chestnut feathers around their head and neck like a pair of exaggerated ears. These ear-like frills were known in the millinery trade as "tippit" and were valued for decorating ladies' hats.

Grebes' lakeside nests were not difficult to find, and grebe eggs were taken regularly for eating, but until at least the mid-nineteenth century no one in Britain seems to have considered shooting them for their feathers. That is rather strange because, until then, grebe skins were imported from central and southern Europe where they were also common.[44]

The starting gun for the British slaughter of great crested grebes was fired in 1851, rather by accident and because of a letter written by a landowner, Richard Strangwayes, to the academic journal *The Zoologist*. In it he described the ease with which he had shot twenty-nine grebes and had noticed that the birds' breast feathers were "a fashionable and beautiful substitute for furs."[45] Robert Clarke & Sons, furriers in London, exhibited some of the pelts from the grebes shot by Strangwayes at the Great Exhibition held in London that year, and interest in them took off. While the soft and fur-like breast feathers—known as "grebe fur" in the trade—were used to line ladies' boas, hats, and muffs, the "tippit" was used to decorate hats.[46]

From being a common bird, within nine years there were just forty-two breeding pairs surviving in Britain, all of them inhabiting the most inaccessible lakes.[47] Largely stimulated by the demise of this elegant, easily recognized, and popular bird, legislation was enacted in Britain between 1870 and 1880 to safeguard water bird populations from hunting. By 1880, shooting from March to July was banned in order to protect such birds in the breeding season. But out of the season, hunters still shot grebes, and the demand did not really cease until 1907.[48]

Other British birds were shot and trapped too, though often more for taxidermy than for hat decoration. The common or Eurasian kingfisher (*Alcedo atthis*), a river, lake, and canal hunting bird with a vivid, iridescent blue head and back combined with orange underparts, was an obvious target. Fast flying and small, Eurasian kingfishers don't make easy targets for a gun, so most were caught more easily and without plumage damage by applying a sticky lime to prominent perching twigs on riverbanks or by placing nets along waterside stretches where they were common. Ironically, what limited their use for hats was the nature of the stunning color of these birds. The kingfisher's feather colors are not so much due to pigmentation as to light striking specially modified layers of cells in each feather. Remove individual feathers and much of the intense color fades away; their vivid blue and orange is dulled.[49]

Eurasian jays (*Garrulus glandarius*) were not so lucky. Common woodland and parkland birds in Britain, like all members of the crow family they were heavily persecuted by sportsmen, farmers, and gamekeepers because they were perceived (wrongly) to be killing game birds, attacking smaller farm livestock, and generally being a nuisance. Some were also shot for hat decoration because milliners were attracted by their checkered azure blue and black wing coverts, a small part of this pale cinnamon-colored crow's wings. The same colorful feathers attracted anglers who used them to make artificial flies, a purpose for which they are still used today. But it is unlikely that hat decoration accounted for a substantial proportion of the jays killed throughout the year in Britain.[50]

Many British seabirds, though, attracted a lot of millinery attention. Several species of tern, mainly small, white and pale gray seabirds that nest colonially on seaside shingle, on sand, or on rocky islets close to shore, were especially vulnerable. Their wings, individual feathers, and sometimes whole birds were used to decorate ladies' hats. Information on the numbers killed is lacking, but the millinery trade has been thought to have reduced substantially the breeding populations of species such as roseate tern (*Sterna dougallii*) in the United Kingdom.[51]

Black-legged kittiwakes (*Rissa tridactyla*) were particularly sought after. Ocean-going gulls, kittiwakes only come ashore to breed in summer on the ledges of high sea cliffs. Light gray in color, their first-year youngsters have a characteristic black, W-shaped marking on the upper side of their otherwise almost white wings (see plate 15). Unfortunately for the kittiwake, and rather inexplicably in fashion terms, this patterning appealed to milliners and their clientele. The result? A full scale assault on many of the hapless gull's breeding colonies. The wings of young kittiwakes were going to sit atop ladies' hats. And they did so in substantial numbers starting around 1860. Vertiginous sea cliffs were certainly not going to get in the way of the needs of fashion and milliners' profits.

Persecution of birds breeding on sea cliffs in various parts of Britain had not started with hats. Through the nineteenth century and long before, large numbers of both the birds and their eggs were taken in summer at their sea cliff breeding sites, particularly on some of the Scottish islands and around Flamborough Head, Yorkshire, on the northeast coast of England. Common guillemot, known as common murres in the United States (*Uria aalge*), and razorbill (*Alca torda*) eggs were particularly favored. They were good eating to supplement an often very restricted diet. The local collectors—known as "climmers" around Flamborough Head—were experienced and worked in groups of four, one man being carefully lowered down the four hundred-feet-high sea cliffs on ropes. Shooting "for sport" was also commonplace. Boats were hired to take shooters out to sea off the cliffs where they took potshots at any seabirds flying in and out of their nesting ledges.

While there are claims that specially chartered trains in the late nineteenth century took members of the public to sea cliffs to harvest as many of these young birds as possible, that seems highly improbable. Close to the Flamborough cliffs, the seaside town of Bridlington was exceedingly popular as a holiday resort. Dealers arriving there by train and wanting to obtain kittiwake wings presumably paid the climmers to get the birds for them. It was not a job for rank amateurs. Taking and selling fledgling kittiwakes was a way of extending the short egg-harvesting season (about forty days a year) to bring in more money for the climmers and their families. After years of persecution, kittiwake numbers plummeted, both here and elsewhere. On Lundy Island in the Bristol Channel, for example, the harvest of birds supplied a dedicated cottage industry in the Devon village of Clovelly. There the kittiwakes were decimated.[52]

The *Manchester Guardian* in 1868 reported:

On a strip of coast eighteen miles long near Flamborough Head, 107,250 seabirds were destroyed by "pleasure parties" in four months; 12,000 by men who shoot them for their feathers to adorn women's hats and 79,500 young birds died of starvation in emptied nests. Commander Knocker . . . who reported these facts saw two boats loaded above the gunwales with dead birds, and one party of eight guns killed 1,100 birds in a week.[53]

Not all of these kills would have been of kittiwakes; common guillemots and razorbills would have been shot too. What's odd about this statement is that the kittiwakes shot as they flew away from or into their breeding ledges would have been mostly adult birds. Adult black-legged kittiwakes do not have the sought-after black W-markings on their otherwise pale grey wings. Killing young birds would have to have been concentrated later in the breeding season when the young kittiwakes take to the sea if the aim had been to obtain them for millinery decoration. If the adults were being shot, the *Manchester Guardian's* anonymous correspondent might have assumed, wrongly, that the adult wings were destined for ladies' hats. Alternatively, the shooting might have been merely for entertainment.

With improved access to parts of the British coast provided by new train routes, thousands of seabirds breeding on sea cliffs were shot for "sport," their bodies not even gathered up but left floating on the water. Adults shot in the summer breeding season left starving young birds to die a slow death or to be taken by predators. So many guillemots and razorbills were being shot indiscriminately that the Flamborough Head climmers had to discontinue their egg collecting for several years.[54]

The climmers seemingly practiced a degree of sustainable exploitation to maintain a decent egg harvest year upon year. They left sections of cliff that had been heavily robbed without exploitation for a subsequent year or two so that populations would recover. And they also stopped collecting at a particular time in the summer to allow the kittiwakes and other breeding seabirds to lay a replacement egg. Whether they were as thoughtful when it came to bagging kittiwake youngsters for feather dealers is not recorded.[55]

There are claims that the wings were sometimes torn off the living birds when they were taken from their nests and their bodies thrown into the sea. This abhorrent practice, quoted by many writers, seems to have its origins in a statement by William Yarrell (1784–1856), an English zoologist, bookseller, and naturalist, an expert respected for his precise scientific work and, therefore, unlikely to be prone to exaggeration. He was commenting on the practice at Lundy Island off the Devon coast in southwest England: "In many cases the wings were torn off the wounded birds before they were dead, the mangled victims being tossed back into the water."[56]

It is highly unlikely that a climmer at Flamborough Head—or in a similar high sea cliff location—dangling on a rope a few hundred feet above an often swirling sea, trying to snatch a young kittiwake off a ledge, is going to grapple with a struggling bird the size of a small crow possessing a sharp beak while trying to tear off its wings. More likely, he is going to kill it quickly by breaking its neck and stuff the dead bird into the canvas bag he has tied to him while he tries his luck grabbing more of the birds.

Killing kittiwakes, some other sea birds, and a few terrestrial species was banned in Britain by the Sea Birds Preservation Act of 1869. The act became law thanks to the lobbying of Henry Barnes-Lawrence (1815–1896), rector of the Priory Church in Bridlington, and of a local member of Parliament, Christopher Sykes (1831–1898). The act made it illegal to kill most wild seabirds in their breeding colonies between 1 April and 1 August anywhere in the United Kingdom with the exception of St. Kilda, the remote Scottish Island where the tiny human population still then in existence depended partly on seabirds and their eggs. The problem with the act was that shooting could begin with impunity on 2 August, an ideal time to find young kittiwakes with their W wing markings on the sea close to shore.

The 1869 act ushered in a series of wider bird protection laws; the first Wild Birds Protection Act became law in 1872, followed by others up until 1896. These measures were partial in the protection they gave to British birds but did nothing to stem the enormous trade in bird skins and plumage imported into Britain from all around the world. That would take considerably longer. Seabird egg collecting at Flamborough Head was not stopped until 1954 when yet another, this time more comprehensive, Protection of Birds Act was passed by Parliament. By that time the numbers of breeding birds on these cliffs had been reduced very dramatically in spite of the climmers' claims of sustainable harvesting.

By 1914, continued killing of birds to decorate ladies' hats on the enormous scale of a few years earlier had been substituted by the appalling human carnage of World War I. The outbreak of hostilities cut off the bulk of feather imports into London, a tax imposed by the British government in 1915 on the import of luxury goods included feathers, and the war had precipitated a wholesale fashion reassessment. With so many human deaths, and so many families grieving, it was no longer appropriate to wear flamboyant hats sporting an array of feathers or whole dead birds. Except, that is, for mourning hats, which were in depressingly heavy demand.

Obviously black in color, many of these still had a bird attached. An example held in the St. Fagans National Museum of History near Cardiff, Wales, dated to 1914–1920, is made of black cotton velvet and is topped with the whole stuffed body of a lesser bird of paradise—the male naturally a striking maroon-brown, green, and yellow bird—dyed completely black, including its gorgeous spray of wispy yellow and white flank plumes. One wonders why go to such expensive bother when a crow, already naturally funereal black in color, would have done the job almost as well, minus the flank plumes of course.

Doughty suggests that without the intervention of World War I, the plumage trade might have continued, at least perhaps well into the 1920s.[57] After all, the trade had fought long and hard against any legislation designed to curtail it; it took twelve years of argument before the Importation of Plumage (Prohibition) Act became law in Britain in 1921.

One event that certainly raised the profile of the cruelty and killing inherent in the feather trade occurred in 1906 in the Murray Basin, New South Wales, Australia, just five years after the United Kingdom had granted the country independence. Photographs sent to the UK's Royal Society for the Protection of Birds by Arthur Mattingley (1870–1950), a pioneer of Australian bird photography and a leading ornithologist on the continent, showed an egret colony decimated by plume hunters with a scatter of dead adults and young birds consequently starving in their nests.[58]

The pictures were displayed on billboards and in shop windows in London and in towns across southern England. The amount of cruelty was made obvious to shoppers, businessmen, and anyone else who walked past. The story was circulated in other European countries and the United States; it received a good deal of publicity in Australia itself. The two species involved, both white with impressive, filamentous breeding plumes, were the intermediate egret (*Egretta intermedia*) and the great white egret. The mixed colony had originally numbered about 750 birds; when Mattingley visited it in 1906 it had been reduced by plume hunters to around 150 birds. It was on a subsequent visit later the same year that he found at least 50 dead adults, their nape plumes removed, and more than 200 young egrets dead or dying of starvation in their nests.

The 1921 Importation of Plumage (Prohibition) Act was the death knell for the London feather market. Domesticated goose and pheasant feathers replaced those of egrets and birds of paradise. But the market for exotic feathers had not subsided entirely; some of the more exotic feathers stockpiled by dealers prior to the act were sold off at a loss to dealers in other European countries where there were no similar restrictions on their use for hats. What really curtailed the trade was a sea change in fashions.

Slowly, very slowly, the tide was starting to turn. To quote Winston Churchill in 1942, albeit in a very different context: this is not the end. It is not even the beginning of the end. But it is, perhaps, the end of the beginning. After World War I, public opinion was beginning to mobilize against the death and destruction wrought on birds worldwide by fashion. Change was in the air, and the days of the killing spree of birds for fashionable hats were beginning to be numbered.

An American Tragedy Unfolds

SOMETIME IN 1886, FRANK CHAPMAN (1864–1945), AN ACCOMPLISHED ORNITHOLOGIST
and a pioneering head of the Department of Birds at the American Museum of Natural History,
decided to take two long afternoon walks to record the birds he spotted in what he referred to as
New York's uptown shopping districts. It was not the kind of place in which Chapman normally
sought out birds.

Nevertheless, he found no fewer than forty species: warblers, woodpeckers, some orange- and
black-colored Baltimore orioles (*Icterus galbula*), jays, grebes, even some cinnamon-hued cedar
waxwings (*Bombycilla cedrorum*) and a couple of northern bobwhites (*Colinus virginianus*), a
species of quail, with their grey- and white-scalloped feathers.[1] He noted fifteen delicate, black
and white snow buntings (*Plectrophenax nivalis*), twenty-one northern flickers (*Colaptes auratus*), a species of woodpecker, even a green heron (*Butorides virescens*), a chestnut and glossy
green bird of the swamps.

None of them, of course, were in the sidewalk trees or perched on buildings. What Chapman was looking at were ladies' hats; three-quarters of the seven hundred hats he noted were
decorated with whole stuffed birds, sometimes several on one hat, or adorned with their most
spectacular feathers. He sent his list to the editors of a popular magazine of the day called *Forest
and Stream*,[2] commenting that there was probably a greater array of species to be found but that
"in most cases mutilation rendered identification impossible."[3]

The American feather trade was at its peak, and precious little thought was being given to the
enormous carnage being wrought on the millions of wild birds supplying such assumed millinery
essentials. Ladies' hats were embellished with the most unusual, flamboyant, and colorful feathers, many decorated with several whole small birds. They might sport egret plumes, owl heads,
sparrow wings, and whole hummingbirds; a single hat could feature all of these plus four or five
warblers. The more ostentatious and exotic the better. "That there should be an owl or ostrich
left with a single feather apiece hardly seems possible," wrote a New York reporter for *Harper's
Bazaar* commenting on the 1897 winter hat season. In the late 1890s, entire terns and pheasants
became popular, their heads complete with beak draped over the hat's front brim. "It will be no
surprise to me," a Chicago reporter remarked in 1900, "to see life-sized turkeys or even farmyard
hens on fashionable bonnets."[4]

The late nineteenth century was an era when almost everyone went outdoors with something
covering their head; what was sitting on top of a lady's hat, and how elaborate was its decoration,

provided a quick first impression about the background and class of the wearer. Style dictated that elegant ladies must powder their faces with swansdown puffs, fan themselves with fancy feather plumes, and adorn their hats with splendid, often highly colorful feathers and whole birds.

It was a fashion that had become established in American cities in the 1860s: gentlemen frequently selected fedoras with a feather trim, and ladies' hats became increasingly lavish following in the fashion footsteps of major European cities such as Paris and Berlin. In 1895, *Vogue* magazine announced that "Women, civilized women, new and 'advanced' women, are all bitten with the craze and show no satiety so far."[5] Uncharacteristically, these ostentatious and sometimes gaudy hats were worn at a time when women dressed in extremely constricting clothes: corsets, long heavy skirts, high-neck shirt collars. After all, a woman at the turn of the nineteenth century was prohibited from voting, discouraged from pursuing a career, and expected to devote herself to managing the home. Maybe a bird, or some very obvious parts of one—the exotic, airy plumes of an egret perhaps—adorning a lady's hat embodied the emancipation and mobility out of her reach. Feathers were perhaps more than a gesture toward freedom; birds could fly where they wished. But only living ones.

While feathers had been used for hundreds of years as fashion accessories, especially in Europe, toward the fading years of the nineteenth century and into the early years of the twentieth their use as hat decorations reached its zenith in North America. Bird plumage had been an entirely elite indulgence until fashion went mass market in the era of mail-order catalogs and a growing middle class. By the 1880s, the latest fashions had become more accessible than ever. While garments made of skins and furs were also popular, it was feathers that seemed to capture the style that fashion-conscious American city women desired.

The millinery trade cast about for increasingly exotic feathers and birds; the more unusual and bizarre they were, the more the nineteenth-century fashionistas loved them. They were ravenous for feathers to adorn their hats: the longer, fuller, and fluffier the better. Soon, the huge array of native American birds—around 650 species sporting a multitude of feather colors and sizes—would not provide an exotic enough range. So the U.S. millinery trade started importing the wings and tails of ostriches from Africa, exotic "jungle" pheasant feathers from India, even whole, stuffed birds of paradise from Borneo, much of it purchased in the London feather auctions.

Sometimes a stylish hat might have a pair of birds arranged on its crown—bluebirds maybe—as if frozen in some kind of mating ritual. Another popular decoration was a single stuffed bird fixed to seem as if it was incubating eggs on its nest. The entire bird was used, often mounted on wires and springs that permitted its head and wings to move about as if the pathetic creature was still alive. Some even went as far as having a landscaped scene—a mini habitat—atop their heads replete with a stuffed bird or two. A *Harper's Bazaar* article in 1868 commented on the first "bird-feathered hats" to reach the United States: "A few of the feather and fur bonnets, now so fashionable in Europe, have just been imported. The feathers used are those of the grebe [presumably Great Crested Grebe, from Europe] and pheasant. The white and pearl grey grebes are bound with green, scarlet or blue velvet, while bonnets of dark pheasant's feathers have a fall of brown lace."[6]

The showiest ladies' hats were adorned with plumes, the long, elegant feathers acquired by birds such as egrets when in their breeding plumage, and known in the millinery trade as "aigrettes" (from the French for "egret"). Historically, such plumes, cut short in gathered bunches and often dyed in a particular color (and known as hackles), were attached to the military helmets of certain infantry regiments or to the feather bonnets worn by Scottish Highland regiments. Many marching bands have them attached to their headgear today.

The late nineteenth-century fashion for plumes to adorn ladies' hats stimulated bird killing in the United States on a scale never witnessed before or since. The most desirable plumes came from large wading birds: egrets, herons, and spoonbills. Populations of the western grebe (*Aechmophorus occidentalis*) and the closely related Clark's grebe (*A. clarkia*)—birds of the shallow waters of marshes and lakes where their elaborate, choreographed springtime courtship displays are a joy to watch—were decimated. In California, their killing began in 1886 and persisted for at least fifteen years. Few were left alive.[7]

No birds in the nineteenth century had any legal protection, larger species were relatively easy to shoot on or near their nests, and—unfortunately for the birds—many of them nested colonially in huge so-called rookeries. Ecologist Gary Gray refers to the slaughter of birds for the hat trade in the late 1800s being "so staggering in its dimensions as to be almost inconceivable. If it were somehow possible to catalogue all the abuses, it is unlikely that many could bear to peruse the full account."[8] An 1886 bulletin of the American Ornithologists' Union (AOU) gave an estimate that five million birds were being killed each year in the United States to decorate ladies' hats.[9] No accurate figures exist, but large-scale killing went on from the 1860s to about 1910, a half century of slaughter for fashion.

Large numbers of smaller American birds were being trapped: belted kingfishers (*Megaceryle alcyon*), northern flickers with their handsome, black-scalloped brown plumage (see plate 16), blue jays (*Cyanocitta cristata*), black and white little snow buntings that spend their winter in the United States, even small coastal wading birds like sanderling (*Calidris alba*) and game birds (presumably plucked for eating) such as northern bobwhites. The AOU concluded:

> Among the smaller birds it is naturally the brighter colored species that furnish most of the victims, especially the orioles, tanagers, grosbeaks, cedar waxwings, bluebirds, meadow-larks, and golden winged woodpeckers. Only their conspicuous abundance on hats and bonnets and their greatly decreased numbers attest the slaughter to which they are subjected.[10]

Snowy egrets (*Egretta thula*), as their name makes clear, are as white as freshly fallen snow; graceful small egrets no more than two feet in height, they have yellow feet that contrast with their black legs (see plate 17). They are entrancing to watch as they feed, seeming to spring, run, and dance on golden slippers in the watery shallows they search. Come springtime, these gorgeous birds develop lacy plumes that hang down from their neck and others that form a Mohican ruff on top of their heads. These elegant plumes are designed to attract a mate, and snowies do it in style. Unfortunately for them, these stylish feathers were also their downfall; what might look more impressive on a ladies' hat than a few of these gorgeous, frothy plumes?

Breeding in huge colonies in trees, often mixed in with other species of egret, with herons, and maybe with some burly wood storks (*Mycteria americana*), breeding male snowies display by pointing their long stabbing beaks skyward while raising their newly grown plumes and pumping their heads up and down, calling at the same time. And if all this is not visible and audible enough for a plume hunter to spot, displaying snowies even fly in small circles above their breeding rookeries and tumble down into its trees.

At the time of European settlement in the early 1600s, the land area that became the United States is estimated to have had about 221 million acres of wetland, around 9 percent of its land area. By the mid-1980s barely half remained; there is less still today.[11] Much of it was probably snowy egret habitat. No one knows how many snowies inhabited these original swamps; maybe as many as a million nested across the southern United States alone, especially on the coast where extensive marshes, swamps, and pools dominated parts of the landscape.

Shot on their nests, dead adult egrets were retrieved from the trees or picked up from the ground where they fell, their plumes and most of their other desirable feathers cut off, and their bodies left to rot. Young egrets in the nests, now with no parents to feed them, were simply left to starve and die; they provided a surfeit of food for predators on the lookout for an easy meal. Deserted egret eggs, too, would have fed plenty of nearby crows, vultures, and gulls. Reports of the heads and necks of young, dying egrets hanging out of their nests by the hundred started to spread and cause concern in natural history circles.

An egret plume shoot was a ghastly business, as the prominent professional American conservationist T. Gilbert Pearson (1873–1943)—himself a shooter of egrets for hat plumes in his youth in Florida—recounted after he visited former egret breeding colonies (he knew them as "herons") in central Florida sometime in the 1890s:

> A few miles north of Waldo, our party came upon a little swamp where we had been told Herons bred in numbers. Upon approaching the place the screams of young birds reached our ears. The cause of this soon became apparent by the buzzing of green flies and the heaps of dead Herons festering in the sun, with the back of each bird raw and bleeding. . . . Young Herons had been left by scores in the nests to perish from exposure and starvation.[12]

An egret plume hunter's life was distinctly unpleasant. In an article in the *San Francisco Call* on 3 April 1898, David Bennett (known as "Egret Bennett") of Pomona, California, a professional plume hunter, describes starting his career in 1873 by shooting a dozen egrets to give their plumes to his sisters in New Orleans. Operating in Mexico, Bennett was paid $4,000 ($89,000 today) for egrets in two years at $5 a time (eight hundred egrets). Living conditions were hard. Long hours in a canoe, burning sun by day, mosquito-infested camping, only canned food, and little company. In his twenty-year career he had "cleared out" Central America with his shooting team and was well on his exterminating way in the Gulf of California and the Pacific coast of Mexico before he retired.

He is quoted as saying:

> If you're crafty and quick and accurate you can sometimes bring down several of the scary birds before they get out of range. But a few of 'em pays big. Everywhere in the regions I have been in (mostly Central America and the north of South America) and ever heard about, a rapidly growing scarcity of egrets is evident. We made the birds mighty scarce down there before we were through.[13]

The number of egrets that would have to be shot to provide one pound of plumes must have been substantial, though estimates vary considerably. One great white egret has around forty to fifty aigrette feathers, the long, silky nape plumes that hang down their backs. A pound of these plumes would require perhaps 450 snowy egrets or between 70 and 140 of the larger egret species to be killed.[14] On that basis the thirty-three thousand pounds of egret plumes recorded as being exported from Argentina, Brazil, and Venezuela between 1899 and 1912 represents somewhere around 15 million smaller egrets or between 2.3 million and nearly 5 million larger egret species killed. And these numbers do not, of course, include the huge numbers of eggs and growing chicks that would have perished in the breeding colonies where the adults were shot.

An 1838 New York State law aimed at reducing bird kills by forbidding the use of batteries of guns (rather than individual firearms) to shoot waterfowl had to be repealed because it was so ineffectual. Such was the value of the trade that commercial shooters had taken to wearing masks to conceal their identities while threatening to murder informers who revealed who they were. Plume hunters would shoot out a rookery of several hundred egrets within a couple of days, collecting up all the dead adults, removing their feathers, and dumping their putrefying corpses. The valuable plumes would be sold through markets in New York or exported to London and Paris. Before the nineteenth century drew to a close, all of the known snowy egret rookeries across the southern United States were devoid of any birds.[15]

Rather like their snowy cousins, much larger great white egrets—standing up to three feet tall—and equally adorned in their breeding plumage with long nape and back plumes that trail below their stubby tails, were hunted avidly too. Reddish egrets (*Egretta rufescens*) with their slate blue plumage and rusty red head and neck—in summer covered in shaggy rufous plumes—and even more exotic roseate spoonbills (*Platalea ajaja*) with their vibrant pink and white plumage were also sought out at their breeding rookeries along the southern U.S. coasts. The birds quickly vanished.

William Scott (1852–1910), a prominent U.S. ornithologist, sailed along parts of the west Florida coast in the spring of 1886 to check out a number of mangrove-dominated keys that he had known previously to hold huge numbers of breeding water birds including egrets and spoonbills.[16] Where he had seen thousands of egrets, storks, and spoonbills on his previous visit six years earlier, few remained. Some rookeries had been completely cleared of breeding birds. He saw a freshly slaughtered colony of over two hundred reddish egrets, great white egrets, tricolored herons (*Egretta tricolor*), and little blue herons (*Egretta caerulea*). Their impressive breeding nape plumes had been cut off; some had their wings removed. Their bodies were left to rot. Scott summarized his feelings like this:

> It would be difficult for me to find words adequate to express not only my amazement but also the increasing horror that grew on me day after day as I sailed southward. The great Maximo rookery at the mouth of Tampa Bay was no longer a rookery; it was a deserted mangrove island.[17]

Although they were shot mainly for their meat and their soft down feathers that were used to fill pillows and bed coverings, and to make face powder puffs, trumpeter swan (*Cygnus buccinators*) feathers were also used to adorn hats. From the early nineteenth century, their killing was at a peak and encouraged by the Hudson's Bay Company who were responsible for many thousands of these huge, northerly breeding birds meeting their end. By the early twentieth century, trumpeters were on the verge of extinction. Less than a hundred remained in the Yellowstone National Park, but they had been eliminated everywhere else. They had nested historically from Alaska and northern Canada to areas south of the Great Lakes and along the St. Lawrence River.[18]

The amazingly colored scarlet ibis (*Eudocimus ruber*) was far too attractive as a millinery proposition to last long. Until about 1890, they were uncommon but possibly regular winter visitors to the southern U.S. coast; John James Audubon certainly recorded them. They bred in the Caribbean and parts of South America. According to William Hornaday, writing in 1913, any ibises that turned up hoping to while away the winter in American waters were shot in the wet shallows they searched for food. Hat décor knew no geographical bounds either. American and European plume hunters went after these attractive birds in their South American breeding sites.[19] The red and pink American flamingo, with a very similar distribution to the scarlet ibis,

Whole wings of seabirds were a popular hat decoration, this one probably from a species of North American tern (National Audubon Society).

was another target but, ironically, a much luckier one. Its brilliantly colored feathers fade rather quickly after they are removed from the birds. So the millinery trade soon lost interest in them.

The wildlife photographer, writer, and ornithologist Herbert Job (1864–1933), who accompanied Theodore Roosevelt on several of his expeditions in the early years of the twentieth century, was one of the first people to publicize how lucrative the plume trade was as a business. In 1903, the price for plumes (from snowy and great white egrets in particular) offered to hunters was $32 ($3,520 today) an ounce, twice the value of gold at that time. Later they became more valuable still, as much as $80 an ounce, reflecting their increasing rarity as the birds were hunted down wherever they nested.[20]

With the demise of most sources of aigrettes, the millinery industry—and thence the plume collectors—turned their attention to the seabirds of the American Atlantic coast: terns, gulls, pelicans, and others. Most were shot after having been attracted down onto the ground by carved wooden decoys made to closely resemble the species of birds most sought after. Between the 1870s and 1900, tens of thousands of terns,[21] especially least terns (*Sternula antillarum*), gull-billed terns (*Gelochelidon nilotica*), Arctic terns (*Sterna paradisaea*), common terns (*S. hirundo*), and roseate terns (*S. dougallii*), as well as other seabirds including black skimmers (*Rynchops niger*) were shot and their wings, sometimes other feathers or even complete birds, used for hat decoration. Tropicbirds, particularly elegant seabirds with their long, white streaming tail feathers used for maneuverability in flight and for display, were never going to be exempt. The red-billed tropicbird (*Phaethon aethereus*), found in coastal waters off the southern United States, the Caribbean, and northern South America where it bred mainly on rocky islands, was especially vulnerable to the plume hunters.[22]

Least terns were almost annihilated; by 1900 a typical seasonal kill would take one hundred thousand of these delicate, yellow-billed birds that nested on readily accessible sand spits, beaches, and sand dunes.[23] A *Forest and Stream* magazine dated 7 August 1884 referred to an unnamed New York lady who had agreed with a Parisian millinery firm to deliver forty thousand or more bird skins in the summer of that year.[242] She had hired gunners to go to Cobb's Island, a low-lying sandy barrier island off the Virginia coast, to kill as many terns as possible at ten cents a skin. Few survived, and by the turn of the nineteenth century, almost all species of tern along the U.S. Atlantic coast had been very nearly exterminated. Less than a century before, they had been incredibly abundant.

The huge range of bird species killed for their feathers beggars belief. On his 1886 visit along the west Florida coast, William Scott reported on one particular day's visit onshore:

> In the morning I went on the beach with Mr Batty and we shot Knots, Black-bellied Sandpipers [black-bellied plover], Sanderlings and Turnstones over decoys, all these species being used by Mr Batty in his feather business. Mr Batty's men were killing Wilson's Plovers, Least Terns, Boat-tailed Blackbirds [boat-tailed grackle], Gray Kingbirds and any other species that came their way. All owls, and particularly the Barred Owl, are desirable. One of Mr Batty's employees told me . . . that Mr Batty was constantly purchasing and trading with native and other gunners for plumes and . . . skins of all the desirable birds of the region. Not less than sixty men were working on the Gulf coast for Mr Batty in this way.[25]

In correspondence written to Scott as a result of his observations along Florida's Gulf coast—which included massacres of herons, egrets, and spoonbills at numerous breeding colonies—it was clear that guns and ammunition were distributed liberally by agents of feather dealers in New York so that those shooting the birds were not restricted in the numbers of birds they could kill.

And while hat decoration can't take the entire hit for the decline and eventual extinction (in the early years of the twentieth century) of the small green parrot with a bright yellow head and reddish orange face known as the Carolina parakeet (*Conuropsis carolinensis*), it most certainly played a part.[26] Deforestation, killing by farmers to protect their crops, collection for the pet trade, and diseases thought to have been picked up from domestic chickens all played a role too.

As public concern about the scale of the slaughter slowly increased, but was very far from universal, one woman told Celia Thaxter writing for *Audubon Magazine* that there was a great deal of sentiment wasted on birds.[27] She assured her that there were so many of them, they would never be missed any more than mosquitoes. Nor did some politicians of the day have any scruples about supporting the continued mass killing; Missouri senator James Reed (1861–1944), referring to egrets, questioned: "Why there should be any sympathy about a long-legged, long-beaked, long-necked bird that lives in swamps and eats tadpoles."[28]

It seems almost surreal to us today, with our heightened concern for wildlife and sustainability, that the public attitude to all this bird killing into the early years of the twentieth century was so laissez faire. There seemed to be a commonly held and naïve belief that there was some self-perpetuating superabundance of birds, as if more and more would appear miraculously year upon year however many were killed. Wild animals on a huge continent such as North America seemed as infinite and varied as the air around; recognizing their limits and urging responsibility for conserving a seemingly unlimited resource was not the way to win friends. But let us examine why that attitude might have prevailed.

Firstly, there seemed to be endless numbers of birds. The early European settlers, moving west across North America, had seen vast numbers of wading birds, ducks, egrets, and herons in wetlands they traveled near. The forests they were riding through were full of bird song and game birds like wild turkeys that were good eating. Flocks of passenger pigeons were so huge they caused the sky to darken as they flew overhead, while their gargantuan numbers roosting for the night were heavy enough to snap branches off trees. Not much more than half a century ago, it was still possible to see flocks of hundreds of thousands of ducks, herons, and egrets take off from the shallows of the Florida Everglades with a noise like a cyclone.

Secondly, birds reappeared year after year, as regular an event as night following day. Forests fell silent in winter, and fewer birds remained. But come springtime—every spring—they filled up again with all manner of summer migrants: warblers, vireos, thrushes, and more, all arriving to breed. Wintering birds headed south for warmer climes; huge feeding flocks of snow geese (*Anser caerulescens*), often many thousands strong, descended on pastures during their annual migration twice every year en route between the Arctic and the central U.S. states. And every winter, vast numbers of wading birds would appear on the coast, on the fringes of southern lakes, or in marshes. It seemed to be a never-ending supply. Why would it matter if some were shot or trapped for their feathers? More would turn up come the next spring, or winter, and the years after that ad infinitum.

By the late nineteenth century, knowledge about birds, their habits, their feeding require-ments, and, above all, their migrations was gaining ground. Experiments in bird banding (known as "ringing" in Europe), which had begun in Europe, were started up in North America soon after 1890; it began to reveal more information about their migrations. It became obvious that birds shot in spring, as many were in the United States and Canada on their way north to their breeding grounds, equaled fewer birds heading south in the fall. That kind of information helped conservationists put up reasonable proposals for protective laws.[29]

Another part of the explanation for this over-optimistic belief in the never-ending bird supply was perhaps the view that human culture reigned supreme over wild nature. It was the strongly held belief of the Puritans, explorers, and Jesuit missionaries that arrived on the New England shore in the seventeenth century. These pioneering European colonizers who set out west a little over two centuries ago from the towns and villages they had built along the American east coast were convinced that they were destined, even divinely ordained, to expand across this vast continent and populate it. Native Indians were simply in the way. Bison and turkeys were there to be hunted for food. The cornucopia of animal life was a divinely provided resource, and human needs always trumped nature.

Birds were not the only animals killed for the American hat industry. The structure of hats, both for men and for women—from the Middle Ages and still today—often consisted of felt, a textile that is produced by matting, condensing, and pressing fibers together. Felt texture varies depending on the fiber used to make it. Sheep's wool or rabbit fur can be used to make cheaper hats, but one fiber was used for better quality hats: beaver fur. It was, for instance, to be the felt of choice for making top hats worn by gentlemen on more formal occasions, not to be replaced by silk until the late nineteenth century. And that was bad news for this large aquatic rodent found in streams, lakes, and rivers across the North American continent. Very bad news indeed.

Between the sixteenth and eighteenth centuries, the Eurasian beaver had been hunted to near extinction across the whole of that continent, partly for hat making and partly for castoreum, a secretion it exudes to mark its territory, which was in demand for perfumery (it conveys an odor of leather) and for some rather dubious medicinal uses. By 1800, the international beaver trade had moved to North America, both French and English colonists trading with various Native American Indian tribes for the pelts to ship across to England and the cities of western Europe. North American beavers were trapped and killed across the United States and Canada, their pelts exported to England where they were used to make the best quality hats, then many reimported into North America for sale. In the United States, cocked beaver felt hats were worn by troops during the American Revolution, and flat-topped beaver hats were commonly worn by eighteenth-century clergy.[30]

As the North American beaver was being trapped to near extinction, fortunes were being made from marketing their pelts. It was a trade that helped John Jacob Astor to become the first U.S. multimillionaire. And it helped a pioneer of the hat trade whose name became synonymous with the cowboy hat he created. John B. Stetson almost certainly based his design on the wide-brimmed, high-crowned Mexican Vaqueros hats worn by the horsemen and cattle herders of Spanish Mexico. Noting the often flea-infested coonskin caps worn by many of the gold prospectors he spent time with in his youth traveling the American West, Stetson was convinced that he could make a more practical hat using lightweight beaver fur felt.

With excellent training from his father, a master hatter, Stetson made his first hat in 1865. It was a time when almost every man wore a hat of some sort. Lighter in weight, retaining their shape, with a wide brim to protect against the sun, a high crown to keep an insulating air pocket above the head, and even able to carry water, the Stetson was an instant success. And a death notice for North American beavers. Each hat took around forty beaver belly pelts to make.

By 1886, Stetson ran the largest hat-making company in the world; it produced almost two million hats a year by 1906, though not all were made of beaver fur. His characteristic "Boss of the Plains" Stetson was durable, waterproof, and elegant but consumed millions of North American beavers in their construction. Many Stetsons are still made with beaver fur today, trapped under license, though cheaper versions use rabbit fur, even straw or leather.[31]

Other fur-bearing animals were hunted too, their fur used for hats as well as for other garments. Raccoons were trapped and shot, in the early twentieth century sometimes hundreds of thousands of them in a year. Red foxes, one of the most abundant mammals in North America, were killed on a massive scale, though mainly for scarves, muffs, jackets, and coats rather than for hats. North American river otters, American marten, coypu, and muskrat fur have all been used for similar purposes.

In 1900, after a considerable amount of campaigning by concerned individuals and by both established and newly formed conservation organizations, the U.S. Congress passed the Lacey Act, named after Representative John Lacey of Iowa who introduced it. The act was the result of increasing public distaste at the killing of wild birds for fashion. It prohibited the sale of wild birds (or their parts) across state boundaries.

But the American plume industry proved tenacious. It altered its focus to searching outside the United States because the milliners knew that more exotic birds were to be found elsewhere, and the Lacey Act only prohibited the killing of American birds. So U.S.-based feather dealers would pay hunters to kill birds in various parts of the world, the more exotic the species they could obtain the better. In South America, huge numbers of hummingbirds were killed as well as larger, fabulously attractive birds including the two species of cock of the rock (*Rupicola sp.*), thrasher-sized birds the males of which are vivid orange and black. Several species of birds of paradise in New Guinea suffered the same fate; captured then killed by local tribesmen, the birds would be skinned and shipped with feathers attached so that they could be stuffed and mounted whole on a hat. In 1913, William Hornaday counted in the store window of E. &. S. Meyers, 688 Broadway, New York, about six hundred plumes and skins of birds of paradise for sale for millinery purposes. He wrote this:

> On October 2, 1912, at Indianapolis, Indiana, in three show-windows within 100 feet of the head-quarters of the Fourth National Conservation Congress, I counted 11 stuffed heads and 11 complete sets of plumes of this bird [the greater bird of paradise], displayed for sale. The prices ranged from $30 to $47.50 each! And while I looked, a large lady approached, pointed her finger at the remains of a Greater Bird of Paradise, and with grim determination, said to her shopping companion: "There! I want one o' them, an' I'm agoin' to have it, too!" No wonder the Greater Bird of Paradise is now almost extinct! With fiendish cunning and enterprise, the shameless feather dealers are ferreting out the birds whose skins and plumes may legally be imported into this country and sold. From the trackless jungles of New Guinea, round the world both ways to the snow-capped peaks of the Andes, no unprotected bird is safe. The humming-birds of Brazil, the egrets of the world at large, the rare birds of paradise, the toucan, the eagle, the condor and the emu, all are being exterminated to swell the annual profits of the millinery trade. The case is far more serious than the world at large knows, or even suspects.[32]

This massive international trade was centered on London, and Hornaday lists over sixty species and whole genera of birds such as grebes, owls, manikins, even vultures, condors, and eagles, the feathers or whole skins of which were available for international buyers to choose from. One sale alone might contain ten thousand or more hummingbird skins. Many were bought by American feather dealers who shipped them to the United States for milliners across the North American continent to decorate their wares.

Birds of paradise from New Guinea were particularly popular to decorate American ladies' hats. The *New York Times* in 1904 included a section on how fashionable women were wearing their bird of paradise plumes:

> Mrs. John Jacob Astor is wearing a chic purple crinoline hat with a small, flat, round crown and a wide brim that curves over a bit at the edges and then rises at the right front and describes a wide, flaring semi-circle to a point back of the left ear. Its sole trimming is a black bird of paradise plume [bird of paradise feathers or whole birds were often dyed black] that starts from the left of the crown and sweeps upward, outward, and backward against both brim and crown.
>
>   Mrs. Clarence Mackay . . . the other evening had on at dinner at Sherry's a charmingly light but large round hat of pearly grey white tulle shirred on invisible wires and quite transparent as to the wide brim. From the front and left of the hat floated a plume of white bird of paradise feathers.[33]

In the early years of the twentieth century, American-based fashion magazines such as *Harper's Bazaar*, *Peterson's Magazine*, and *Graham's Magazine* were still heavily promoting feathers from a variety of birds. Another similar publication, the monthly *Delineator* magazine, a "journal of fashion culture and fine arts," in autumn 1903 contained an article titled "Winter Edwardian Millinery." It gave this advice about the current fashion:

> Never have hats been more attractive or so generally becoming, and while a great deal of lace and other trimming characterizes some of the smartest importations, so cleverly is it employed that, in most

instances, a simple effect results. Plumes are to have a triumphal career during the entire season. They are shown in all lengths, from tips to long plumes formed by joining two invisibly.

There is a variety of ways in which to arrange plumes, but the preference is to place them low at the back; they start underneath the brim or on its upper side and are bunched at one side of the front, or fall low over the left shoulder in Cavalier fashion. A single plume may be used or one starting from each side of the front and drooping low at the back.

Bird of Paradise plumes distinguish many of the best creations, and little other trimming is used with them. They are shown in exquisite colors, some shading from the palest tone to the darkest. Purple is especially favored, and when used to trim a hat of dark purple velvet or chenille is wonderfully pleasing.

The felt hat has attained a position it has not held for some time and is even a dressy affair when richly trimmed. The long-nap beaver adapts itself to curves and graceful lines. The large white beaver hat with its trimming of white plumes is intended for carriage and calling wear.[34]

Dying highly colorful bird of paradise feathers black would seem rather illogical, but it might have reflected the convention in elite social circles to have extended periods of mourning. Dying was a labor-intensive—and thereby expensive—process, something only those moving in select social circles could afford, and perhaps an obvious visual symbol of their status and wealth.

With the printing of sales catalogs by department stores in the last years of the nineteenth century, a huge array of exotic feathers, including birds of paradise, became available for the first time to those who could afford them throughout the United States and Canada. A catalog of 1914 from Eaton's Department Store in Toronto lists an array of "fancy feathers and wings" including those of herons, grebes, and parrots, many selling for less than Can$1, but with a single set of bird of paradise feathers priced at Can$12 (Can$264 today), a considerable expense at the time.[35]

In 1870 millinery was the fourth largest occupation for women in the United States. By the turn of the nineteenth century as demand fell it had fallen to fourteenth place but was still employing nearly eighty-three thousand women. The trade stood fast against claims of cruelty and exploitation. It explained carefully that the bulk of the plume collecting was limited to those feathers egrets shed naturally when the breeding season was over, feathers to be found scattered in the rookery trees or on the ground about. It was, of course, utter rubbish. Anyone picking up molted plumes can easily see that they are worn and damaged (and known in the trade as "dead plumes"), the inevitable result of everyday wear and tear through a breeding season. In truth, discarded plumes brought only one-fifth the price of the live, unblemished, hardly worn plumes cut from birds that were shot early in the season. The other excuse propounded by the millinery trade was that most feather decoration on hats was either artificial or produced on foreign farms that exported naturally molted feathers. This was equally untrue.[36]

A sworn statement provided by a Mr. A. H. Meyer to the National Association of Audubon Societies and subsequently laid before the legislature of the state of New York in 1911 is particularly revealing. For nine years Meyer had been obtaining plumes in Venezuela, collecting them for American feather wholesalers. His testimony included this:

The natives of the country, who do virtually all of the hunting for feathers, are not provident in their nature, and their practices are of a most cruel and brutal nature. I have seen them frequently pull the plumes from wounded birds, leaving the crippled birds to die of starvation, unable to respond to the cries of their young in the nests above which were calling for food. I have known these people to tie and prop up wounded egrets on the marsh where they would attract the attention of other birds flying by.

These decoys they keep in this position until they die of their wounds, or from the attacks of insects. I have seen the terrible red ants of that country actually eating out the eyes of these wounded, helpless birds that were tied up by the plume-hunters. I could write you many pages of the horrors practiced in gathering aigrette feathers in Venezuela by the natives for the millinery trade of Paris and New York.

To illustrate the comparatively small number of dead feathers which are collected, I will mention that in one year I and my associates shipped to New York eighty pounds of the plumes of the large heron [great white egret] and twelve pounds of the little recurved plumes of the snowy heron [snowy egret]. In this whole lot there were not over five pounds of plumes that had been gathered from the ground—and these were of little value. The plume-birds have been nearly exterminated in the United States and Mexico, and the same condition of affairs will soon exist in tropical America. This extermination will come about because of the fact that the young are left to starve in the nest when the old birds are killed.[37]

Plumes were being collected in countries such as Venezuela simply because there were so few egret rookeries left in the United States. In 1899 the *Millinery Trade Review* published the opinion of a British consul about the hunting of egrets in Venezuela.[38] He warned that their populations were declining rapidly, estimating that the number of egrets killed in 1898 was over 1.5 million. He also claimed that 870 birds had to be killed to obtain two and a quarter pounds of the feathers milliners wanted. The *Review* in an editorial comment scoffed at the figures, complaining that they were "the usual Audubon scare."[39]

How determined the plume hunters had become, attracted by easy money to be made, became brutally clear one hot July day in 1905. Guy Bradley (1870–1905) was a game warden and deputy sheriff for Monroe County, Florida. Born in Chicago, his family had relocated to Florida when Guy was a boy. They eventually settled in Flamingo at the southern tip of the state where the vast, wildlife-rich marshes of the Everglades metamorphose into the shallows of Florida Bay. Life then in Flamingo could be very unpleasant; a small village of wooden dwellings on stilts to protect them against storm surges, the place was apparently infested with fleas and mosquitoes. One visiting naturalist even claimed to have seen an oil lamp extinguished by a cloud of mosquitoes.[40]

As a boy, Bradley often served as guide to visiting fishermen and plume hunters. In 1885 when he was fifteen, he and his older brother Louis worked as scouts for the noted French plume hunter Jean Chevalier on his trip to the Everglades; the two youths and Chevalier killed 1,397 individual birds of thirty-six different species over a few weeks. But, as with so many boyhood bird egg collectors that become conservationists in adulthood, in 1902 Bradley was hired by the AOU at the request of the Florida Audubon Society to become one of the country's first game wardens.[41] He had given up plume hunting after the Lacey Act became law, describing it as a cruel calling.

Bradley took his job seriously; he educated locals about the newly implemented Lacey Act that made plume hunting a punishable offense if those plumes were then traded outside the source state, he spoke to hunters directly, and he posted warning signs. He also set up a network of spies who watched for suspicious behavior and employed his brother Louis and others close to him to work as assistant wardens during the height of the plume season. He patrolled a vast area, mainly by boat, the only practicable means of travel; it stretched from Florida's west coast, through the Everglades, to Key West.[42]

But the conservationists of the newly formed AOU and Audubon were complacent, believing naively that the presence of their armed wardens upholding the law was enough to deter the most ardent plume hunter. It was not. Bradley became a vilified figure in southern Florida; working mostly alone with few reinforcements, he had been shot at more than once. In 1904, he alerted visiting ornithologist and author Frank Chapman to one of the most isolated rookeries that had been "shot out" despite previously having been found in good condition. He told Chapman that after the plume hunters had finished their grisly work he could have walked right around it on the birds' bodies, between four and five hundred of them. Bradley took the slaughter to mean that he was being watched by local hunters because they could have discovered the rookery only by tracking his movements.

On 8 July 1905, Bradley heard gunshots close to his waterfront home. He set sail in his small skiff and encountered a father by the name of Smith and his two sons shooting up a rookery. The families had known each other for years, but Civil War veteran Walter Smith had a reputation for being troublesome, and Bradley had previously had altercations with him. According to Walter Smith's account, Bradley encountered the three men as they were loading dead plume birds, mostly egrets, onto their boat. An argument ensued, and as the warden attempted to arrest one of the young men, Smith opened fire with his hunting rifle, fatally wounding Bradley. His body was found in his boat by his brother's search party the next day ten miles from the scene of the crime. He had bled to death.[43] He was just thirty-five years old.

Smith turned himself in to the authorities the next day. Despite evidence found by the prosecution that Bradley had not fired his weapon, Smith claimed self-defense. He maintained that the warden had fired first, but missed, hitting Smith's boat even though Bradley was known to be a superb shot. Nevertheless, the jury decided there was insufficient evidence to convict Smith of murder. He served five months in jail, convicted on a lesser charge. Bradley's death and Smith's acquittal of the murder charge made national headlines. With no one to replace Bradley, lawlessness continued in the Everglades, and rookeries were devastated for several more years.

Other murders followed. In November 1908, Audubon warden and deputy sheriff Columbus G. McLeod of DeSoto County, Florida, went missing near Charlotte Harbor. A month later, his boat was found weighted down and sunk; inside, police found the warden's bloodstained hat, long gashes cut into its crown with what appeared to be an axe. It was suspected that he had been killed by plume hunters, but his body was never found and the perpetrators were not caught.

Guy Bradley's untimely death in particular not only galvanized conservationists and helped move public opinion against the plume trade, but it led in part to stronger bird protection laws and helped to get the Everglades designated a national park.

Even though by the early years of the twentieth century it was widely appreciated that some plume and feather hunters would kill anyone trying to stop them, and bird protection laws were on the statute book, feather-decorated hats were still popular and very fashionable. But there was a difference compared with similar hats a decade or two earlier. Fewer of these latest designs were garnished with the feathers of American birds. Since the 1880s in particular, imported ostrich plumes had become even more popular for well-dressed ladies' hats after Congress passed the Lacey Act in 1900 followed in 1913 by the Weeks-McLean Act. The latter banned the spring shooting of migratory game and insectivorous birds, declaring them to be "under the custody and protection of the federal government."[44]

When the ostrich feather market was booming, many contemporary observers compared them with diamonds in terms of their durability as fashion items, noting that ostrich plumes had been used to decorate ladies' hats for centuries, especially in the fashion centers of Europe. There was no indication then that plumes would have a more finite appeal than diamonds for the well-to-do and well-dressed lady. They were often dyed in a variety of colors and transformed into fanciful, sculpted shapes, sinuous and sensual according to some fashion critics of the time.[45]

Prior to the 1860s, all of the ostrich feathers for the American market would have been taken from wild ostriches that were chased down and shot on the semiarid plains of much of North, sub-Saharan, and southern Africa and in parts of the Middle East. Huge numbers were being killed, their feathers transported north through the Sahara, overseas to London, and many then purchased by New York feather dealers. Feathers from ostriches in Sudan were particularly valued; they were robust, taut, and glossy, just what the market desired. Later in the nineteenth century and up to the outbreak of World War I, most ostrich plumes for sale in North America had been imported from South African ostrich farms; lesser numbers were still being obtained from the rapidly depleting resource of wild African birds.

The farms that were set up from the mid-1800s on, most of them at first in the Little Karoo region of South Africa, an arid area inland from the country's southern coast, saved the wild birds from annihilation. Ostriches, though dangerous—a single slashing kick with their powerful feet can disembowel or kill a person—are relatively easy to breed in captivity to provide a supply of plumes without killing the birds. And the feather trade made the most of its claim that farmed ostriches lived a long and pampered life, simply having their most desired feathers clipped off every nine months or so, a process compared with ladies and gentlemen periodically trimming their toenails.

At its peak in the early years of the twentieth century, South Africa's farms, by then set up in many parts of the country, held over a quarter of a million birds. In the four years to 1911, between $1.1 million and $5 million ($130 million today) of ostrich plumes were imported annually into the United States, mostly from South African farms but some maybe from farms set up subsequently in Algeria, Sicily, France, Australia, and elsewhere. When the *Titanic* sank in 1912 it was carrying, among much else, a consignment of ostrich feathers purchased at London feather dealers en route to the U.S. market.[46]

Ostrich farming became a successful enterprise by the 1890s in California, Arizona, Texas, Arkansas, and Florida following its earlier success in South Africa. The consumer benefited too; imported ostrich feathers were heavily taxed, so the home-grown variety was distinctly cheaper. Feathers clipped from these farmed birds satisfied American millinery demands because the Lacey Act did not apply to captive-reared animals. Ostrich feathers were deemed highly acceptable embellishments for hat wearers young and old and of all sizes and complexions.

In spite of fashion commentators in earlier decades having declared that plumes could outlast diamonds as a fashion accessory, by the outbreak of World War I ostrich feathers had come to be viewed as fragile, dated, and tawdry. Diamonds, meanwhile, remained a girl's best friend. But it was perhaps not so much the growing revulsion at the past excesses of wild bird killing, the growth of conservation movements, the introduction of more effective laws protecting birds, and a more responsible attitude to wildlife—or even the killing of Guy Bradley—that would call a halt to this horrendous trade.

One New York City–based writer and culture commentator argued that there were other factors involved such as World War I cutting off international trade routes and promoting austerity and practicality.[47] Women had less time and money for frivolities; adorning oneself with sumptuous feathers would have been seen as unpatriotic. Utilitarian clothing—hats included—was in; feather décor was out. Ostrich feathers were consigned to the making of feather dusters and the adorning of cheap kewpie dolls. The ostrich farming industry collapsed in the United States and in South Africa; large numbers of investors, farmers, and dealers went bankrupt. There were revivals in the fortunes of ostrich plumes after World War I and well into the twentieth century, but the industry never got back to more than a shadow of its peak.

Practical changes were afoot as well. Automobiles such as the "high-wheelers" popular in the United States until Ford's Model T took over in the 1920s—open-topped or with small hooded cabs—made it impossible to wear a hat the size of a small coffee table in such a confined space or to keep it in place while traveling along bumpy roads or on a windy day. By the 1920s, form had followed function, and women's hairstyles had been minimized to the point that they simply could no longer support a large hat decorated with a proliferation of plumage and bird parts.

In came more streamlined and austere ladies' hat styles, though still partly reliant on beaver fur: a simple, almost brimless toque, adorned maybe with a ribbon band. After World War I, hemlines went up, women got the vote, and hair got shorter. Hair styles like the bob and the pageboy demanded smaller hats such as the bell-shaped cloche. The age of exotic, feather-adorned headgear was over.

Ladies with Influence

IN THE LATE NINETEENTH CENTURY, WELL-TO-DO SOCIETY LADIES IN THE UNITED States and in Britain frequently busied themselves by inviting other ladies to afternoon tea. It was not deemed acceptable for them to involve themselves in politics, except maybe by having quiet asides with their far more worldly wise and life-experienced husbands. Ladies most certainly did not take up employment. In Britain, women could not own property, it was not until 1918 that a minority of women were able to vote, and it was another decade again before all British women could do so. In the United States, women did not win that fundamental right until 1920.

So it is all the more surprising that a well-to-do American society lady, Harriet Hemenway (1858–1960) of Boston, Massachusetts, galvanized early public opinion so effectively against the enormous trade in bird killing for hat decoration that laws were eventually passed across the United States to ban it. Not only that, but her brave and formative efforts resulted eventually in the creation of one of the largest voluntary societies for bird conservation worldwide, Audubon.

Married to a Boston philanthropist and public servant who was heir to a shipping fortune, Harriet Hemenway was part of that city's elite. Her concern at the assemblage of whole birds, wings, and plumes of feathers decorating most ladies' hats she saw was growing by the day. She would observe them diligently to try and identify what precisely had been killed for each fashion statement when she passed yet another lady walking past on a Boston street. But her rage was growing. One day, out walking with her maid, "Harriet squinted her eyes as the lady of fashion walked proudly by. 'Arctic Tern, I believe,' Harriet whispered. 'Looks ready to fly away,' said the parlour maid. 'It won't,' Harriet replied sadly."[1]

One January afternoon in 1896 when she read an article about the decimation of Florida's egret rookeries by plume hunters supplying the millinery trade, she became incensed. Inviting her like-minded cousin, Miss Minna Hall (1851–1941) to afternoon tea, the two women combed through the "Blue Book"—Boston's society register—and set out to contact the most fashionable Bostonian ladies with the idea of starting a boycott of hats decorated with feathers. A whole series of afternoon teas would be the next step.

Harriet Hemenway had always been something of an iconoclast. She once invited as a houseguest Booker T. Washington, the black American educator, author, and orator who was the de facto leader of the African American community at the time. Boston hotels had refused him accommodation. She was also a passionate naturalist, setting out on bird expeditions in unthinkably unfashionable white sneakers.

Tea drinking clearly galvanized many of Boston's great and good ladies into action. Before

Harriet Hemenway who began the antiplumage movement in the United States and the establishment of Audubon, painted by John Singer Sargent, 1890 (Adelson Galleries, New York).

long, the pair had persuaded around nine hundred of them to boycott feather-decorated hats and to set up an organization for bird protection. "We sent out circulars," Minna Hall later recalled, "asking the women to join a society for the protection of birds, especially the egret. Some women joined and some who preferred to wear feathers wouldn't join."[2] But why was it that many society ladies would not contemplate forsaking their bird- and feather-decorated hats? Maybe it was because they were convinced that the millinery trade's (false) claim that the feathers were removed only from birds that had died naturally was in fact true. Or they had believed stories that many fancy feathers were obtained from birds that were farmed just like ostriches. Or, perhaps more likely, they had decided not to give the birds' origins too much thought when they purchased the latest fashion creations.

Hemenway and Hall named their new society after one set up in New York a decade earlier by George Grinnell (1849–1938). George Bird Grinnell (yes, his middle name actually was Bird) was a New York–born anthropologist, naturalist, and writer who became a prominent early conservationist and was a key promoter of movements to conserve the wildlife and wild places of the American West. But Grinnell's Audubon Society, named after the famous naturalist and painter John James Audubon, had grown too quickly for him to manage, and in 1888 it had collapsed from its own success. Earlier attempts to limit the plumage trade had failed too. In 1876, for instance, Joel A. Allen (1838–1921), an eminent zoologist and ornithologist who was a cofounder of the American Ornithologists' Union (AOU), influenced many others from different walks of life to support his opposition to the plume trade. But their efforts fell on deaf ears.[3]

Now, thanks to the initiative of Hemenway and Hall, the Massachusetts Audubon Society, the first of many, came into being. This one would never collapse. Other ladies of means picked up the baton from Hemenway and Hall; by 1898, sixteen states across the country had followed suit and set up their own Audubon Societies. Men started to join too, and the roster of honorary

Emily Williamson who began the anti-plumage movement in Britain in 1889 (Bateson family archive).

vice presidents boasted Grinnell, Frank Chapman, and Theodore Roosevelt in New York alone. In Massachusetts, the doughty pair of ladies recruited William Brewster (1851–1919), an eminent ornithologist of his day and president of the AOU, to be the first president of Massachusetts Audubon.[4]

Reflecting the times and the need for these societies to be influential and realistic, men were slotted into key positions, the societal norm at the time for any organization. By 1899, on average, men made up half of the Audubon leadership overall, and women comprised 80 percent of the membership.[5]

Laws to protect certain groups of birds had already been enacted in several states, but they were piecemeal, generally poorly enforced, and had plenty of exceptions built in. Massachusetts had been the first, as early as 1818. It protected several species of small bird but only in the breeding season. Connecticut brought in year-round protection in 1850, but only for insectivorous birds. Iowa prohibited Sunday hunting in 1855. West Virginia protected all birds all year, except woodpeckers, blackbirds, and some predators. But protection from killing birds for their feathers gets mentioned only after 1870: Florida brought in a plume bird law to protect egrets and some other birds in 1877, and Wisconsin did likewise a decade later.[6] They made little difference, and their enforcement was lax.

Afternoon teas had also certainly figured prominently in the home of Emily Williamson (1855–1936), another well-to-do lady who lived in Manchester, England. Seven years before Harriet Hemenway, she had also garnered together a group of like-minded ladies who were equally appalled at the destruction of birds worldwide merely to decorate the hats of ladies like them. Dispensing tea and fruit cake with the help of her housemaid, Annie, she frequently filled her drawing room with ladies of her social class. In 1889 when she convened her first meeting, Mrs. Williamson would have been thirty-four years old.[7]

Some significant efforts had already been made in the United Kingdom to limit the plumage trade, but they were distinctly partial and limited. As early as 1869, the Sea Birds Preservation Act became law in the United Kingdom. The act made it illegal to kill thirty-three species of wild seabird in their breeding colonies between 1 April and 1 August anywhere in the United Kingdom.

The act was aimed at stopping the wanton killing of seabirds for sport and for their eggs and feathers, a concentration of destruction that was threatening the very survival of some cliff-nesting species. But the act proved difficult to enforce. Each summer, as soon as the ban ended, many of the seabirds, especially fledged youngsters, remained on the sea near their breeding cliffs and were shot mercilessly. The act was also of little consequence to the plumage trade because it could still legally import the feathers and wings of seabirds such as gulls and terns from outside the United Kingdom.

Walk today around the impressive Fletcher Moss Gardens in Didsbury, a suburb of Manchester—part botanic garden with a wealth of trees and shrubs, part wildlife habitat—and the large, ivy-covered house named "The Croft" overlooking the Gardens is not immediately obvious. Donated to the people of Manchester in 1919, this was Emily Williamson's home from 1882 until 1912 where she had settled after her marriage to Robert Wood Williamson (1856–1932), a British solicitor and anthropologist.[8]

Superficially, the nineteenth-century industrial and mercantile city of Manchester might not seem an obvious center of more liberal and iconoclastic views. But that would be a misunderstanding. It was actually the British center of radical, intellectual life: antislavery, pacifist, free-thinking, nonconformist, and suffragist. It was the city in which Emmeline Pankhurst (1858–1928), the leader of the British suffragette movement, was born and lived. She and Emily Williamson were contemporaries. More than that, they were each very determined contemporaries—though on very different missions—and there is no evidence that they ever met.

In 1889, Emily Williamson founded the Society for the Protection of Birds to campaign against their enormous slaughter; two years later it joined forces with the Fur and Feather League (sometimes known as the Fur, Fin and Feather Folk), founded in the same year by Eliza Phillips (1823–1916), Etta (Margaretta) Smith (1860–1953), and Catherine Hall (1838–1924), close neighbors living in Croydon near London who had very similar concerns. Their activism seems to have been inspired in different ways: Eliza Phillips's by witnessing the sufferings of cattle on a sea voyage and Etta Smith's by reading about egrets killed for their plumes.[9]

The coming together of the two groups to create the Society for the Protection of Birds (SPB) was facilitated by the Royal Society for the Prevention of Cruelty to Animals (RSPCA), an organization that traces its origins back to 1824. The RSPCA, though, was adopting a neutral stance on the feather debate. Their U.S. equivalent, the American Society for the Prevention of Cruelty to Animals (created in 1866 primarily to help protect domesticated and farm animals) was certainly not neutral; they were supporting the new Audubon movement and invoking God on their side into the bargain.

SPB members, charged two pennies to join, were required to sign a pledge not to wear feathers except those of ostrich (by that time mainly farmed) and game birds that were shot for meat (and for sport by British society's upper classes). A letter in 1890 from Emily Williamson to *Punch* magazine seemed to fire up that publication's enthusiasm for their cause,[10] their editorials over many months suggesting that giving up feathers was not exactly "a severe, self-denying ordnance" for ladies anyway.[11] There was another piece of happenstance too. December 1890 was a ferociously cold, ice-covered month in Britain. It was a death sentence for very many small birds. As a result, bird feeding became established as a British pastime, and the plight of birds in general struck a chord with British people, a chord that continues to this day.[12] The fledgling SPB—excuse the pun—was attracting the public attention that it needed if it was to close down the lucrative trade in bird feathers for hats.

But by no means everyone was backing Emily Williamson's cause. Not even all ornithologists of the day. She had attempted to join the British Ornithologists' Union (BOU), the senior ornithological society in Britain. But the BOU was then a bastion of exclusive male membership; it reckoned that no women could be considered to be serious ornithologists. And it wasn't going to change its rules to allow some upstart lady from a Manchester suburb, whose only interest was to ban feather wearing, to join its hallowed ranks. Angry and unable to lodge a protest there about the killing of birds for hat décor, she sought retribution and banned BOU members from joining her SPB.[13]

By early 1891, the SPB already had a few thousand members. It was attracting an increasing amount of attention. Maybe Mrs. Williamson thought that her creative task was complete. She had fired the starting gun, and the new anti-feather, bird-protection organization she had envisaged was on its way. Whatever the reasons, in May 1891, just two years after she set it up, she relinquished her status as secretary, accepted the offer of a vice presidency, and spoke only once at a national SPB meeting in the next forty-five years. She continued to run the small local branch she had set up in Didsbury, Manchester, but devoted herself to social work where she was remembered for her "quiet dignity" and "lovable disposition." Emily Williamson was not one for the limelight.[14]

Or was there another reason for her move to the shadows? Had the astute Emily Williamson realized that her fellow activist Etta Smith was by now a formidable driving force who would press the cause for which the SPB had been set up harder and more effectively than she ever could? In 1892, Etta Smith married Frank Lemon (1859–1935), the barrister who wrote the constitution for the newly created SPB. From then on, Mrs. Lemon (she was never referred to as "Etta") propelled the SPB forward, tolerating no criticism, and with a single-minded purposefulness almost impossible to match.

In the United States, meanwhile, progress was also accelerating. The late 1890s saw a frenzy of new Audubon clubs springing up across the country. The movement was going from strength to strength. But these germinating groups still had plenty of vociferous, often highly sexist critics. "Nature made woman beautiful and the earth and the sea give up their gems for her. Let the air do the same," ranted one anti-Audubon man at the time. Another came up with this: "Killing is the law of nature. Except for the vegetarians and they, being obviously mad, do not count!"[15]

But Audubon ladies were not easily cowed; one, Margaret T. Olmstead of the Iowa Audubon, believed it was "woman's sacred mission to be the conservator of beauty and not its destroyer. Dead and mutilated bodies, charnel houses of beaks and claws, and bones and feathers and glass eyes. Does any woman imagine these withered corpses are beautiful?"[16] Doubtless, though, Marie Antoinette and the Duchess of Devonshire—and many other ladies—would have had to have answered yes.

Criticism or not, their constituent base continued to grow. They appointed local secretaries to organize an Audubon club in every town. The women members set up traveling libraries on birds and bird protection. They spoke to women's clubs. They spoke in schools. They offered public lectures on such topics as "Woman as a Bird Enemy." They erected Audubon-approved, bird-free millinery displays. They created "white lists" of milliners who sold feather-free hats. And, of course, they hosted afternoon teas.

Male members did the more "masculine" things: creating bird charts; carrying out bird surveys to get data on species declines; prowling around railway goods yards to spot any bird shipments; and arguing the need for bird-protection legislation by brandishing science, objective reasoning, and the law.

The women promoted the moral argument. A Miss Mary Thatcher, writing in *Harper's Bazaar* on 22 May 1875, for example, titled her article "The Slaughter of the Innocents" and began her discussion with the most visible example of what she felt to be a problematic use of bird life: on ladies' hats. While she complemented the beauty of the avian form, she lamented the loss of the bird lives. She wrote:

> But alas! These brilliant visions have been only ghosts of birds, mute warblers, little captives deprived of life and light and song. The outspread wings have lost their magic power, and the little feet, instead of clasping some swaying bough, have been hopelessly entangled in meshes of velvet and lace.[17]

It was a writing style echoed in the voices of many later women nature writers.

The Audubons started to attract influential support, not the least from President Theodore Roosevelt, a strong sympathizer who took office in 1901. Across the United States, women were refusing to buy feather- and bird-decorated hats, and many were either burning those they already owned or squirreling them away out of sight. Within just a few years the Audubon movement had garnered enormous public support, had gained the ear of many politicians, and had won most of the moral and scientific argument. It was everything that George Grinnell's first Audubon a decade earlier had lacked.

Back in 1886, the AOU had written a "model law" for non–game bird protection whose possession, purchase, and sale would be prohibited. Several states implemented versions of it over the next few years, but local exemptions were commonplace and some states later repealed or emasculated the legislation they had enacted. It was, in common parlance, a dog's breakfast of poorly protective measures that had no significant effect on the plumage trade.

Then, in May 1900, after considerable lobbying by the Audubons and with other societies in support, only four years after Harriet Hemenway and Minna Hall had convened the first of very many afternoon teas, the U.S. Congress passed the Lacey Act. Introduced into Congress by John F. Lacey (1841–1913), an Iowa Republican and lawyer, it regulated federally the introduction of birds and other animals to places where they had never existed and prohibited the transportation of illegally captured animals—and, crucially, their parts—across state lines. But it didn't ban the importation of foreign bird skins and feathers.[18]

It was a start, but in spite of several seizures of plumage—including large numbers of dead gulls whose wings were being transported across states and were destined for hats—the law, poorly enforced, did little to slow overall commerce in plumage. Getting in the way of plume hunters could be dangerous too; the murder of Guy Bradley in 1905 as he attempted to arrest a plume hunter in the Florida Everglades had proved that. When his killer was found innocent, it bolstered the Audubon cause even further. But with continued opposition from the millinery trade, compromise began to achieve some traction among increasing numbers of ornithologists. Even Frank Chapman who, in 1886, had drawn public attention to the carnage of American birds to decorate ladies' hats, showed himself open to doing a deal. He wrote:

> We cannot hope to abolish the trade in feathers, but, if by a concession, we can so control it that our native birds shall be exempt from its demands, we shall have afforded them a measure of protection we had not expected to secure in this generation nor the next.[19]

In spite of a few state Audubons agreeing to such a compromise, at least temporarily, the movement overall was rapidly gaining strength in numbers; there was no chance that they were going to agree to a deal protecting only American birds. In 1905 their growing numbers joined forces to create the National Association of Audubon Societies; it adopted the snowy egret, one of the species decimated by the plumage trade, as its emblem. William Dutcher (1846–1920), a businessman and keen ornithologist, became its first president, and T. Gilbert Pearson, an academic and ardent conservationist who in his youth had shot birds for their plumes, became its secretary.

Increasing lobbying of politicians to get effective plumage legislation brought about what seemed like a watershed moment in 1913. It was the year in which Audubon membership U.S.-wide reached one hundred thousand. The Weeks-McLean Act, jointly sponsored by Republican Massachusetts representative John Weeks (1860–1926) in the House and by Connecticut senator George McLean (1857–1932) in the Senate, got approval. A strong case had been made by Pearson and Hornaday representing the Audubon Societies; Hornaday received a medal from the RSPB in the United Kingdom and another from the French Société d'Acclimation as a result of his efforts.[20]

Effectively ending the plume trade, the new law prohibited spring hunting and the marketing of migratory birds as well as prohibiting the importation of feathers from wild birds into the United States. It gave the secretary of agriculture the power to set hunting seasons nationwide, and it was the first U.S. law to regulate the shooting of migratory birds. It resulted in many U.S. citizens, returning home from abroad, having their feather hat trims or even whole hats confiscated at entry ports. A public outcry resulted in legal amendments to the act to rein in the customs officials provided that the wearer could prove that ownership predated the act. More constructively, it also resulted in regular seizures of plumage imported illegally into the United States.

One major smuggling episode was detected in 1916 when a crewman from the ocean liner *Kroonland* was apprehended wearing a belt holding no less than 150 bird of paradise plumes. Jailed for eleven months, he admitted to being part of a smuggling ring based in the United Kingdom. After he implicated others, $100,000 of illegal plumage was seized from a feather company.[21]

But difficulties soon arose. The Weeks-McLean legislation had been added into a much larger bill about agricultural funding; President Woodrow Wilson (1856–1924) claimed to have signed it into law without realizing that the Weeks-McLean provisions were included. Legal challenges ensued, though all of them were rather inconclusive. At least one court ruled that individual states, not the federal government, "owned" the wildlife within their borders. The case went eventually to the U.S. Supreme Court where it sat without resolution for years.

The matter was settled finally when the Weeks-McLean Act was replaced by the Migratory Bird Treaty Act, 1918, which is on the U.S. federal statutes to this day and which currently protects over one thousand native bird species in the United States including full protection of their parts such as feathers. Since it became law, the United States has signed treaties with Mexico,

Japan, and Russia in addition to an earlier treaty with Canada protecting migrant birds entering American territory.[22]

Milliners and plumassiers across the United States were ordered to burn their plumage stocks after the act became law. Entire contents of millinery stockrooms were often confiscated and turned into feather bonfires by officials enforcing the act because it was difficult to tell from which species the feathers came. The act was rigorously enforced.[23]

Impassioned speeches by conservationists to politicians in Congress had played a big part in getting this legislation on the U.S. federal statute book. Henry Oldys (1859–1924), a prominent ornithologist who referred Congress to the implications of continuing bird killing, was one:

> "History will not listen to the plea: It was not my business," he said. "It will answer: You were there and could have prevented it; therefore, it is your business. You failed to do your duty. The only explanation is that you were corrupt, ignorant or weak."[24]

It was direct and passionate.

Progress was faster in the United States than that being achieved by the SPB in Britain, which had to put up with a great deal of carping and criticism as well as a large dose of indifference from most politicians. Cartoons appeared in magazines and newspapers of the day mocking the SPB's ideas. Commenting on a letter written in 1891 by the Reverend Francis Orpen Morris (1810–1893), a clergyman and respected naturalist, sent to the journal *Nature Notes* about his ultimately unsuccessful attempt four years earlier to set up a Plumage League, the journal's editor, James Britten (1846–1924), a botanist at London's British Museum, added condescendingly:

> As to the name of such a society [the SPB], that suggested by Rev Morris is immeasurably the better [The Plumage League]. To assume such a very ambitious title as the Society for the Protection of Birds for a band of ladies who do nothing but abstain from personal iniquity in the matter of bonnets, may give occasion for the unrighteous to scoff.[25]

But Britten was proved very wrong. Within six months, the SPB had five thousand members, and that number had doubled by 1893. It was sending out more than fifteen thousand letters and fifty thousand leaflets annually. The RSPCA, which was supplying moral support, was moved to comment that it was growing laterally like a branching taproot. Its focus was unerring; it was going to stop the plumage trade. The indomitable Mrs. Lemon would see to that. It had garnered help from other societies too: the more academic Linnean Society, the Zoological Society, and others had heard the clarion call and joined in. Even the BOU came onboard.

And successes there were. Hats with birds and feathers atop were still on sale, but not in every millinery shop. By the autumn of 1892 many of the smarter London premises had ceased using birds or bird parts. Tessa Boase quotes a wildfowler in that year who was complaining in *The Times* that his annual shooting of thousands of kittiwakes had dwindled to nothing. He blamed what he referred to as "this ladies' association."[26] But the decline in bird-decorated hats might have been merely a pause. Surreptitiously, the redoubtable Mrs. Lemon was in the habit of obtaining an auction catalog for the feather and bird-skin sales at the London warehouses. They were not publicly available. In 1892 she recorded a single shipment alone that contained thirty-two thousand hummingbirds, eighty thousand "waterbirds," and eight hundred thousand pairs of wings imported by just one London dealer. A year later, feathers were again all the rage. Mrs. Lemon had far more work to do yet.[27]

The adolescent SPB had another problem to overcome too: it had few men as members; fewer still were active members. Most influential ornithologists in Britain were men; the plumage trade was run by men; the fashion industry was owned by men; and the press was a male preserve. So influential men were asked to join the SPB as "Life Associates." Many did; senior members of the clergy, politicians, artists, senior military men, and others from a range of professional backgrounds joined up. So, too, did some leading ornithologists including Professor Alfred Newton (1829–1907), an internationally recognized zoologist and ornithologist.

All the same, some of its staunchest supporters were ladies from the top echelons of Britain's still very hierarchical society, many of whom had given up their feather- and bird-bedecked hats. The Duchess of Portland, Winifred Anna Cavendish-Bentinck (1863–1954), became the SPB's first (and longest serving) president. She was a lifelong humanitarian and animal welfare activist who had links to members of the British royal family. In 1897, the SPB obtained offices and a small staff in High Holborn, London. Two years later their membership had reached twenty thousand, the year in which Queen Victoria—personally abhorrent of cruelty—confirmed an order to prohibit the wearing of egret feather sprays (so-called ospreys) by the military. They were to be replaced with (farmed) ostrich feathers.

Into the twentieth century the SPB's campaigning continued. But it did not seem to be substantially reducing the demand for feathers and dead birds on ladies' heads. SPB membership had leveled out at around twenty thousand. A law had been passed in 1902 in the United Kingdom banning the export of bird skins from (then imperial) India, but no one much bothered to enforce it. And plenty of skins and feathers from a plethora of southern Asian birds were still to be found in London feather sales even though Australia had banned such exports in 1912 and Indonesia (then the Dutch East Indies) in 1913.[28]

An initiative launched by Mrs. Lemon to get an acknowledged expert to check out the veracity of the many "fake" egret feather sprays the millinery trade were promoting and supposedly using (rather than real feathers) proved that most were taken from wild birds. Various claims of horsehair, whalebone, bleached grasses, or ivorine (a kind of imitation ivory) were shown to be fallacious; the trade was still consuming vast quantities of feathers, and many ladies still wore feather-decorated hats.

Artificial feathers for millinery were on sale; after all, ladies not wishing to adorn their hats with the real thing provided a new market. Walking through London's West End as early as 1896, Adolphe Boucard (1839–1905), a French ornithologist, taxidermist, and feather merchant, spotted strings of birds made of artificial feathers, "badly made, some badly dyed and with the most unnatural and grotesque appearance." M. Boucard was a strong advocate of killing birds to adorn ladies with the real thing, the "most brilliant jewels of Creation" as he called them.[29]

Come the twentieth century, the SPB decided it should direct its energies to getting royal rather than direct political support for a ban on birds and feathers on hats; it surmised that royal patronage would help its case. Eventually it succeeded. The SPB became the *R*SPB—the Royal Society for the Protection of Birds (as it remains today)—on receipt in 1904 of a royal charter from King Edward VII. The publicity value, both in the United Kingdom and in the United States, was enormous. Much of the effort to get it this far had been due to the formidable Mrs. Lemon, who became the driving force of the RSPB for more than half a century, all of it unpaid. A tireless and redoubtable campaigner, she did not make a lot of friends in part because she was deeply mistrustful of ornithologists, believing them to be hostile to the efforts of the RSPB to curb the activities of bird egg and skin collectors.[30]

Tessa Boase, who researched Etta Lemon's track record on the plumage debate and the rise of the RSPB, concluded that she was a Victorian fanatic, utterly dedicated to her goals with tremendous drive and a ruthlessness of purpose. Boase mentions one incident in which a then director of London's Natural History Museum hid on a stairwell rather than be harangued by the formidable Mrs. Lemon for some perceived bird protection failure. In her early days with the Fur and Feather League she had even written individual and intrusive letters to large numbers of ladies she had spotted in Sunday church sporting hats decorated with feathers (other than ostrich), informing them of the deaths they were causing and of the error of their ways in wearing them.[31]

In 1906 Queen Alexandra, King Edward VII's wife, wrote a letter to the society expressing her disapproval at the wearing of plumes. Fashion leader, a pin-up of the day, and extremely popular, her support was a substantial boost to the RSPB in gaining parliamentary influence. In 1908 Lord Avebury successfully steered a bill through the House of Lords in the British Parliament to ban the importation into Britain of wild birds' plumage. It gained a good deal of support across the political parties, and several peers spoke in support. But it ran out of time at its all-important House of Commons stage and was shelved.[32]

The problem was that every argument put forward by conservationists for a ban was countermanded by the millinery trade and its supporters who claimed that such impacts were either plain wrong or that the birds would have died anyway. It was, argues the modern historian Richard Moore-Colyer in his analysis of the struggle against the trade,

> a debate in which the Victorian notions of freedom of trade and the encouragement of entrepreneurship encountered an expanding groundswell of concern for wildlife based both on sentimental and scientific motives. On either side the devices of special pleading, exaggeration and distortion of the truth were tendentiously adopted, while arguments grounded upon quite breathtaking assumptions were shamelessly advanced.
>
> The issue of hunting to extinction typified the difficulty of arguing a case in the absence of reliable information. While this matter was being aired by the 1908 House of Lords Select Committee, Lord Strathmore, formerly Governor of a number of overseas territories including Fiji, Ceylon and Trinidad, offered evidence to the effect that numerous species of birds previously common to the countries were now rarely to be seen.
>
> But this anecdotal evidence was refuted by plumage trade witnesses who made the quite reasonable point that if various exotic bird species were on the brink of extinction why was [feather] supply not in decline? It was widely accepted that there was a case for restricting trade in lyrebirds, but with respect to other popular species, including birds of paradise, egrets and parakeets, the supply showed no sign of diminishing.
>
> Special pleading was employed by the plumage trade . . . to counter the "hunting to extinction" arguments. If wild birds were left in their natural state, it was averred, they would probably be eliminated by local natives, so that the best way to ensure their future survival would be to create a demand for their plumage! Since supply would follow that demand and human ingenuity knew no bounds, steps would be taken to husband these economically valuable and aesthetically desirable species. After all, had it not been for the commercial importance of its feathers, the South African ostrich would have been eliminated by hunters before successful programmes of domestication had been undertaken.[33]

The RSPB and like-minded conservation groups were most emphatically not for giving up the struggle in Britain. They bombarded potential supporters with letters and pamphlets to get them on side. Harold Massingham (1888–1952), a prolific British writer on rural issues, set up a Plumage Bill Group that lobbied hard to get legislation through the UK Parliament. It attracted wide

Men hired by the then Society for the Protection of Birds to publicize the killing of egrets, probably about 1910 (RSPB Images).

support, including from literary and intellectual figures such as Thomas Hardy, W. H. Hudson, and John Galsworthy. They wrote to the press, spoke at meetings, and petitioned Members of Parliament.

But the plumage industry fought back yet again with counterarguments led by the equally determined Mr. C. F. Downham, a prominent feather merchant and managing director of Sciana & Co., ostrich and fancy feather merchants. He rivaled Massingham for the numbers of letters he wrote to the press, the amount of public speaking he did, and how many pamphlets he distributed. He also played a prominent role in frustrating several private members' bills brought to the House of Commons between 1908 and 1921. How was it, he argued, that killing wild game birds such as duck and partridge merely for sport was acceptable, yet killing for adornment was not? And he challenged the conservation lobby to provide evidence to show that imported exotic birds were declining because of the millinery market rather than due to agricultural expansion and habitat destruction. They were difficult questions to answer.[34]

Nonetheless, pressure for a ban on feather imports mounted after 1908, partly because some sound ecological arguments were propounded by Massingham and his fellow abolitionists including the essential need to retain insect-eating birds worldwide because of their vital role in controlling insect pests. There was a large element of British self-interest in this argument of course: much of Britain's food was imported from its colonies. Mrs. Lemon was in full swing, doing all she could to garner support for a bill to go through the UK Parliament. But she had a real struggle on her hands; 1912 was the peak year for shop window breaking by the British suffragette movement, and their glass-shattering campaign attracted international press attention. On one day alone, 1 March, 121 women were arrested. They had smashed nearly four hundred shop windows in some of the prime shopping streets in London's West End. There was public uproar. What politician was going to listen to some bird lovers droning on about feathers and bird skins now? The leadership of the RSPB was furious with the suffragettes (whom they did not support anyway), but more furious still with the government.[35]

Predictably, the UK government did not take any feather-related action. And then World War I intervened. In 1920, Colonel Sir Charles Yate (1849–1940), an English soldier, administrator in colonial India, and MP, introduced a plumage bill in the House of Commons. Again it was defeated in spite of many MPs being supportive. Other attempts followed until, in 1921, the Importation of Plumage (Prohibition) Act was eventually passed by the British Parliament. It applied throughout Ireland, too, then part of the United Kingdom.

Inevitably there had been compromises; instead of a blanket prohibition there was a comprehensive schedule of prohibited species and an advisory body was to be formed—including ornithologists and feather merchants—that would draw up a list of exempted species and advise on a system of import licenses for these. At the time of the passing of the act, only ostrich and eider duck (the nests of which are the source of eiderdown that was harvested without killing the birds) were on the exemption schedule, but by 1951 another nine species were added including the Eurasian jay, golden pheasant, and mute swan. It was, though, a mere fraction of the number of species for which the millinery trade had wanted exemptions. A working compromise had been reached.[36] The Plumage Act became law the following year, thirty-three years from Emily Williamson's original initiative. It had been an inordinate time in gestation.

Other countries were beginning to take action too, although passing legislation was the easier option than endeavoring to enforce it. U.S. president Theodore Roosevelt, an early member of Audubon, issued an executive order in 1909 protecting most of the Hawaiian Islands as a breeding ground for albatrosses and other native birds. It was a start for the protection of albatrosses across the oceans they inhabit. In New Zealand the Animal Protection and Game Act of 1921 gave protection to two albatross species followed by a third in 1931, and the Wildlife Act of 1953 protected all albatross species across all New Zealand territory including their important offshore breeding islands.

Feather gathering was banned by the Japanese government in 1906, but it continued illegally until 1932 by which time there were maybe 1,400 short-tailed albatrosses left out of an original population of millions.[37] But much of the legislation was rather piecemeal, sometimes protecting just one exploited species such as the superb lyrebird (whose tails were exceedingly popular for hats), which was given full protection in Australian states at different times: Victoria in 1887, New South Wales in the early 1900s, and Queensland in 1922, although the fines imposed for breaking the Queensland act were insignificant.[38]

In reality, the United Kingdom's Plumage Act, just like protective legislation around the world, was a classic example of closing the stable door after the horse had bolted. The peak of demand for exotic feathers had been several decades earlier when the redoubtable ladies in Boston and Manchester had begun their campaigns. By the 1920s, their use had greatly diminished. Fashions had moved on. After the United Kingdom's 1921 Plumage Act, customs officials were seizing and confiscating illegal ornamental feather imports when they could be sure that they could identify the species concerned. That was often difficult. But the quantities imported illegally slowly declined into the 1930s. The plumage trade in the United Kingdom and most of Europe had been virtually eliminated by World War I, and it did not recover on any significant scale thereafter. Times had changed, and so had attitudes.

Richard Moore-Colyer put it neatly when he wrote: "The post-war younger generation reacted against the ludicrous and tasteless feathers and plumes of their parents just as they reacted against many of their social, moral, political and aesthetic viewpoints."[39]

But what explains the almost total disregard for the wild species so cruelly exploited by millions of ladies wanting birds and their feathers for hat decoration and gentlemen equally eager to obtain the best hats they could afford made from beaver fur? Did they assume, as many in the millinery trade tried to argue, that the birds' feathers could be painlessly removed before the birds were released or that the feathers had been naturally molted? And that beavers needed to be killed anyway because of their supposedly destructive habits? Or was there a far more deeply held belief—much as held by the early European pioneers moving west in North America—that wildlife was placed on Earth by a generous Creator for them to exploit as they saw fit, just as Genesis 1:26 stated: "Let us make man in our image, after our likeness. And let them have dominion over the fish of the sea and over the birds of the heavens and over the livestock and over all the earth and over every creeping thing that creeps on the earth." The thirteenth-century philosopher and priest Thomas Aquinas (1225–1274) stated that cruelty to animals was not wrong in itself and that it should be condemned only if it encouraged cruelty to humans. An opposing view was held by St. Francis of Assisi (1181–1226) who argued that animals were worthy of human kindness because of their status as fellow creatures of God.

Pastor James Rimbach (1939–2009), writing about the Judeo-Christian tradition and the human–animal bond, made these comments:

> Some have found in the scriptural material the impetus for great acts of kindness, others the justification for unspeakable cruelty. In truth, the bible represents an open tradition . . . only by the most heavy-handed and insensitive treatment can the bible be used to support the view that the natural world is "at our disposal." What place and what value the animal world and the rest of the created order have is inextricably bound to the question, "What values do we have, and why?" H. Paul Santmire [a long-established expert in ecological theology] has written, "Nothing comparable to modern exploitation of nature was known in biblical times. Exploitation and compulsive manipulation were simply not possible on so vast a scale." The fundamental picture that emerges from a study of the Judeo-Christian tradition is that humankind is not only to respect nature's rights in a passive way, but to act positively to preserve and defend them. The attitude of superiority and contempt for nature is quite foreign, not only to the biblical world, but to the ancient world in general.[40]

That is a view endorsed by Robin Attfield, professor of philosophy at Cardiff University: "There is much more evidence than is usually acknowledged for other, more beneficent Christian attitudes to the environment and non-human nature. The evidence for gentler attitudes is underplayed."[41] Rooted in religious beliefs or not, a recognizable and more organized beneficent attitude to wild creatures only manifested itself in the late eighteenth century and well into the nineteenth century when the first humane societies in the world were set up. Even then they restricted themselves very much to the well-being of domesticated and farmed animals. Only with the establishment of Audubon and similar groups in the very late nineteenth century did concern for wild creatures start to get wider public support.

Today, attitudes about how we treat other animals are so very different. Tessa Boase, researching her book *Mrs Pankhurst's Purple Feather*, recalls the reaction of a group of visitors on a "behind the scenes" tour of the V&A Museum's Clothworkers' Centre in Kensington, London. A set of early twentieth-century hats was set out on a table, some decorated with whole birds of paradise. The keen visitors immediately dashed across to see them close up. As Boase recounted:

Then, suddenly, they faltered. What was this? Whole dead birds? On top of hats? Birds with beaks and eyes, and scrabbling little claws. Was this really a fashion? One woman reached out her finger and compulsively touched the yellow, staring taxidermist's glass eye of the bird of paradise [a green, black and maroon Raggiana Bird of Paradise adorned with gossamer-fine flank plumes] and shuddered. The white-coated conservationist led her away.[42]

And as a consequence of what they helped achieve, how are the early pioneers of the American and British movements to ban feather adornments on hats remembered and celebrated today?

Unlike Harriet Hemenway and Minna Hall in the United States, Emily Williamson has been largely forgotten. So, too, have Eliza Phillips and Catherine Hall. Etta Smith, the pugnacious and combative Mrs. Lemon, made the early SPB and RSPB a popular and influential organization but, it seems, upset, frightened, and annoyed too many people to gain her rightful place in any list of honors. Today's RSPB acknowledges their formative mission in publications about the origins of the society but has lost much detail of these influential pioneers because of bomb damage in World War II at their then London offices that destroyed much of their early archive.

Yet some of the RSPB's male pioneers are remembered, and large oil paintings of a few are much in evidence in the wood-paneled entrance hall in their headquarters at Sandy in Bedfordshire. In 1989 when a plaque was affixed to Emily Williamson's house, "The Croft," in Manchester to commemorate the RSPB's centenary, it did not even include her name. That of its then president, Magnus Magnusson (1929–2007) is, though, particularly boldly displayed. In June 2019, though, a plaque in her memory was unveiled at her former home.

Richard Moore-Colyer in his otherwise thorough analysis of the struggle against the plumage trade does not mention *any* of these early female pioneers.[43] And Emily Williamson as "Mrs Robert W. Williamson," Eliza Phillips as "Mrs Edward Phillips" and Etta Smith as "Mrs Frank E. Lemon" get just seven lines of text by Robin Doughty in his lengthy study of the development of bird protection to curtail the feather trade and no entry of their names in his book's index.[44] Professor Doughty, though, does accept that he did not give them sufficient credit when he wrote his book back in the 1970s.[45]

Harriet Hemenway's achievements in the United States are much more positively commemorated. Audubon (as the National Audubon Society is now called) makes copious reference to her and Minna Hall as the two people who started the organization. And there are frequent references in a range of publications to both ladies' achievements. Harriet Hemenway's home in Clarendon Street, Boston, is a stop on the city's Women's Heritage Trail. This is the house in which she and Minna Hall arranged their tea parties to influence the ladies of Boston to forsake their feathered and bird-endowed hats. And the three quarters of a mile long Hemenway Street, in Boston's Fenway neighborhood bordering the Back Bay Fens, is named in her honor. It is quite a contrast to the half-hidden achievements of Emily Williamson and her colleagues.

In the annals of the origins of Audubon at state level, other inspiring ladies are recognized for their achievements too. Reflecting on the first quarter century of Audubon Florida, for example, Dr. Hiram Byrd, its president from 1924 to 1928, noted:

Clara Dommerich, at whose home the first meeting was held in 1900, was probably the leading spirit in the movement, but as so frequently happens in this world of affairs, the hand that presses the button is not seen. All too often the unseen hand was that of the women whose stories often were ignored or relegated to short references or footnotes. At first glance, the story of the Florida Audubon Society appears to follow that same course. Its early presidents were well-educated and prestigious men who easily mixed with business and government officials in making pleas for greater protection of the state's non-game birds. However, their successes were built upon the work of many progressive-minded women whose energy and club-women connections were vital to the founding, organization and early achievements of the organization.[46]

Without doubt, the creation of Audubon (membership today 1.4 million) and the RSPB (membership over 1.2 million) has been a substantial success. Both organizations today play a significant role in influencing government environmental and wildlife policy in the United States and the United Kingdom, in directly protecting large numbers of wildlife reserves, and in providing educational resources for young people.

A question, though, remains. None of this effort by progressively minded men and women over the course of a century, and none of the legislation that has been put on the statute books in the United States and the United Kingdom as a result, was aimed at addressing the plight of the many wild mammals killed on an enormous scale to manufacture hats, either directly from their pelts or by making hat felt from their fur. They gained no legal protection. Two species of beaver were driven to the brink of extinction; sea otters, sables, martens, foxes, and many other species were exploited mercilessly and often unsustainably.

In the United Kingdom, legislation introduced in the nineteenth century was aimed solely at preventing cruelty to farmed animals; it did not apply to wild species. Bull, bear, and badger baiting—as well as cockerel and dog fighting—was made illegal in 1835. But in 1880, the Ground Game Act, still in force today, gave landowners the right to kill rabbits and hares at any time of year though they cannot shoot at night, use poison, or employ spring traps. The first effective protective UK legislation didn't get on the statute book until the Conservation of Seals Act in 1970 followed by the Salmon and Freshwater Fisheries Act five years later. And it was not until as comparatively recently as the Wildlife and Countryside Act, 1981—a requirement on the United Kingdom of European Union legislation—that a comprehensive list of wild mammals (reviewed every five years) gained proper protection in the United Kingdom. The list omitted common species such as red fox but did limit the means of killing them. The legal regulations were consolidated after numerous modifications in 1994.[47]

Legislation to give some protection to mammals was enacted very much earlier in the United States. The Lacey Act of 1900 applied to all wildlife, not just birds. But it did not provide protection for indigenous mammals within individual states; that was the responsibility of the individual states themselves. The act—still in active use today though much amended—protects wild mammals by making it an offense to "take, possess, transport or sell" any species taken in violation of state laws.[48]

Federally, the next significant step was the Endangered Species Act, which became law in 1973; it protects and aims to recover a list of imperiled species and the ecosystems they depend upon. The list includes some species used historically for making head coverings including Steller's sea lion and sea otter. Individual U.S. states control all aspects of animal hunting. Each has different rules and regulations including what firearms and other killing methods can be used, what species can be taken and during which annual seasons (or all year for many common species such as raccoons), whether—and in what circumstances—dogs can be used, and the requirements for hunting licenses and any other restrictions.

Did Eliza Phillips, Etta Smith, and Catherine Hall have the plight of many of these fur-bearing mammals in mind—and presumably also the exploitation of fish by anglers—when they set up their Fur, Fin and Feather Folk, as it was sometimes called, before they merged it with

Emily Williamson's Plumage League? Did that presumed concern for the fate of mammals used in hat making get diluted out by the overwhelming concerns over the plumage trade? We shall never know. What we do know is that a wholly unexpected revival in mammal fur became big business in the 1950s both in the United Kingdom and in the United States. And it was the result of a myth.

The Davy Crockett Revival

THE YEAR WAS 1955. IN BRITAIN THOSE FEW PEOPLE LUCKY ENOUGH TO HAVE SMALL BUT constantly flickering, sound-crackling, and ill-focused, black-and-white television pictures were mesmerized by "Westerns": cowboys and what were then referred to as "Indians"—indigenous Americans—in stories of derring-do replete with revolvers, cowboy boots, bandannas, and Stetson hats. There were ranchers and, more exotic still, people called bounty hunters. The American West in the late nineteenth century seemed to British preadolescents a place of incredible excitement, mystery, and allure where cowboys lived by their wits and the gun. For young children growing up in spartan, post-World War II Britain—and this author was one of them—Westerns symbolized a world so far away and remote compared with our own limited experiences, we all emulated it in play, as best we could.

Among the mesmerizing episodes of *The Lone Ranger*, *Hopalong Cassidy*, and the *Cisco Kid* was another, even more incredible, all-American hero. He was *Davy Crockett, King of the Wild Frontier*. Crockett (1786–1836) was a folk hero, a frontiersman, soldier, and politician who died in somewhat obscure circumstances at the Battle of the Alamo. There were only a few episodes of his incredible adventures, but every 1950s child in Britain seemed to want a Crockett buckskin shirt, Crockett-style moccasins, and a toy rifle. Most of all they yearned for a coonskin cap: a fur hat made from a northern raccoon (*Procyon lotor*), a medium-sized, gray-furred mammal with a characteristic ringed tail native to North America (see plate 18). That was terribly exotic too.[1]

The Crockett obsession was just as great among urban American youngsters. It had begun there on 15 December 1954 when the first of three episodes produced by Walt Disney, "Davy Crockett, Indian Fighter," was broadcast on the ABC Network. Crockett was portrayed by a young actor named Fess Parker, and over forty million viewers tuned into the TV program that first night. For the subsequent two episodes, viewing figures ballooned. By the time that the last of the three episodes was broadcast on 23 February 1955 ("Davy Crockett at the Alamo"), the United States was in a Crockett frenzy. Children wore coonskin caps to school and slept with them on their heads in bed.[2]

The first three episodes were edited into the 1955 film *Davy Crockett, King of the Wild Frontier*, filmed partly in the scenically beautiful Great Smoky Mountains in North Carolina. Another film appeared in 1956. But no one wanted to even consider that this larger-than-life folk hero owed more to Disney and Fess Parker's acting than to Davy Crockett in reality.

Merchandising of "Davy Crockett wear" became big business. We did not know it at the time, but while probably the majority of the Davy Crockett caps were made of faux fur (though many had a real raccoon tail attached), at the height of their appeal the Crockett fashion phenomenon resulted in around five thousand coonskin caps being sold each and every day in the United States alone.[3] The coonskin cap became the look that every little boy wanted, and the frenzied demand boosted the price for raccoon tails from 25 cents per pound to $6 and, in a few cases, to $8 ($75 at today's value).

The coonskin cap worn by Fess Parker in all of the TV episodes and in the film was made from the skin and fur of a wild northern raccoon complete with head and luxuriant tail. In 2004, he donated it to the National Museum of American History where it remains on show. But according to a contemporary report in the *New York Times*, caps sold to consumers might have been made of almost any mammal bearing fur: useless scraps of opossum, muskrat, rabbit, wolf, fox, and skunk were often substituted for raccoon to get the hats on the market.[4] The subterfuge relied on the vast majority of purchasers not being able to tell the difference. A girl's version, the Polly Crocket hat (Crockett's first wife was Polly Finley), made of white faux fur, was also marketed.

The profit-driven, unrestricted wildlife killings of previous centuries had returned. Northern raccoons and other mammals were being killed in large numbers across much of the United States. Dealers would no doubt have driven it well along the near extinction route of the North American beaver had the market for "Davy Crockett" hats endured (see plate 19).

By the early decades of the twentieth century, using feathers from wild birds to decorate hats had been banned, and fewer hats of any description were being made out of beaver fur—mainly because beavers were few and far between—but the sudden and wholly unexpected success of the Davy Crockett story gave the fur hat trade an unpredicted and completely unexpected boost.

Not that Crockett-type hats were anything new. Coonskin caps were originally worn by some indigenous American tribes. Raccoons were often killed for their pelts in order to make warm winter clothing. Spotted Tail (ca. 1823–1881), a famous Brulé Lakota tribal chief, took his name from a raccoon skin hat—with the tail attached—that he had acquired from a fur trader. European pioneers that settled in Tennessee, Kentucky, and North Carolina in the eighteenth and nineteenth centuries saw what the local indigenous people were wearing for warmth, adopted them, and wore them as hunting caps. Their rough-hewn look became an iconic part of the American frontiersman image.[5]

Crockett was born in what is today Greene County near the community of Limestone in Tennessee, though it was part of North Carolina at the time. Always known as "David" and not "Davy," David Crockett was a frontiersman never more at home than when he was out in the forests and canebrakes (dense stands of tough grasses over twenty feet high) hunting with dogs and shooting any edible animal or farmland pest: squirrels and rabbits as well as wolves and bears.

Married twice (Polly Crockett died after a short illness in 1815) with six children, he was a charismatic and amusing raconteur who could hold a crowd of people spellbound. He was also a soldier in his youth, volunteering with the Tennessee Militia led by Major General (later President) Andrew Jackson (1767–1845) and fighting in the controversial and bloody wars against the Creek indigenous nation. Crockett later turned local politician and was elected in 1821 to the Tennessee State legislature. An outspoken representative, he championed the rights of ordinary settlers and the poor against big landowning interests.

In 1827 he was elected to the U.S. Congress where he served intermittently until 1835, often vehemently opposing many of the policies promulgated by Jackson, especially the Indian Removal Act of 1830. In 1836 he took part in the Texas Revolution (the armed rebellion by U.S. colonists and Texas Mexicans against the Mexican government) and was killed at the Battle of the Alamo that year. After his death, the precise circumstances of which have never been clear, Crockett's exploits at hunting and as a frontiersman assumed mythical proportions; he became one of the best-known American folk heroes.[6]

But hype far outstripped reality. There is no evidence that Crockett ever wore a coonskin cap when he was out hunting; the Fess Parker version of the Crockett persona owed little to reality and much to the box office. Ironically, it was after his early death that the first drawing of Crockett in a fur cap appeared; more ironically still, the hat in the drawing was not made of raccoon skin but of the skin of a wildcat, possibly a bobcat (*Lynx rufus*). It appeared on the cover of the *Davy Crockett's 1837 Almanack*, one of a large number of such publications (none of them written by Crockett) that appeared in numerous cities across the United States between 1835 and 1841. No one knows who wrote them, but they use a pastiche of Crockett's voice to tell amusing, seemingly firsthand tales of life in the backwoods in which the hero wins fights with panthers, bears, and snakes, to name but a few. When it came to publicizing his own book, written with the help of Kentucky congressman Thomas Chilton (1798–1854) and titled *A Narrative of the Life of David Crockett, Written by Himself* (published in 1834 by E. L. Carey and A. Hart), he was known to wear a coonskin cap for the occasion to address an audience in his inimitable folksy and amusing style.[7]

Daniel Boone (1734–1820), another well-known—and well promoted by the media—American pioneer, frontiersman, explorer, and woodsman who was exploring Kentucky before Crockett was active in Tennessee, is also portrayed in films wearing a coonskin cap. According to the Boone Society, Boone never wore a coonskin cap either;[8] he wore a beaver fur felt hat, Quaker style with a wide, slightly upturned brim. It was Fess Parker again, this time portraying Boone in a television series in the 1960s, who gave his Boone character a coonskin cap just as he had with Davy Crockett. It seems as if the media image of any American frontiersman had to incorporate a coonskin cap.

The name "raccoon" is derived from an Algonquian Indian word, "arakun," though it is often spelled in different ways. Translated, it means "he who scratches with his hands," a probable reference to the raccoon's forepaws that are shaped very much like tiny human hands with five fingers and have amazing dexterity. The Sioux called this masked animal "wica," which means "little man." European colonists on the North American continent dropped the beginning from "arakun," and the mammal became the raccoon.[9] When the first European colonizers entered North America, raccoons were common in most habitats except the higher, and thereby colder, mountains and were distributed from what became southern Canada down through the United States and into Central America.

Raccoons were first hunted by indigenous Americans for their fur and meat, and European settlers soon took up raccoon killing and started using specially bred hounds for the purpose.[10] George Washington is usually credited with owning some of the first coon-hunting dogs, seemingly foxhounds or mongrels with hound ancestry, imported from Europe. They had to be trained and bred to follow raccoons at night (raccoons are mainly nocturnal) to trees that they would readily climb to seek refuge, stay put at the base, and wait until the hunter dispatched the hapless animal by shooting it.[11]

In the nineteenth century, several thousand were being killed annually in the United States, but the numbers rose substantially when coonskin coats became popular into the twentieth century, including becoming de rigueur with college students in the 1920s. At least 388,000 were killed in the 1934/35 hunting season (the length of which varied state to state), but that burgeoned to around one million animals being killed annually in 1946/47 and two million by

1962/63. Information on the numbers killed just to make Davy Crockett–style hats is impossible to unravel from estimates of the numbers killed for all other purposes: to make warm winter coats, or because they were considered urban and agricultural pests, overturning refuse containers, raiding fruit trees and other crops, and breaking into poultry houses to take eggs and chicks.

An all-time killing high was reached in 1976/77 with 5.2 million killed, though this is well after the Davy Crockett craze had faded away,[12] suggesting strongly that most raccoons were still being killed for their pelts to make fur coats, for "sport," or because of the damage they often cause.

The American and British boyhood obsession with the coonskin cap was short-lived. By the end of 1956, interest in it was fading. It fizzled out as rapidly as it had taken off. The ephemeral Davy Crockett craze was the last fling on any substantial scale of the widespread killing of a fur-bearing mammal solely to make hats.

Through the twentieth century in the coldest climates in the world—the Arctic and sub-arctic and mountainous regions of central Asia, for instance—a wide range of mammal species continued to be hunted for clothing including hats. Much later in the century, synthetic fur substitutes started to become more available and would eventually form a significant sector of the fur market.

Ladies' hat decoration with feathers, wings, and whole wild birds—which reached its zenith in the late nineteenth and early twentieth centuries—had been at least temporarily curtailed by World War I when it became unseemly to wear bird-laden hats, at least in public. The wings, tails, heads, and all manner of feathers that were the everyday wear of so many ladies in the 1880s both in Europe and North America were regarded as bizarre and wholly inappropriate before the 1920s. Those that retained them hid them away in boxes in wardrobes and cupboards, some never to be worn again. Public opinion against the killing of birds, both native and from overseas, had gathered substantial pace, and legislation on both sides of the Atlantic would eventually curtail permanently the trade in most species.

But there was something of a revival in feather-bedecked hats in the melee of celebration and relief when World War I was over. The British Empire Exhibition of 1924/25 held in London saw the South African pavilion display a twenty-foot replica of the crest of the Prince of Wales, three white ostrich feathers emerging from a gold coronet. The huge replica consisted of thousands of ostrich feathers; there were live ostriches on site, and feathers could be plucked from them by anyone willing to spend six shillings a go ($24 today).[13] The South African ostrich feather industry (using farmed birds) was regaining some of its glory days; an "osprey"—a few clipped egret feathers (some from captive birds but maybe not all)—or an ostrich plume or two, and even an occasional bird of paradise, made a regular appearance on otherwise plainer hat styles that were still in vogue into the early 1920s.

Overall, less decorated hat styles had become fashionable. The sheer impracticality of some of the most flamboyant, bird-trussed, and glitzy headwear had also become obvious when the automobile became a much more sought-after status symbol in the 1920s. Some hats, though, managed to combine practicality with a show of exotic feathers; one such, made in the 1930s by Lucienne Rabaté for the House of Reboux, Paris, is constructed around a simple, cloche-style, unlined suede cap that fits close to the head (see plate 20). The brim of the hat is composed entirely of iridescent Himalayan monal pheasant feathers and sweeps from a peak at the center of the forehead to a curved point at either side of the face. A small group of feathers stands vertically on the hat to form a small crest; these are actually the feather crest of the pheasant itself.

With the Importation of Plumage (Prohibition) Act in the United Kingdom coming into law in 1922, no hummingbirds, birds of paradise, or Himalayan monals were any longer legally available; milliners had to start to make the best they could out of much less showy and very much more homespun goose, cockerel, and pheasant feathers. In the United States, hat trimmings were confined to farmed ostrich, pheasant, cockerel, artificial aigrettes (seemingly made of fur), and other feathers of farm birds, often dyed to make them more exotic in appearance.[14]

According to Madeleine Ginsburg, a former curator of costume at London's V&A Museum, ladies waving soldiers off in the United Kingdom at the outbreak of World War I wore small neat hats, mostly cloches and toques, close-fitting, bell-shaped hats with limited trimming.[15] They were, said some commentators, "rammed on the head" and "singularly ugly," though after the first year or so of war, some spiky feathers made an appearance, presumably farmed ostrich feathers. Into the 1920s, hats were worn straight and pulled low over the forehead; according to Edna Woolman Chase (1877–1957), editor in chief at *Vogue* magazine for nearly forty years, "chic started at the eyebrows" and Loelia, Duchess of Westminster was almost reduced to recognizing her friends by their teeth! A tiny jewel, a tuft of flowers or feathers, or even a plastic clip was the sole ornamentation.[16]

Nevertheless, customs officials in the United Kingdom implementing the 1921 Importation of Plumage (Prohibition) Act, were still occasionally seizing quantities of illegally imported feathers. In 1923, for example, two Frenchmen were charged with concealing in egg boxes a load of bird of paradise skins valued at £7,500. The case was dismissed, seemingly because of a lack of evidence. But there was another seizure the following year in which an incredible 136,000 grebe skins (of three different species) were seized, coinciding with an upsurge of interest in these fine "furs" by the millinery trade.[17]

By the later 1920s and early 1930s, hats with wider brims became more fashionable; called "picture hats" or "Gainsboroughs," they were semiformal wear for garden parties and such. A few feathers and ribbons lying along the brim were all that was needed to banish the unsentimental cloche.

In trend-setting Paris at around the same time, ladies' hats were bulkier than in Britain or in the United States. Even when France was under German occupation in World War II, a pillbox style (upright with straight sides and no brim) decorated with whatever was available—some farmyard bird feathers from geese, ducks, and chickens, scraps of fabric, even old newspaper—combined with skill and panache made the look far more dazzling than elsewhere in the 1940s. It signaled a determination not to be cowed, rather to defy the occupiers, a sign of normality under repressive circumstances.[18]

In the United Kingdom, World War II brought government control over the output of hats. A "make do and mend" philosophy got drilled deeply into the British psyche; combined with the inflated cost of materials, it ensured that many people had stopped wearing hats of any kind by the end of the war. Much the same attitude started to pervade U.S. culture too, and wearing anything approaching a formal hat as everyday clothing is one fashion style that has not returned. Not that going hatless was accepted everywhere. In the early 1940s, the National Audubon Society found that New York and Philadelphia millinery companies were still selling large amounts of wild bird feathers. Long, "Robin Hood" type plumes had become popular, and the undercover representatives of Audubon found no less than twenty-four milliners selling large feathers from foreign birds of prey. Some offered native eagle feathers from golden and bald eagles shot or trapped in western U.S. states. Imported feathers of twenty other species were found including Oriental storks (*Ciconia boyciana*) from Southeast Asia, great bustard (*Otis tarda*), probably from Russia, and crested screamers (*Chauna torquata*) from South America. Confiscations and prosecutions followed.[19]

When the war was over, just as happened after World War I, the ban on wearing evening dress in Paris theaters was lifted and the extravagances of the 1880s reappeared for a while. Aigrettes (egret plumes), panaches of bird of paradise tail feathers, ostrich plumes often dyed in a range of colors, wings, and whole small birds were again to be seen. The hats had, presumably, been boxed up for the duration of the German occupation and were released from their safe keeping once again.

In general, though, more and more people in the West were going outdoors hatless, except perhaps for more formal social occasions. Ginsburg quotes a Mass-Observation survey in 1948 that found that only a third of sixteen- to twenty-five-year-olds in the United Kingdom were likely to wear a hat.[20] The prewar conventions were being abandoned along with what was considered to be unnecessary expense. When President John Kennedy was inaugurated on a cold January day in 1961, neither he nor Jackie Kennedy, an elegant fashion icon of the time, wore hats. Kennedy did not wear a hat throughout his short presidency. On just a few occasions, Jackie Kennedy did wear a pillbox-style hat: head hugging, no brim, and cylindrical. It had no ornamentation, and there most certainly was not a feather to be seen.

The Survivors' Story

LOOKING DOWN THE ARID ROCKY HILLSIDE, WHAT LOOKS LIKE ANOTHER DUST DEVIL IS sending up a small spiral of sand into the air on the Acacia-dotted savanna below. A closer look and a large shape appears gradually as the pale orange sand-cloud fades: a single common ostrich. Reintroduced in the 1980s here in the Bou Hedma National Park on the northern fringes of the Sahara in Tunisia, these huge flightless birds were common across almost all of North Africa until they were decimated by the feather trade, which peaked around 1880. The nearest wild ostriches today to those at Bou Hedma are 1,600 miles south on the southern fringes of this mighty desert.

Although the four subspecies of the common ostrich are very similar in appearance (differentiated mainly by the color of their bare-skinned necks and legs), their fates are rather different. The North African subspecies occurs today in only six of the eighteen countries in North Africa where it once roamed. At the other end of the continent, in southern Africa, the South African subspecies is confined mainly to the very northwest of its historic range, although escapes of feral birds from ostrich farms have bolstered its numbers. A third subspecies is today restricted to the savannas of southern Kenya and eastern Tanzania, almost entirely within protected national parks. A fourth subspecies, known as the Arabian ostrich, was formerly common across the Middle East and western Asia. It was driven to extinction by hunting for food and for its plumes. The last individual was found dying in Jordan in 1966.[1]

Hunted over many centuries for its meat and eggs, as well as for its skin for leather making, these might all have been factors in the early decline of the common ostrich over much of its former range. A more significant decline probably began in the Middle Ages when ostrich feathers became fashion items for the wealthy and for senior military officers in Europe. But it was the intensive hunting for the hat market in the nineteenth century in particular, spurred on by the huge profits that were being made from the trade, that substantially reduced its numbers and caused the enormous contraction in its distribution (see plate 21).

Today the common ostrich inhabits less than half of the territory it occupied historically. Nevertheless, the overall population of common ostriches is considered to be large, often bolstered by ostrich farm escapes—though there are no estimates of numbers—and, although it is declining slowly today because of habitat degradation and hunting, it is considered by IUCN to be "of least concern," defined as "not threatened or near threatened."[2]

Ostriches might well have become extinct—or reduced to very few, scattered populations at best—if ostrich farming had not begun in the 1860s in South Africa and subsequently started up in other countries. Reintroductions of ostriches to parts of their historic range in the Middle

East and in a few protected areas in North Africa (such as Bou Hedma) have been attempted but have been very limited in their success. That success depends on convincing local people to desist from exploiting them. In many areas, too, degradation of desert habitats due to overgrazing by goats and camels has substantially damaged the habitat required to support them. All of this does not augur well for returning this much exploited bird to more than a tiny fraction of its previous range. It remains one of the major casualties of the feather trade.

The Somali ostrich, found only in northeast Africa, was once considered a subspecies of the common ostrich, but since 2014 it has been recognized as a separate species. It has declined substantially, and its populations have become highly fragmented, because of hunting for meat, collecting of its eggs for consumption and other uses, and killing for its feathers. Today, habitat degradation is perhaps even more of a threat, and the species is considered to be "vulnerable," defined by IUCN as "likely to become endangered." This veritable cocktail of problems faced by the Somali ostrich is not one that suggests it will survive long term.[3]

Equally or even more heavily exploited than ostriches, the fate of egrets whose nuptial display feathers were ruthlessly sought by the plume trade could not be more different from the fate of the two species of ostrich. Three egret species, in particular, the great white egret found across much of the Southern Hemisphere, the snowy egret of the southern United States and South America, and the very similar little egret of southern Europe, Asia, and much of Africa were driven to the edge of extinction across much of their historic ranges. Huge numbers of the breeding colonies of all three species were annihilated. It was not until legislation banning imports of feathers to the United States and the United Kingdom was introduced in the early decades of the twentieth century—and there was a substantial change in fashion—that the killing ceased. Today, however, all three species have bounced back: they are common once again across their historic ranges, all three are extending their breeding areas, and all three are considered by IUCN to be of "least concern," not considered as "threatened" or even as "near threatened." Their recoveries have been nothing short of spectacular.[4]

The great white egret's recovery in the United States has been rapid. In 1912, the largest surviving Florida breeding colony contained only four hundred nests; twenty years later the state had eighty thousand birds. Overall in the southern states of the United States where it breeds, there has been a 29 percent increase in numbers on average per decade in the last forty years. It is also abundant once again in Central and South America after many decades of plume hunting there in the nineteenth century in particular. Its range is also expanding in Europe—where the population was estimated in 2015 to be between forty-one thousand and seventy thousand individuals—partly perhaps encouraged by climate warming, though unexplained population fluctuations might limit its further permanent expansion.[5]

The snowy egret was particularly badly hit because it was the more numerous egret across vast swathes of the lowlands of South America and much of the southern United States. It was also less shy and, thereby, easier to approach and shoot. And its aigrettes—its nuptial display plumes—were even more sought after than those of other species. By 1900 it was extinct in Florida where previously it had been abundant at numerous large breeding colonies. A successful attempt was made in Louisiana by Ned McIlhenny (1872–1949), an American businessman, explorer, and conservationist, as early as 1892 to captive breed snowies in order to begin re-establishing populations in protected locations. By 1909 he was able to release three thousand snowies to other parts of Florida.[6]

Today, the snowy egret is common once more throughout its historic range, and it still appears to be increasing in numbers. In the United States, its breeding range is extending to new locations along the Atlantic coast.[7] The *North American Waterbird Conservation Plan* published in 2002 estimates a U.S. continental population of over 143,000 birds, although drainage of wetlands they rely on for feeding continues to be a problem across their range.[8]

The fortunes of the little egret since the banning of the feather trade have been very similar to those of the snowy. They have regained abundance across their historic range, in large parts of which they had been decimated. Today there are estimated to be between 660,000 and 3.15 million little egrets in total, a rather wide variation in assessments but the best available. Partly confined to lowland marshes and coastal plains as well as using wet farmland habitats such as rice fields, the European population within this total is estimated at between 133,000 and 170,000 (although die-offs occur in cold winters), and the birds seem to be generally expanding their mainly southern European range.

Since the early 1980s, the species has gradually colonized the southern half of the United Kingdom and much of southern Ireland where it was previously a rare visitor. Breeding mainly among grey herons (*Ardea cinerea*) in woodland heronries, the expansion of the little egret in the United Kingdom and Ireland is one of the most phenomenal shifts in abundance and distribution of any bird in western Europe over the past two decades.[9]

The fate of other egrets and herons whose feathers were sought for millinery has been far less positive. Reddish egrets, for instance, were exterminated in Florida at the beginning of the twentieth century; small numbers of these attractive wading birds with their auburn nape plumes that were the original cause of their downfall have returned to breed, but overall their numbers in the very south of the United States have never recovered. Much the same appears to apply to their Central American breeding colonies where they were exploited for eating and for their plumes; they remain depleted and very patchily distributed. The reddish egret is classified by IUCN as "near threatened," and its population numbers between fifteen thousand and thirty thousand birds. It might be increasing slowly overall, but poorly understood declines at several colonies are reported too.[10]

The Chinese egret is even more imperiled. It was also exploited for its wispy, white nape and chest nuptial plumes. Breeding in scattered small colonies mainly in the coastal zones of southeast China and Korea and a few other places, its total population now might number less than one thousand pairs. Prior to wide-scale killing for its plumes, the Chinese egret was considered to have been far more abundant. It has never recovered from this onslaught. With present-day threats of habitat destruction and some egg collecting for food, the future of this species is bleak. It is considered by IUCN as "vulnerable to extinction."[11]

While one or two other species of heron and egret suffered some depredations at the hands of plume hunters, the impact on their populations appears to have been small and impossible to quantify. They include the intermediate egret of central and southern Africa and much of southern Asia, the great blue heron (which in its white plumage form has lacy neck plumes) of North and Central America, the little blue heron of the southern United States and South America, the tricolored heron mainly found in Central America, and the little squacco heron found in much of Africa and in southern Europe. All are today regarded as being of "least concern" by IUCN.

The greater adjutant stork and its close relative, the lesser adjutant, were the source, according to contemporary records from the early nineteenth century in India, of the so-called marabou feathers used by milliners. But these accounts make no claim that the birds were shot. Instead, they were seemingly captured in some way (both species often feed close to human habitation and refuse), and a bunch of the soft, white under-tail feathers pulled out before the birds were released. Painful certainly, but it probably led to few deaths of either species. Compared with the wide-scale threats both species continue to face in recent decades in Southeast Asia where both were historically common—felling of tree nesting sites, pesticide poisoning, habitat destruction, and more—any impact from the plumage trade was insignificant. The greater adjutant is today considered by IUCN to be "endangered" and in serious decline; the lesser adjutant is classified as "vulnerable" but not as a result of the feather trade.[12]

Another large wading bird persecuted by the feather trade was the roseate spoonbill. Its pink and pink-tinged white plumage was too much of an attraction for milliners; in consequence it was frequently shot at its tree-breeding colonies in the very south of the United States and across parts of its extensive Central and South American range. It was virtually exterminated along the whole of the U.S. Gulf Coast in the late nineteenth and early twentieth centuries. As it became eliminated in the United States, hunters started to eliminate it from parts of northern South America too. By the 1970s, this attractive spoonbill had recovered its numbers in much of the southern United States and in Central and South America. Listed by IUCN as of "least concern," its populations are considered to be stable overall though with habitat destruction and illegal hunting outside the United States still affecting some colonies.[13]

Rather like the roseate spoonbill, the most colorful ibis in the world most certainly did not escape the attention of the millinery industry. The scarlet ibis, a vibrant pink-red in color, breeding in large colonies in the very north of South America, has recovered from depredations by nineteenth-century plume hunters and is considered abundant and of "least concern" by Birdlife International today,[14] although several colonies are in decline because of more recent habitat changes such as wetland drainage and the destruction of coastal mangrove forests.[15] Scarlet ibis feathers are still obtained by hunting in parts of French Guiana where a large industry prospers making artificial flowers from them for sale to tourists. This ibis can be hunted legally in French Guiana during the winter months, and the flowers can be sold throughout the year. It has become an important part of the local economy in the town of Sinnamary, and the only means of eradicating the trade might be to encourage the use of substitute feathers obtained from domesticated farmed birds that are then dyed to match those of the ibis.[16]

Grebes were sought by the millinery trade for a very different product that the industry referred to as "grebe fur," their thick under pelt of downy feathers. The great crested grebe breeding in the United Kingdom, southern Europe, and southern Asia and the western grebe and Clark's grebe in the United States were shot in large numbers, mostly for lining coats and capes, but the millinery trade also made use of them.

In the case of the great crested grebe, its showy ear tuft feathers were particularly sought after for hat decoration as well as its "grebe fur." In the United Kingdom, by the early 1900s the great crested grebe was on the brink of extinction as a breeding bird, but numbers recovered well through that century after persecution ceased. It is now abundant again on larger inland waters throughout its range; its European population has expanded north in recent decades and numbers in the hundreds of thousands of pairs, while its UK population continues to expand.[17]

Many thousands of western grebes were shot in the nineteenth and early twentieth centuries for their down, but protection subsequently promoted their recovery. Today there are good populations across most of their historic territory in the west of the United States and southwest Canada, though their habit of wintering in coastal waters has made them susceptible to oil spills in recent decades and they have largely disappeared from many Californian lakes where they were formerly common, seemingly due to pesticide poisoning. The very similar Clark's grebe, always a much less common species inhabiting a similar U.S. zone to the western grebe, has also recovered from feather hunting—though it was never persecuted to the same degree—but is confronted with the same issues that are impacting its lookalike.[18]

Of the many seabirds exploited for their feathers, several species of albatross suffered enormous depredation and cruelty. Mostly their feathers were used for mundane purposes other than for decorating hats—even for stuffing mattresses—but some wing plumes and the wings themselves were occasionally used as hat décor through the nineteenth century and into the first part of the twentieth. At least eleven breeding islands for the short-tailed albatross in the North Pacific were recorded before the killing began, and although the precise size of their original population is not known, it is estimated at several million. The killing was banned by the Japanese government (who owned most of the breeding islands) in 1906, but it carried on illegally until 1932. By 1929, the short-tailed had been reduced to 1,400 birds on its sole surviving breeding island, Torishima off southeast Japan, and volcanic eruptions there later finished off the population. The species was declared extinct until 1950 when a few birds surprisingly returned; breeding began soon after, and their world population stands at around four hundred birds today, a mere shadow of their original population size.[19]

In the Hawaiian Islands, tens of thousands of Laysan and black-footed albatrosses were killed by Japanese feather hunters and their eggs taken for eating. And the once huge colony of shy albatrosses off Tasmania was reduced to just three hundred nests by 1909. Today, the Laysan albatross has recovered and numbers between 1.2 and 1.4 million birds, though many thousands are killed each year by getting trapped in gill nets and possibly by ingesting discarded plastics. Black-footed albatrosses (also a North Pacific species) have also recovered, the bulk of its world population—perhaps two hundred thousand birds—breeding again on the Hawaiian Islands. But some of its colonies are declining, seemingly the result of predation by introduced land mammals such as rats and because of habitat degradation, disturbance, fishing entanglements, and plastic ingestion. Populations of the shy albatross are still recovering, and the species today has a total population across the Southern Ocean of maybe one million birds. Mortality from commercial fisheries appears to be declining as countries gradually introduce more seabird-friendly fishing systems.[20]

Tropicbirds, with their long and elegant tail streamers, were an obvious visual attraction for the millinery trade. The two more numerous species of the three that exist, the red-tailed and white-tailed tropicbird found across the mid and South Pacific and the Indian Oceans, were both exploited, but they were also hunted for their meat and eggs. No tropicbirds are globally threatened today, and many of their breeding sites, usually steep cliffs, would have been largely inaccessible to hunters. There is, though, little information on the size of their historic populations, so it is difficult to establish real trends. Some populations today appear to be increasing; others have been lost, possibly because of continued harvesting for their meat and eggs plus the introduction of non-native mammal predators to some breeding islands. Red-tailed tropicbirds today number probably several tens of thousands of pairs, with their white-tailed cousins, seemingly always more common, numbering very many more.[21]

Black-legged kittiwakes, the juveniles of which were sought after for their wings to decorate ladies' hats, recovered rapidly from the persecution they suffered on many of their breeding cliffs in the United Kingdom in the early years of the twentieth century. An oceangoing seabird traversing the North Atlantic and North Pacific Oceans, its global population is today estimated as maybe sixteen million birds. But it has declined rapidly since the 1980s, the decline is ongoing, and the species is now categorized as "vulnerable." Overfishing depleting its food supplies, oil pollution, and bycatches in commercial fisheries appear to be the main factors that are having much more impact than the millinery trade ever did.[22]

Several species of tern were depleted by plumage hunters, both in Europe and in the Americas. Almost all terns breed on open areas of land, many on shorelines, so they are particularly vulnerable because they can easily be trapped or shot.

The roseate tern's pale pink breast feathers when in its breeding plumage attracted the attention of milliners, and many of its coastal breeding colonies were ravaged as a result. This tern has an almost worldwide but exceedingly scattered distribution in the North Atlantic, in the Caribbean, and in parts of the southern Asian and Australian coasts. It has recovered from the ravages of the hat industry; its global population today is estimated to be up to 220,000 individuals, and it is classified by IUCN as not under threat. But its overall population trend is uncertain: some populations are decreasing, others (including its European population) are increasing, and several are stable. Hunting in its South American and African winter quarters, together with human disturbance and predation at its seashore breeding colonies and their natural vulnerability to events such as storm surges, means that the roseate tern still has a somewhat precarious existence.[23]

Least terns, formerly exploited on a semi-industrial scale for the hat industry, have recovered their numbers and are today not considered under threat. Breeding on seashores, rivers, and lakesides in the United States, they winter in the Caribbean and along the northern coast of South America. Vulnerable, like many tern species, to human disturbance, unpredictable high tides, urban development, and ground predators, their numbers often fluctuate wildly year to year; they are declining slowly, and their total breeding population is a fraction of that of their roseate cousin.[24]

Sooty terns, gull-billed terns, and other species were exploited too. Today there is no evidence of the impact of their killing for feathers. Sooty terns number as many as twenty-two million birds and breed on tropical islands through most of the world's oceans. The number of gull-billed terns, always far less common, might be four hundred thousand; they are widely distributed around the globe, although because many nest inland at wetlands and lakesides, they are prone to the impacts of drainage and other habitat changes, which are factors in their steady decline.[25]

Birds of paradise have been among the species most exploited for their feathers, probably sustainably by New Guinea native tribes over maybe thousands of years but almost certainly unsustainably in the nineteenth and early twentieth centuries by feather dealers eager to obtain the impressively decorated males of several species. Hunting for sale and export was eventually banned in the 1920s; limited hunting in New Guinea has been allowed since then to meet the ceremonial requirements of native society, but some birds are still hunted illegally and the skins sold to tourists.

Of the forty-four species in existence today, just four are considered as "vulnerable to extinction" in the IUCN classification while eight others are classified as "near threatened," a lesser threat category. While hunting for their plumes almost certainly depleted some species or populations of some species—several are distributed on other islands in the Indonesian archipelago as well as in Papua New Guinea—today the main threats they face are the destruction of their rainforest habitat and other implications of a growing human population.[26]

Information on precisely which species of birds of paradise, and what numbers, were killed and their skins exported—many through London auctions—is rarely recorded in sales documents. Dealers were seemingly far less interested in identification than they were in colorful feathers, nuptial plumes, and what prices their valuable prizes would attain. What we do know is that many of the skins were of the greater bird of paradise, the lesser bird of paradise, the Raggiana bird of paradise, and the red bird of paradise, but other species were doubtless exploited and added into the cargoes too. The first three are today regarded by IUCN as of "least concern"; they remain widely distributed and common, though there are no estimates of their population sizes.

The red bird of paradise, though, is classified as "near threatened" because it has a much more restricted range (four islands only) than the other three. It probably always had a far smaller population, but now its forest habitat is shrinking while collecting for its feathers (for local tribal use) might also be contributing to its decline.[27]

Although there is no record of its skins being sold at the London auction houses, the blue bird of paradise has historically been killed by local tribesmen for its feathers, especially its magnificent tail plumes. Confined to the central eastern portion of Papua New Guinea where the growing human population is reducing the area of forest, collecting for feather use locally—and some illegal selling of skins to tourists—might be a factor in this species' decline too.[28]

The tragic effects of multiple pressures on species' populations can be illustrated best by the example of Hawaii. No place on Earth is home to more bird species under threat of extinction, and the Hawaiian Islands have the very dubious distinction of being the bird extinction capital of the world. According to the American Bird Conservancy, since humans arrived there (maybe around 300 A.D.), 95 of their 142 endemic bird species have become extinct. Thirty-three of Hawaii's remaining endemic birds are listed as under threat; several might already be extinct. Habitat destruction, invasive predatory species, the spread of disease brought by introduced mosquitoes, and, in many cases, the capture or killing of birds to lavishly feather the robes and headdresses of Polynesian kings are all factors in their demise.

One example is the Hawaii mamo (*Drepanis pacifica*), one of several honeycreepers in Hawaii, which was extinct by 1898. Its vibrant black and yellow plumage guaranteed that its feathers were highly prized for feathered capes and head coverings for Polynesian royalty. Naturally tame, it was easily captured using a sticky paste to trap its feet or by holding up a flower, waiting for a mamo to dip its long, downcurved beak inside, then trapping it by squeezing the flower around its beak. In spite of this widespread hunting, it is possible that forest destruction and introduced disease might have been the primary reasons for its eventual extinction.[29]

It is not surprising that many ground-inhabiting birds with colorful plumage that appealed to feather dealers were often comparatively easy to trap and kill. Pheasants are an excellent example; several are some of the world's most visually impressive larger birds. They include the red junglefowl (*Gallus gallus*), the wild ancestor of all domestic chickens and an inhabitant, originally, of Southeast Asia. There is evidence that junglefowl feathers were sometimes for sale in the London feather auctions—probably imported from colonial India—but some might have been obtained from domesticated cockerels, which can be equally colorful. Feathers from many of the more colorful varieties bred today (and known in the trade as "coq") are frequently used to decorate contemporary hats.

The Indian peafowl, introduced as a kind of exotic living architectural feature to many parks, stately gardens, and country estates across the world, but native only to India and Sri Lanka, was very much sought after for the long train of eye-spotted, multicolored tail feathers sported by the male bird. Revered in India but often regarded as a pest for damaging farm crops, the peacock's tail feathers obtained from killed birds (the molted feathers would have been too damaged to sell) were certainly available at London feather auctions. They might well have been supplemented from occasional birds killed closer to home in parks and gardens to which they had been introduced. In the wild, the Indian peafowl remains common, and its populations are seemingly stable.[30]

Found only in Australia, the superb lyrebird, another large forest-inhabiting ground bird, was exploited solely for the long, lyre-shaped, and lacy tail feathers of the male. Today the superb lyrebird is confined to eucalyptus forests in southeast Australia. Formerly more widespread on that continent, their distributional decline is very largely the result of habitat destruction; shooting for their tails might not have been a substantial factor in this because only mature birds at least six years old could have developed the fine tail plumes so sought after. Superb lyrebirds are reasonably common today and are considered of "least concern."[31]

Other much more colorful ground birds—especially the golden pheasant, which is confined to just one area of southern China, and the Himalayan monal of the high mountains of southern China, Pakistan, and Nepal—were exploited for their exotically colored plumage and exported to the feather auctions of London mainly in the late nineteenth century. The golden pheasant, although still reasonably common, is declining because of timber extraction, hunting for food, and capture for the cage-bird trade. Whether or not the feather trade in the past also contributed to this steady decline is not clear. Introduced to many other countries across the world, including the United Kingdom where they are declining and maybe now below one thousand breeding pairs, golden pheasants are not considered to be under any serious threat.[32]

Himalayan monals are incredibly exotic-looking, large pheasants, the multicolored male possessing a blue-green feather crest that was too much of a temptation for milliners to ignore. There was an international trade in its feathers, its crest in particular, in the London auctions through the nineteenth and into the early twentieth centuries. "Crest hunting" for local use has always been common across much of its Himalayan range too, the feathers worn in hats and caps as a status symbol. There is, though, some evidence that the practice is declining. In Pakistan, the crests aren't recognized as such symbols; the monal is hunted instead for its meat.[33] Still considered to be widespread and common, this attractive pheasant is seemingly declining because of hunting and habitat degradation rather than because of any millinery use.[34]

Reeves's pheasant, found only in evergreen forests in central and eastern China, has been exploited in the past for its long, silvery white and chestnut-barred tail feathers that can reach over four feet in length. They were used traditionally to adorn headdresses in Peking opera (a form of Chinese stylized opera dating from the eighteenth century), but plastic imitations are now used because this pheasant is vulnerable to extinction. Hunting for meat, and probably for its feathers for local use, combined with forest clearance is seemingly continuing to cause an enormous fragmentation of its population.[35]

Other ground-dwelling birds heavily exploited in the past for their feathers include the four crowned pigeons that inhabit the forests of parts of New Guinea and one or two nearby islands. All are incredibly attractive, blue-grey or blue in color, and possess a fan-shaped crest of fine blue feathers. They have long been hunted by indigenous peoples for their meat and to use their feathers, the crest feathers especially. All four species—the Victoria crowned pigeon, western crowned pigeon, Scheepmaker's crowned pigeon, and Sclater's crowned pigeon—are today regarded by IUCN either as "near threatened" or as "vulnerable to extinction" in spite of having legal protection. The skins of these birds were sold in the London auctions, especially during the latter half of the nineteenth century, but the species are not recorded. Feather dealers—and maybe not even the local hunters—were not bothered about which particular pigeon they were trapping; provided it was blue and had a crest, it was highly marketable and sought after by milliners. That trade has doubtless contributed to the decline of these impressive birds, but other factors are responsible too: forest felling to plant palm oil crops, for food (crowned pigeons are large and meaty), for illegal sale to aviaries and zoos, and for feather use locally.[36]

Many other birds, both large and small, have been exploited for the feather trade, but there is very limited or no information about which species were involved. In many cases, a family name is all that appears in the sales records; for example, "kingfishers" of which there are ninety-two different species worldwide. Hummingbirds and tanagers are others. It is very likely that millions of these tiny birds were killed for their feathers and exported as skins to the markets in North America and Europe over several decades. But few records exist to record which species were trapped and killed.

Today, of the 245 species of tanager, 40 are known to be vulnerable or endangered, though information on some species is rather scant. The main problems they face are forest destruction to convert more land to agriculture and their wide-scale capture in many parts of South America as cage birds. Most of the 330 or so species of hummingbird are not under immediate threat either, but 29 are considered to be "vulnerable to extinction" or "endangered."[37] One that is mentioned by name in dealers' records is the ruby topaz hummingbird, a species found in much of northern South America. Thought to be uncommon today (there is no systematic data), it has a very wide geographical distribution, and although it appears to be declining slowly because of habitat loss, it is considered of "least concern."[38]

At the other extreme, there are some species recorded in feather auctions by name that seem rather odd; one such is the little spotted kiwi, a small, flightless New Zealand bird formerly much more widespread there than its currently very restricted distribution. Its feathers are rather shaggy in appearance, attractively mottled but a rather dull grey and white. They do not appear to be attractive to a milliner, certainly not when so many other far more exotically colored and textured feathers were available. Maybe kiwi feathers did not enthuse the millinery trade as much as early hunters thought they might, and New Zealand's kiwis—under substantial threat in so many other ways—were at least relieved of this one assault on their numbers.

There are other birds whose absence from the sales lists seems inexplicable. No bee-eaters or rollers are named, yet almost all species are common, most are widely distributed across much of Africa, Southeast Asia, and southern Europe, they are well known to many indigenous peoples, they can be captured quite easily because they are colonial breeders, and they are among the most colorful and glamorous birds in the world. Is it possible that they were labeled as kingfishers (equally colorful) by mistake, simply because hunters might not always know their names and dealers would not have recognized them anyway? Most species of bee-eater have historically been netted, shot, and poisoned because they were perceived as menaces at beehives, yet there is no record of their often gorgeously colored feathers being harvested for any purpose.[39]

Many species of bee-eater would have been easier to trap than many of the kingfisher family. The only kingfisher named in auctions appears to be the white-throated kingfisher (presuming it was identified correctly) found across southern Asia and in parts of the Middle East. Its populations today are either stable or increasing as this adaptable species penetrates new habitats. It has presumably recovered entirely from any depletion due to its killing for feathers; today the issues it faces are habitat degradation in parts of its range and the possibility of indirect pesticide poisoning.[40]

It is particularly odd that there is no mention of the cinnamon-pink, black, and white hoopoe (*Upupa epops*), another very common and easily distinguished bird found across southern Europe, southern Asia, and much of Africa or of the exotically colored jacamars of Central and South America. Why, too, were hummingbirds so sought after in the Caribbean while the tiny, vivid green todies, the dwarfs and hobgoblins of West Indian forests, were not?

By comparison, trogons—equally glamorous birds of the tropics across South America, southern Asia, and parts of Africa—do get at least a very occasional mention in auction lists in spite of being skulking forest birds that are difficult to trap. But there is no record of which species (there are thirty-nine of them) were sometimes obtained for their feathers. All remain relatively common today. Of the six species of quetzal (all of which are classified as trogons) restricted to South America—used in particular by the Aztec and Mayan civilizations in headdresses—five species today remain moderately common; one, the resplendent quetzal, is classified by IUCN as "near threatened," but that is because of forest felling increasingly restricting its habitat.[41]

Of the many mammals exploited over several centuries, even millennia, to provide fur for hats, either directly or for making into hat felt, the only two species of beaver in the world suffered catastrophically. Both the North American beaver and the Eurasian beaver were extirpated over the majority of their historic ranges, the former mainly because of its fur used to make the best quality hat felt as well as by wetland drainage, the latter by the millinery industry, because of wetland drainage, and for its castoreum.

North American beavers are today abundant again across the bulk of Canada and the United States, inhabiting almost every river and lake. Protection programs that began in the 1920s, combined with translocations of animals from pockets of remaining populations to repopulate rivers and other water bodies from which they had been lost, have achieved such success that beavers are the cause of localized problems caused by their dam construction. Prior to human settlement of the continent, the North American beaver population has been estimated at between sixty and four hundred million. By 1930 it had fallen to maybe one hundred thousand; most of those remained in the least accessible parts of Canada. Today the North American population might be six to twelve million. The far lower population than prehuman days is considered to be due to a range of factors, especially wetland drainage, pollution of rivers, engineering changes to waterways, and overhunting for their pelts.[42]

Today, North American beavers are hunted and trapped for their pelts throughout their range, but all hunting is licensed by each U.S. state or Canadian region. Annually today, about half a million North American beavers are trapped and killed under license across North America, their fur used for clothing including hat felts.[43] Some of the most expensive hat felts available today are made from beaver fur. Regulations vary, but most regulators define methods of killing and capture, seasons, bag limits, and other rules. There is no suggestion that hunting is depleting their numbers, and the North American beaver is considered to be of "least concern" by IUCN.[44]

The recovery of the Eurasian beaver is still ongoing. The fur trade had reduced its population in Europe to the brink of extinction by the start of the twentieth century; only eight populations survived totaling 1,200 animals. Protection for Eurasian beavers began in Norway in 1845, and other countries slowly followed suit. Equally importantly, a series of habitat management improvement schemes, especially water pollution reduction, combined with reintroductions to many rivers in western Europe have allowed the beaver to return to much of its former range. Most of these populations—in the Netherlands, France, and Spain, in eastern Europe and European Russia, and in parts of Scandinavia—are expanding, but several countries still remain without significant numbers or any beavers, the United Kingdom included.

By 1998, the population Europe-wide had reached 430,000. Today there are in excess of 640,000, maybe many more. While there are concerns that their numbers are not recovering in southern Asia where they existed historically, overall they are regarded as being of "least concern." Eurasian beavers are protected by European Union law implemented in all member states, and only very limited, licensed hunting is legal in a few countries with strong populations.[45]

The coypu, known as "nutria" in the millinery trade, was another aquatic mammal exploited for its fur to make lesser-quality felts than those made from beaver fur. Large numbers were trapped in the nineteenth century until coypu were farmed intensively in South America. Native to rivers and wetlands across the southern half of that continent, it was introduced in the nineteenth century to parts of several other continents for breeding in fur farms. Many subsequently escaped or were abandoned when farms outside South America closed down due to limited breeding success and a declining market.[46]

Regarded as a pest in most regions where it is non-native, coypu can cause substantial damage because they dig large burrows in riverbanks and flood banks and consume copious amounts of native vegetation and underground plant rhizomes. Eradication programs are frequent. In the wild, the coypu is considered reasonably common although decreasing and is categorized as of "least concern" because of its wide native distribution.[47]

Rabbit fur was widely used historically for hatting felt and is still used commonly today. The quality of their fur was more coarse than that of beaver, but rabbits were much more abundant, and they were easy to catch in the wild or to breed in captivity and farm. As a result, hats made of rabbit fur were considerably cheaper and available to a much wider hat-wearing public. Of the thirty-six species in the world, the European rabbit was the species most frequently used. Native only to Iberia, western France, and a sliver of North Africa, it is today considered to be "near threatened" by IUCN across its native range where its numbers have declined by up to 95 percent in recent decades. None of this is the result of harvesting for their fur; it is due, instead, to disease, habitat loss, killing for sport, and eradication by farmers. In the nineteenth century and before, it was still common in its native range and was regularly harvested for its fur.

The European rabbit has been introduced to many countries—a process begun in parts of Europe by the Romans for food—including all of Europe, Australia, and New Zealand, and parts of the United States and South America. Often abundant, though periodically controlled by outbreaks of disease, they are considered an agricultural pest and are widely killed. Historically, most fur for hat making came from rabbits kept in protected colonies in the wild (so-called warrens), from semi-domesticated populations often kept on farms, or from those shot in the wild. They were "farmed" in this way as a source of meat and fur. Gradually, a range of different rabbit breeds were developed from the original wild species.

Today, the world's output of farmed rabbits is estimated at 1.2 million carcasses a year, most of it for food; the French and Italians eat more rabbit meat than any other nation. Europe is the center of world production, and there is clearly no shortage of rabbit fur for the hat trade.[48] Consequently, the impact of the hat industry on the European rabbit has been insignificant.[49]

Fur from the European hare was often used historically to make hatting felt, often mixed with the fur of rabbit or of beaver. Some high-quality gentlemen's hatmakers still use hare fur today, either on its own or mixed with beaver fur. The most widely distributed species of hare in Europe (of thirty-two species worldwide) and introduced as a game species to parts of South America, Australia, and New Zealand, it is classified as of "least concern" by IUCN in spite of a declining population overall. Heavily exploited in the past for its meat especially, the pressures on the European hare population today are very different. Farm intensification is destroying its habitat, and sometimes exacerbated by excessive hunting, in several European countries the hare is considered to be under threat. In some countries, it is a protected species.[50]

Closely related and widespread U.S. species of jackrabbit such as the black-tailed and the white-tailed jackrabbit, the latter found also in a large part of southern Canada, were both killed on a large scale and used for hatting felt (as well as for their meat). Both remain abundant and are not considered to be under threat, but there have been some largely inexplicable local declines of the white-tailed. Both species remain widely hunted for sport and for their meat while the white-tailed is still valued for its fur, some of which is used for hat felts.[51]

In northern latitudes across North America, Scandinavia, northern Russia, and other colder regions, fur-bearing animals including Arctic hares, mountain hares, Arctic foxes, red foxes, corsac foxes, muskrats, sables, pine martens, American martens, wolverines, Arctic ground squirrels, and Arctic wolves have long been trapped for their fur to make various forms of highly insulating hats and/or trims on hooded parkas. Historically, the killing of these important fur-bearing mammals has been sustainable; northern-living peoples had a very well-developed sense of sustainability because the continued availability of such furs was a requirement for continued living at such global climatic extremes. Today, all of these mammals remain widely distributed and categorized by IUCN as being of "least concern," though some are subject to considerable local exploitation.

Arctic hares inhabit northern Canada and Greenland where their populations are widespread and healthy; small numbers are killed for their meat and for using the fur locally.[52] The closely related mountain hare remains reasonably abundant across a huge expanse of northern Europe and northern Russia. Some populations are fluctuating or are in longer-term decline, although the causes—which might include disease—are not understood. A popular game species, its fur is rarely used.[53]

Arctic foxes have a circumpolar northern distribution and a total population of maybe several hundred thousand animals. Numbers fluctuate annually depending on the abundance of their main rodent prey, lemmings. It remains the most important terrestrial game species for indigenous peoples who today mainly use shooting and leg-hold traps to capture them for their fur. Used locally, the furs are also an important trade item, though the market has declined in recent decades, and farmed Arctic foxes now predominate. Because of their large reproductive capacity, Arctic foxes have been found quite capable of sustaining high levels of harvesting and can still maintain their populations. Only in parts of Scandinavia is their population in seemingly irreversible decline, though the causes—maybe disease—are unclear. In most of its range the Arctic fox is not protected; the exceptions are full protection in Sweden (since 1928) as well as Finland and Norway plus partial protection in a few other countries including Russia.[54]

The red fox occurs naturally across the whole of Europe and most of Asia into the Arctic. It was introduced into North America in the seventeenth century for fox hunting and to Australia in the 1800s. A highly adaptable opportunist able to prosper in habitats as diverse as Arctic tundra and city centers, its population is huge and is stable overall though subject to significant fluctuation locally. Generally not a protected species, most countries in which trapping for fur and killing as farm pests take place have regulated open seasons and controls on the methods of capture. The number of red foxes raised in farms for their fur exceeds that of any other species except, possibly, American mink (whose fur is used for jackets, coats, capes, and scarves but not hats) and far exceeds the number of wild red foxes killed for their fur.[55]

The corsac fox is confined to a large area of southern Russia and northern Asia where it inhabits vast arid steppes. Generally common and widespread, increasing killing, illegal trade, and habitat changes might soon affect its overall numbers. The intensity of trapping or shooting for its fur varies between regions and is intense enough to substantially reduce populations at least locally (see plate 22). Hunting for their fur has long been a traditional and commercial activity; hunting bans have been implemented periodically in Mongolia and Russia to allow their populations to recover following intense periods of hunting, although for many years after the collapse of the

USSR controls there were poorly implemented. Some countries impose seasonal hunting restrictions and certain hunting methods are banned, but the corsac fox is not otherwise protected.[56]

The muskrat of North America was introduced as a fur farm animal into northern Europe in 1905, subsequently escaped, and has spread incredibly fast into much of northern Asia. It can be abundant and widespread throughout its original and new ranges. Extensively trapped for their dark fur, muskrats are often also trapped, hunted, or poisoned because they cause considerable damage by burrowing into riverbanks and other structures. In the United States, over 1.6 million muskrats were trapped in 2013, and there is no reason to assume that numbers trapped have fallen since.[57] Unsurprisingly, it is not protected anywhere.

The sable of northern Russia and northern China is closely related to the American marten of the northern United States, Canada, and Alaska and the pine marten of Europe and western Russia, none of which is under threat. Possessing the crème de la crème of furs, more lustrous and silky than others, the sable has the misfortune to be assiduously hunted throughout most of its range as a result. However, because Russia limits hunting to wintertime and implements scientifically substantiated quotas, sables are actually increasing in numbers. They are also strictly protected in Russian state reserves, game reserves, and national parks. In China they are fully protected too.[58]

By the early twentieth century excessive trapping had severely depleted the similar American marten in Alaska, Canada, and the western United States, while logging of mature forests has also removed much of its habitat. Reintroduction since then has helped boost populations in many areas, and its total numbers are probably at least several hundred thousand today. It is still legally trapped for its fur in the western U.S. states.[59]

The pine marten of Europe and western Russia is stable in numbers and generally widespread, though local declines are recorded. Heavily exploited for its fur in Russia up until the 1920s, its population there has since been increasing, and hunting quotas are rigidly enforced. Across much of Europe, hunting controls are reversing earlier declines, but the marten is often still the subject of persecution where it is legally protected. Current introductions of martens from strong populations in Scotland are successfully bolstering depleted populations in Wales.[60]

With a huge circumpolar northerly distribution, the aggressive wolverine occurs at a low density throughout most of its range. Declining overall, the falls are particularly notable in its European range but are offset by large populations, seemingly stable, in North America and northern Asia; hence its "least concern" overall categorization by IUCN. It is still killed for its fur in Russia, Canada, and parts of the northern United States; wolverine fur is often used for the trim on parka hoods by Arctic-living peoples, and wolverine fur hats remain popular in the United States and Canada. Killing of wolverine in many parts of its range (though it is a protected species in several countries and is subject to considerable population monitoring) is the result of its frequent attacks on livestock including sheep (up to ten thousand each summer in Norway alone) and even reindeer/caribou. Wolverine (no more than four feet long) will even attack moose/elk, which can be six feet in height.[61]

The very much smaller and colonial Arctic ground squirrel of northern Canada and the Russian Far East is today common to abundant throughout its range. Trapped historically, and currently, for its meat and fur for mainly local trade, the species is not threatened. In Alaska, they are often called "parka squirrels" to reflect the frequent use of their fur to make the important ruff around the edge of a parka hood. Trapping doesn't appear to be reducing its numbers, but overgrazing by livestock and more frequent drought might cause future declines. IUCN classifies this squirrel as being "of least concern."[62]

The northern raccoon, whose killing was substantially stimulated by the Davy Crockett hat craze in the 1950s, remains abundant throughout the United States, southern Canada, and Central America. From the 1930s on, it was introduced to parts of Europe and Western Asia. Adaptable and common, the northern raccoon is increasing especially in urban areas where it can be a pest. The substantial numbers killed historically for their pelts—including for Davy Crockett hats—do not seem to have had any long-term impact on its numbers.[63]

The tails of sables, pine martens, American martens, beech martens, gray foxes, and fishers were used to make shtreimels worn by male Orthodox Jews on special occasions. Killed for their body pelts, the tails were largely surplus to requirement and were worth far less. Beech martens, found across Europe and parts of southern Asia, are reasonably common with populations either stable or increasing. Today they are trapped for their fur in Russia and probably elsewhere, but there is no indication of a decline as a result.[64]

The gray fox of the United States and Central America is also widespread, and its populations are stable. Not a prime source of pelts because its fur is of lower quality compared with other mammals, nevertheless thousands are probably killed legally (they are not a protected species) for their pelts annually. The gray fox is regarded as of "least concern" by IUCN.[65]

The fisher, closely related to, but larger than, the American marten, is found mainly in southern Canada and the very north of the United States. During the nineteenth and early twentieth centuries it was trapped excessively for its fur. Forest felling also reduced its numbers. But its populations have rebounded, and it probably has a total population today of hundreds of thousands. It is still trapped for its fur but in smaller numbers. Efforts are underway to reintroduce the fisher to some parts of its range where numbers remain low. It is categorized as being of "least concern."[66]

Across their enormous, circumpolar Arctic range, wild caribou/reindeer have declined by about 40 percent over the last few decades and today number under three million. Although obviously still a large population, they are classified by IUCN as "vulnerable" because the decline continues. It is caused probably by habitat changes, by unregulated hunting that has become more intensive, and because of infrastructure and tourist developments such as gas installations posing barriers and thereby modifying their natural migration. Some of the largest range contractions have been in Arctic Canada. The situation is complicated further by many domesticated caribou/reindeer herds causing competition with wild animals.[67]

The American black bear is today found across much of Canada and the northern United States, but it has been extirpated from its previous range in much of the southern United States and the north of Central America. Not all black bears are black; those in the west of its range tend to be very much browner. Widespread, its numbers are roughly double that of the two other bear species in the United States, the polar bear and the brown or grizzly bear. Its population is generally increasing, and hunting for sport and its pelts is strictly controlled under license in every range state, although in Mexico hunting black bears is illegal. Loss of forest habitat and unregulated hunting and persecution resulted in their extirpation across large parts of their range by the early twentieth century, but the species continues to expand today and recolonize parts of its former range. There are probably as many as 950,000 black bears today; around 40,000 to 50,000 are killed for sport and pelts annually, hunting that is controlled and licensed. The mammal is categorized as of "least concern."[68]

Of the sea mammals exploited for their fur, none have come closer to extinction than the sea otter (see plate 23). Categorized today as "endangered," the species recovered through the decades after trade was banned by international treaty in 1911 from the few small populations that remained breeding on islands in the Bering Sea off the U.S. west coast and the Russian east coast. Since the 1980s, translocation of animals to re-establish lost breeding colonies, and regulations imposed by several governments to protect them, has seen further recovery, but some recovering populations have suffered serious setbacks, the result of oil spills—the Exxon Valdez spill in 1989 killed hundreds—competition with fisheries and entanglement in nets, increased predation by orcas, and disease.

Today there are an estimated 126,000 sea otters. Their illegal killing remains a problem, and pelts get onto the black market and probably end up in China where high prices are paid for them. In Alaska, coastal indigenous peoples are allowed to hunt otters for local use and, perhaps more controversially, for creating and selling a limited number of handicrafts and clothing items that they can sell. Monitored by the U.S. Fish and Wildlife Service, the five-year mean annual harvest is 765 otters. There is considerable pressure from some Alaskan indigenous groups to increase levels of sea otter hunting and the marketing of pelts, pressure that has so far been resisted.[69]

The cleaned intestines of bearded seals and walrus were often used by the Yupik peoples of western Alaska and the Russian Far East to make waterproof parkas with hoods. Both species today inhabit extensive areas of the circumpolar northern oceans around the Arctic. The bearded seal is categorized as of "least concern" (based very largely on its wide distribution) although the size of its population—thought to be hundreds of thousands—is poorly known, as is any reliable information on population trends. Indigenous peoples in the Arctic still hunt them for their meat and pelts; numbers killed are poorly known but might well exceed ten thousand annually although there is no evidence that this is causing any population declines. Longer term, the impact of sea ice melt due to climate warming is potentially a major concern for bearded seals because they spend a substantial amount of time—including for pupping—hauled out on ice.[70]

The walrus has not fared well in more recent times. Categorized as "vulnerable to extinction," its population declined by 50 percent between 1980 and 2000, and there is ongoing concern about female body condition and calf survival. The reasons are unclear but might include disturbance at their communal haul-out sites, commercial fisheries reducing their food supplies, and a decline in sea ice as hunting platforms. Longer term, the walrus is likely to suffer considerably if sea ice melt increases substantially. Estimates suggest a total population today of around 225,000. Local indigenous people have long exploited them for their meat, hides, ivory, and bones; more locally for their intestines. Commercial hunting from the eighteenth through to the mid-twentieth centuries killed large numbers, and the walrus has never recovered fully. Protected now, only some subsistence hunting on a small scale continues.[71]

Drawing conclusions about the residual impact of the fur and feather trades for ladies' and gentlemen's hats on the very large list of species exploited is exceedingly difficult. Firstly, several animals were not exploited solely for hats; many furs, especially, were used for other clothing items too. And secondly, the impact of numerous other factors—habitat destruction or habitat modification in particular—combined with killing for fur or feathers makes an analysis of cause and effect difficult at best or even impossible.

Some exploited species have, though, shown spectacular recoveries. Three species of egret in particular—great white, snowy, and little—are once again common in their historic ranges (or even expanding their ranges) after an unprecedented onslaught by feather hunters. Great crested and western grebes have rebounded exceptionally, too. The North American beaver is now well re-established, though its Eurasian cousin still has substantial parts of its former range to recolonize. American black bears are seemingly highly resilient and on the increase still; so, too, are northern raccoons in spite of the inroads that the Davy Crockett infatuation made on its numbers. Several coastal birds have recovered well, too, especially the much exploited least tern in the United States.

A couple of species have fared well in spite of the fur and feather onslaught because their wild populations have been augmented by domestication. The European rabbit clearly falls into this category (though it is declining for unrelated reasons in its original Iberian range) and so, to a lesser extent, does the flamboyant peafowl.

But there are several others whose recovery is no more than partial. The common and Somali ostriches today have a considerably restricted range very largely because of the feather trade. Reddish and Chinese egrets have never recovered fully either. And the short-tailed albatross, reduced to the very brink of extinction, will probably never become more than a mere shadow of its original numbers. Likewise, the chances of the enigmatic sea otter ever regaining its historic numbers seem particularly low.

Fashion, and an unwillingness to adopt alternative materials in the case of furs, sent many species into a near terminal decline. But their resilience has nurtured a comeback for many. Now, a good number are threatened again long term because of the many other environmental and ecological pressures, including habitat destruction, climate warming, and pollution, that are taking yet another toll.

Today's Hats

"THE FEATHER IS SO MUCH PART OF LADIES' MILLINERY THAT I CANNOT EVER SEE IT GO-ing away; it's a vital component of what we do," comments Ellen Colon-Lugo, president of the U.S. Milliners Guild and owner of Ellen Christine Couture Inc., based in New York City, the couture designer behind some of the most iconic hats often featured on the pages of the prestigious fashion magazines in the world.[1] It is a view echoed by Lindsay Whitehead, owner of Torb and Reiner, a large supplier of millinery materials based in Melbourne, Australia. "I can't see using feathers will stop. I don't think there has been a revival. Feathers never went out of fashion really," he says.[2]

But today's ladies' hats are not replete with a coterie of hummingbirds, the occasional whole bird of paradise, or an eye-catching panache of egret feathers. Often dyed, trimmed, and otherwise modified in shape and style, today's feathers are from domesticated birds only.

"All the feathers we supply are by-products from the meat farming industry, which includes chicken, goose, ostrich, and pheasant. We also supply peacock feathers, which are naturally shed annually," says Phil Sykes, sales director of Parkin, based in Oldham, UK, a supplier of quality fabrics, feathers, and accessories to milliners worldwide.[3] Ellen Colon-Lugo adds in turkeys and guinea fowl (the domesticated form of the helmeted guinea fowl, *Numida meleagris*, of Africa). "Curled, burnt or stripped versions of any of these feathers of domesticated birds have become the mainstays of the millinery trade," she says (see plate 24).

There are hundreds of breeds of domesticated chicken in existence, some of which have incredibly attractive plumage in a wide range of colors; some even possess crests or have showy, elongated tail feathers (see plate 25). A number of pheasant species, including the ring-necked pheasant that has been widely introduced in the United States and Europe for game shooting, are particularly valuable as a source of attractive and unusual feathers. Lady Amherst's, golden, and Reeves's pheasants—all with stunningly attractive plumage and long tail plumes—have been introduced in the United Kingdom, and the molted feathers or feathers plucked from dead birds are valued by most milliners.

Amy Money, a British hat designer and hatmaker, who counts the Duchess of Cambridge among her clients, uses feathers in many of the ladies' hats she makes. She lives on a farm where she hand rears guinea fowl, turkeys, and chickens, so she uses many of her birds' feathers in her designs. "People don't realize how beautiful the feathers from everyday domesticated birds are; the variety of shapes, colors, and textures you can find on a single bird is extraordinary. The tail feathers of a cockerel are particularly striking; sometimes I cut them to leave just a tip to create an arrow shape. The feathers from a goose wing make really pretty feather 'flowers,' and they take up dye very easily," she says.[4]

"One of my favorite birds is Lady Amherst's pheasant; the tail feathers are over a meter long and are black and white striped with a gold tip. Nature can't be bettered. Hats with big brims are particularly fashionable at the moment, which allows all the more scope to experiment with lots of fabulous feathers," adds Money.

Military uniforms have also very largely substituted the feathers of domesticated birds for the wild bird feathers many used historically. "We make military hackles and Scots pipers' bonnets using mainly goose, turkey, chicken, cockerel, and ostrich feathers," says Dr. Benjamin Jaffé of Jaffé et Fils Ltd., based at Axminster in the United Kingdom, a long-established company who supply millinery and other feathers and feather products internationally.[5]

"One example of the sort of changes the industry has made concerns Blackcock [a male Black Grouse, *Tetrao tetrix*] feathers to fit on a soldier's ceremonial uniform cap in certain Scottish regiments. These were originally taken direct from black grouse that were shot in Scotland. Each feather mount was a whole Blackcock's lyre-shaped tail. My parents were approached by the [UK government's] Ministry of Defence in the 1970s to develop an alternative because it became illegal to take them from wild birds. We make them from chicken and goose feathers that are dyed black, constructing the lyre-shape as they're made. They're worn today on the ceremonial uniform caps of the Royal Regiment of Scotland," adds Jaffé.

The feather bonnet, used mainly by Scottish Highland infantry regiments of the British army from the late eighteenth century until World War I, and now mostly worn only by Scottish pipers and drummers, has also converted entirely to domesticated birds (see plate 26). "We use black-dyed ostrich feathers for all ranks; today, of course they are from farmed ostriches. The hackles on the side of the bonnet can be made from goose, turkey, or chicken feathers and dyed to the appropriate color to denote regiment. The Royal Horse Guards [who, in ceremonial dress, wear a metal helmet with draped red plumes] have the plumes made of yak hair for officers and horse hair for other ranks," comments Louis Chalmers of the Plumery in London who manufacture horsehair, feather, and military plumes.[6]

Not all military units have forsaken wild bird feathers and substituted them with those of domesticated birds. On their ceremonial hats, the Italian army's Bersaglieri Regiment still uses the purple- and green-hued, black feathers of capercaillie that have been shot for sport, though they have not attached the feathers to their fighting helmets since World War I, apparently to make them less obvious targets for enemy snipers.[7] About four hundred capercaillie feathers are attached to each ceremonial hat. Although its populations are declining across its range, these large forest grouse inhabit a huge land area across northern Europe and most of Russia; its numbers total between three million and five million birds. Its decline is attributed to changes in forest management, disturbance by forest operations, and possibly to predation and climate warming. There is no suggestion that limited hunting, where this is legal, is having any significant impact.[8]

Pageantry and tradition remain significant components of English society, and that often requires the wearing of historic uniforms for those involved. One such is the Order of the Garter, an order of chivalry established (though its origins are rather obscure) by King Edward III (1312–1377) and dedicated to St. George, England's patron saint. Members of the order—of which there are very few—wear a black velvet Tudor bonnet (a soft-crowned, round-brimmed cap) sporting a large plume of white feathers.

Peter O'Donoghue, York Herald at the College of Arms (the official heraldic authority for

England, Wales, Northern Ireland, and much of the Commonwealth) refers to the standard work on the history of the order that states:

> from Elizabethan times it was adorned with a plume of feathers, a decoration which became more elaborate in Stuart and later times. Charles II had a number of black and white herons' feathers together with ten ostrich feathers, a pattern which was to continue.... In 1842 the hat was of black velvet with a plume of sixteen ostrich feathers surmounted by one heron's feather.[9]

"King George V had changes made in 1911 both to the shape of the hat and to the feathers; from then on the hat retained the white ostrich feathers but not the heron's feather," says O'Donoghue.[10]

While the use of feathers and whole birds, mostly exotic species, as decoration on ladies' hats has almost completely given way to feathers from domesticated birds, substitution of mammal fur by synthetic alternatives to make hats—so-called faux fur—has not undergone such a paradigm shift. That is especially true in the coldest inhabited parts of the world.

"Sámi people still use furs for their hats, especially for winter hats. The fur is mostly from reindeer/caribou, which is the main material of Sámi handcrafts and, on a larger scale, the basis of the Sámi culture. Nowadays most Sámi wear Western-style clothing in everyday life, but during the winter many use traditional hats with Western-style winter gear. In addition to reindeer/caribou fur, hats can be made of the fur of domesticated young goats or sheep, and for some parts of a hat, or as a decoration, Sámi might use red fox, American mink or mountain hare," says Anni Guttorm, curator at SIIDA, the Sámi Museum in Finland.[11]

For the Inuvialuit of the western Canadian Arctic region, modern fabric parkas, trimmed with fur for protection from wind and snow, are more popular than those made entirely from animal furs and hides. Dr. Bernadette Driscoll Engelstad, who researches the cultural history of Arctic fur clothing design and is based at the Arctic Studies Center, Smithsonian Institution in Washington, DC, notes:

> Although there has been tremendous change in Arctic clothing styles throughout the past century, animal fur remains an essential clothing material generally amongst Arctic peoples. Calico [made from cotton] and duffle [a thick, wool-based material for warmth] are available for purchase in community stores and online. They were introduced by whalers and traders at least a century ago and are used in a traditional, two-layer design: an inner layer of wool duffle and a calico outer layer.
>
> Inuit women in Alaska adopted the style in the late nineteenth century but added a hood with a "sunburst" fur ruff often of Gray Wolf or Wolverine fur creating a halo-like appearance around the woman's face. Although this had a practical application [keeping frost off the face], it also creates a natural "glow" around the woman. Synthetic materials like Gore-Tex [a waterproof but breathable fabric] have been adopted much more recently by hunters for wind- and water-resistance, especially as covers over duffle.".
>
> Given contemporary housing and greater time spent in settled communities today, probably 100 percent of northern peoples make use of so called non-traditional fabrics at some time or another. But they also continue to rely on caribou fur and sealskin clothing while hunting and camping on the land. Some men also continue to wear hats made of muskrat fur.[12]

The Canadian Mounties also continue to wear Klondike-style hats made of muskrat fur for winter warmth, insisting on the best-quality fur. It takes two or three pelts to make one hat, and muskrats are trapped in the wild; each year around three thousand new muskrat hats have to be manufactured for their officers. Their decision to stay with muskrat fur rather than use woolen hats has fueled controversy in Canada with animal rights groups there such as the Fur-Bearers (the Association for the Protection of Fur-Bearing Animals) claiming that the leg-hold traps sometimes used are inhumane and cause some trapped muskrats to gnaw off their own leg as a result. Body-hold traps eliminate that possibility but are still considered inhumane by the Fur-Bearers. Because of the controversy, individual Mounties are given the choice of either material. A synthetic fur alternative has been ruled out; the national police force found that it didn't perform as well in cold, wet conditions. According to a spokesman for the Fur Council of Canada,[13] fur trappers made $1.7 million from trapping around 315,000 muskrats in 2016. Nevertheless, muskrats remain common.

Finding a synthetic fur alternative to the bearskins worn by the five Guards' regiments in the UK Army has also proved impossible in spite of long-term campaigning by humane organizations such as People for the Ethical Treatment of Animals (PETA). The UK government's Ministry of Defence (MOD) has rejected a faux-fur alternative designed by fashion designer Stella McCartney that PETA claims met the rigorous water-repellency tests set by the MOD and that incorporated tiny air vents to keep the wearer cooler on hot days. PETA also claims that the faux-fur hats are lighter in weight and cheaper than a real fur bearskin.

"The MOD does not have a specific policy on replacing bearskin pelts with a synthetic alternative. We have always adopted a neutral position on the use of real fur in ceremonial dress and are open to the use of faux fur where this provides a suitable and affordable alternative. If samples are received, they would be tested and trialled," said a spokesperson for the MOD's Army Secretariat in 2018.[14]

It seems as if an impasse has been reached. Humane organizations want to see an end to hunting black bears because they claim that a proportion of bears are wounded rather than killed outright, while the MOD is not actively seeking an alternative to the bearskin but claims that it will test any that are supplied to it. Whether or not the United Kingdom's Guards' regiments continue to use bearskins, hunting black bears for sport and for their pelts is certain to continue under license in both Canada and the United States, and black bear numbers are either steady or increasing.

One hat that is today less reliant on wild-caught mammals is the shtreimel worn by married Haredi Jewish men on special occasions (see plate 27). Two of the mammals—the sable and the gray fox—whose tail tips are used in their making are farmed as well as trapped in the wild. Beech martens, European pine martens, American martens, and fishers, all wild trapped and not farmed, can sometimes be used to make shtreimels too, depending whether they are hunted in Russia, Canada, or the north of the United States.

Although many wild sables are trapped in Russia, the country also has around seventy sable farms with many thousands of the ferret-like, dark-brown-furred mammals kept at each. Rarely open to public gaze, a single farm can produce seventy thousand sable pelts in a year, and many also breed gray and Arctic foxes.[15] Most pelts end up as fur coats, and the tails can find a ready market for shtreimel making.

Shtreimels are made only in major Hasidic centers such as Jerusalem and New York by Hasidim who carefully guard the professional secrets of their craft.[16] Trying to obtain information on which mammal tails are most commonly used and the method of construction of a shtreimel is shrouded in secrecy, though why that should be so is not obvious. A high-quality shtreimel consists of perhaps thirty animals' tail ends and can cost around $5,000. Some wealthier Hasidic Jews might possess several.

It is that cost, and the use of some wild mammals to make them, that has stimulated questions about producing cheaper faux-fur versions that retail for around $600. Some rabbis have openly campaigned to promote faux fur shtreimels. One such is Shlomo Pappenheim, chairman of Ha'edah Hacharedit, an anti-Zionist faction in the Haredi community in Israel with between fifty thousand and one hundred thousand followers. He argues that causing pain to animals is unacceptable.[17] Others, such as Rabbi Menachem Mendel Schneerson (1902–1994), leader of the Chabad-Lubavitch movement, famously argued that wearing a shtreimel was unnecessary and alienated secular from Hasidic Jews. So far, expense and animal-cruelty arguments have lost out to a seemingly more overriding factor: regard for the shtreimel as a status symbol; the more expensive, the higher the wearer's status in his particular community.[18]

By far the biggest change to hats in the last four or five decades in those parts of the world with a more temperate climate is that far more of us go outdoors hatless or wearing informal headgear such as caps and beanies instead of a more formal hat. Unthinkable until almost the middle of the twentieth century, before which no one of whatever financial means, male or female, would venture out without some sort of head covering, the stimulus for the modern gentlemen's hatless trend is usually ascribed to President John F. Kennedy. He wore a traditional, black top hat en route to his inauguration but left it off for his inauguration speech and never wore a hat thereafter. But there are other much more likely explanations for our modern hatless trend: the growth of a more informal society in the West from the 1960s on; increasing car travel keeping people "indoors"; younger people wanting to show off their more adventurous haircuts rather than cover them up; and soldiers returning home from World War II fed up with constantly wearing headgear.

More formal ladies' hats are less frequently worn too, both in the United States and in Europe, also the result of Western society becoming notably more informal. Many women would only contemplate wearing a formal hat for a wedding, for a garden party maybe, or for some special social occasion such as the annual, week-long Ascot horse races in England where fashion attracts more publicity than the races themselves. The Ascot fashion pinnacle is reached on Gold Cup Day, known since 1807 as Ladies Day, when men wear traditional top hats and well-dressed ladies wear spectacular and large picture hats, some of them over-extravagantly decorated. The Melbourne Cup, Australia's premier horse-racing event, and the Kentucky Derby in the United States are also events that continue to provide opportunities for those who want to sport ostentatious headwear.

In stark contrast to the U.S. white community, who generally reserve highly decorous hats for a few very special occasions, urban African American women never stopped wearing them. They continue the tradition of adorning the head for church worship; their hats remain colorful and flamboyant, and they frequently sport a few feathers too.[19] The tradition dates back to the days of slavery when black women who worked as maids and servants broke away from their uniforms on Sundays and wore decorated hats to church. It was a black slave's one day of individualism, and she would decorate her hat with ribbons, bows, and flowers. Since that time, black ladies' church hats have become much bigger and bolder.

In Western society more widely, conventional, more formal gentlemen's hats in classic styles—the fedora, trilby, homburg, pork pie, and many others—are far less frequently seen. More informal head coverings—beanies, flat caps, hoodies, and baseball caps—are de rigueur, much to the despair of milliners. Most women wear hats far less often, too, unless a hat is a required part of a uniform.

Established in 1773, Christys' factory in Witney, UK, produces a wide range of formal and casual gentlemen's and ladies' hats. It is one of the very few traditional hatmakers remaining from the fifty-three hat-making companies based originally in Stockport, UK, in the mid-nineteenth century. In 1843, Christys' was the largest hat and cap maker in the world. Today it makes around nine thousand traditional felt hats annually in various styles (plus seventeen thousand panamas and eleven thousand police helmets).

"Of our felt hats, 70 percent use wool felt and 30 percent use fur, almost all of it rabbit," says Craig Sallis, their production manager. "We buy in the felt 'hoods' [brimless cones of felt] and capelines [like hoods but with brims] ready made, but all the rest of the hat making is due to the skill of the staff here and our machinery, most of which dates from the 19th century. We make a few hats out of beaver fur hoods; I think it's imported from Canada. But they're expensive: about £400 [$520] each compared with maybe £90 [$117] for a wool felt hat and £150 [$195] for a rabbit fur hat."[20]

Stetson in the United States uses beaver (wild trapped), mink, and chinchilla fur plus other furs (presumably mostly farmed rabbit but probably some hare too) in their best-quality hats, the highest quality having the most beaver fur. But the company is unwilling to give more detail.

Around 85 percent of the mammal fur used for clothing today (hats included) originates from farmed mammals rather than being wild trapped. But whatever its origins, the continued use of natural fur is highly contentious in many parts of the world. Strong arguments, mainly on the basis of animal welfare, are propounded by those wanting to see all natural fur replaced with faux fur (made mainly from acrylic fibers) set against a highly organized fur trade arguing that fur is a natural product, the use of which does not harm wild mammal populations. The International Fur Federation and the fur industry in general claims that using natural fur is using a sustainable product, that standards are in use internationally for wild trapping and for fur farms, that trapping is a long tradition in many cultures, that wild animal populations are not being depleted, that some of the exploited mammals would be shot or trapped anyway as pests, and that both trapping and fur farming provide jobs in otherwise work-deprived rural areas.[21]

There is little doubt that most of their arguments are factually correct. Legislation and regulation by licensing is used in the countries where trapping is permitted in order to control its impact and to ensure that populations of the targeted mammals are not depleted. But the argument that some species would be shot or trapped whether or not their pelts were valuable applies to only a couple of exploited species. North American beavers can be problematic locally because their dam building sometimes causes unacceptable levels of flooding and because they fell small trees. But the small amount of damage they cause is usually outweighed longer term by the benefits to fish stocks and other wildlife, and most felled trees re-grow anyway. In most cases, North American beavers do not *need* to be killed; as a last resort they can be live trapped and relocated to waterways where populations are low.[22]

Black bears rarely attack people, and most incidents have been connected to bears becoming habituated to receiving food left for them in spite of advice to the contrary. Human fatalities are very rare. They sometimes cause damage to agricultural crops and kill smaller livestock, but otherwise black bears cause few problems. Small numbers might need to be shot to eliminate any serious damage, although compensation is an obvious alternative. Nevertheless, large numbers of black bears are killed under license every year in Canada and the United States, both for sport and for their pelts,[23] but in general, there is no necessity to kill them.

Of the large range of charitable organizations campaigning actively to end the use of natural fur, PETA,[24] U.S.-based but operating internationally, claims to be the largest animal rights group in the world with over six million members and supporters. The Humane Society of the United

States, another large animal welfare charity, is affiliated to the Humane Society International that has branches in seventeen countries. And many other organizations exist across a spectrum from those campaigning solely for the ending of the fur trade to many others embracing a much wider concern for animal welfare standards of farmed and pet animals to those seeking to take more aggressive direct action.

There is seemingly little constructive discourse between the two standpoints; those for and against the fur trade have a greater tendency to exchange strongly held opinions, sometimes insults. Photographs apparently showing squalid conditions in fur farms and the mistreatment and suffering of animals abound on the Internet. These are dismissed as unrepresentative or as fake by the fur industry. In this melee of claim, counterclaim, and distrust, apart from statistics (which might be impartial) my consideration of this contentious topic is based entirely on what I deem to be independent information and investigations.

Since the 1990s when the ethical considerations of fur farming and fur use influenced public opinion and fur sales fell, the international fur trade has been generally on an upturn; markets, sales volumes, and prices have been growing, though not in recent years. Certification and labeling programs, animal welfare projects, ever-changing fashion, and clearly thought-through marketing strategies targeting younger generation consumers have all served as key factors in the fur industry's recovery. Emerging markets in China and Russia are today the main consumers of fur. Nevertheless, future prospects for the fur industry are not very clear; the market is volatile and difficult to forecast, ethical disputes continue, and new regulations may be imposed, at least by some countries.[25]

The scale of the fur-farming industry is huge according to International Fur Trade Federation figures (the only source of such data). Worldwide it was worth $30 billion in 2017, although this is a significant fall since 2013 when it was reputedly worth $40 billion. Its economic relevance in certain countries where fur farming is commonplace is particularly significant. Producing over twelve million mink skins annually, fur farming was worth 514 million Euros ($583 million) to Danish farmers in 2002, making it the country's third largest agricultural export product after their better-known bacon and cheese. In Finland, where over two million fox pelts were produced in the same year, the annual value of fur production at 250 million Euros ($283 million) is greater than that of beef. Fur farming is also important in the Netherlands where three million skins were produced in 2002, and in some of the central and eastern European countries.[26]

In Canada, the fur trade contributes Can$800 million (US$605 million) to the Canadian economy, employing over seventy-five thousand Canadians in total. In the United States the value of the fur industry was $1.8 billion in 2003/4. In Russia, the value of the fur trade is over $2.5 billion, contributing around 0.6-0.8 percent of the turnover of all consumer goods. In the United Kingdom, fur brokers are responsible for buying the majority of the world's fur traded wholesale, with a turnover of some $750 million per annum, while Hong Kong is the world's largest importer of farmed fur skins and remains the leading exporter of fur garments.[27]

In 2001, the European Union's Scientific Committee on Animal Health and Animal Welfare launched an examination of the welfare of animals kept for fur production.[28] It concentrated on farmed mink (farmed mainly in Denmark) and foxes (kept mainly in Finland and Norway) since these were, and remain, the principle fur-bearing mammals farmed in the European Union. While Norway is not a EU Member State, it has a close association with the EU and is a member of the European Economic Area. Like almost all mammals farmed for their fur, mink and foxes are kept in wire mesh cages, usually indoors, for the whole of their short lives. Only coypu are farmed in outdoor pens where they have more room to move around. Compared with most farm animals, the committee concluded that farmed mink and foxes have not been bred to select for domesticated attributes such as calmness and reduced fear of humans. Consequently, they are not well adapted to a caged environment. Killing methods vary with species, but in general, foxes are electrocuted while mink are gassed.

For farmed mink the committee reported that a range of nonfatal conditions that affect animal welfare are sometimes widespread and that animals showing abnormal movement disorders are frequent. They also concluded that self-biting of parts of their pelt is common and that the animals have very little room for any significant exercise or stimulation. For foxes they found that their restricted caged environment also limits their physical exercise leading to limb weakness and prevents their natural digging behavior. Farmed foxes are notably fearful of humans, another significant welfare problem.[29]

For species of mammal such as foxes that in the wild roam over significant areas of land to hunt and mink that naturally frequently hunt in water, keeping them in small wire cages with little room for exercise is completely unnatural, especially if, as the EU committee's report concludes, these mammals have not been subject to selective breeding to encourage domesticated traits. This is not the case for farmed rabbits because rabbits have been domesticated for centuries and particular fur-bearing breeds are reared that are docile and accustomed to human presence.

With wild-caught, fur-bearing mammals, trappers profit through the sale of furs for market and the production of ancillary products such as meat that may be used for human and pet consumption. Besides the trappers, the fur trade also consists of those who manage the flow of furs from collection through the processes of dressing, manufacturing, and retailing, activities that provide over two hundred thousand jobs in North America, many of them in poor rural areas, while subsistence trapping remains a traditional and culturally important part of the life of some northern indigenous peoples.

This has led to changes in trapping regulations in various jurisdictions. For example, Canada has a program in place to test and certify traps permitted for furbearer capture. With few exceptions, the use of foothold traps is no longer permitted. Most U.S. states allow the use of a wider range of animal capture devices including various sizes of foothold traps. Eight U.S. states, however, have highly restrictive trapping laws or regulations, in some cases banning the use of foothold traps altogether.[30]

After several years of negotiations, an Agreement on International Humane Trapping Standards (IHTS) was concluded in 1998 between the EU, Canada, and the Russian Federation (with a similar agreement with the United States). They apply to the types of traps used for killing or restraining and cover nineteen wild species of mammal (though more can be added by agreement) including beaver, martens, muskrat, wolf, and sable. While welcomed by most organizations dedicated to the humane treatment of animals, local implementation of the agreement's requirements, appropriate training for trappers, and thorough inspections on the ground will be essential if the IHTS is to work in practice. Regulation is a step forward, but its enforcement is essential.

The EU has banned the importation of furs from wild animals caught in leg-hold traps or from countries where wild trapping standards do not conform to the IHTS. At the other extreme, China, where the number of fur farms is growing rapidly—many of them comparatively small, family-run businesses—is not a party to the IHTS agreement, and allegations of animal cruelty and poor standards abound.[31]

The first fake or faux fur was made in 1929 using hair from alpacas, a domesticated South American animal closely related to the llama. But synthetic textile technology in the 1950s started to produce acrylic polymers that today can be manufactured and dyed to very closely resemble natural furs from a number of mammals. Increasing numbers of clothing designers and manufacturers, particularly in Western countries, are claiming that faux fur is becoming the fashion staple and that natural fur is being increasingly shunned. The fur trade criticizes faux fur because it's synthesized from oil, thereby wasting finite natural resources and risking pollution in its manufacture, and because it doesn't decompose when it's disposed of.

Drapers Magazine, the international business magazine for the fashion retail trade that is often referred to as the "fashion industry bible," recently ran a feature that listed the prominent fashion labels that have become natural fur–free. It included Calvin Klein in 1994, Tommy Hilfiger in 2007, Armani in 2016, and Donna Karan, Versace, Gucci, and DKNY in 2019. Chanel has also recently declared natural fur to be off limits. And luxury e-commerce site Net-a-Porter also announced in 2017 that it would stop selling natural fur. Animal rights' charities claim that this substantial move away from fur by major fashion chains reflects growing consumer revulsion that animals are still being used to make clothing, increasing environmental awareness, and the more mainstream attitude toward vegan lifestyles. A more cynical explanation is that the fashion houses simply want to be rid of the constant barrage of criticism from animal rights and humane charities. When checks have been done, some less reputable companies have been found selling real fur trims on clothing but labeling it as faux fur a practice that requires tighter labeling regulations.[32]

Some cities have also designated themselves "fur-free": West Hollywood in the United States has been fur-free since 2013, and São Paulo, Brazil, has done the same since 2015. San Francisco's ban is due in 2019. In 2017, India banned the import of mink, fox, and chinchilla skins and in 2018 banned the import of seal fur and skin. The United Kingdom banned fur farming in 2003, but it remains legal to import fur or fur products into the United Kingdom provided they accord with EU law concerning IHTS standards.

In another important signal, in 2018 the British Fashion Council announced that it will no longer allow clothing designers to use animal fur in its fashion shows. Caroline Rush, its chief executive, said at the time:

> Our decision highlights a trend we have seen over the past few years with more and more brands deciding to use alternative materials to fur. We're seeing a cultural change based on ideals and choices made within brands. The fur dialogue is ongoing and the stance of brands such as Burberry, Stella McCartney, Gucci, Yoox Net-A-Porter, Versace and Vivienne Westwood, among others, to look at alternative options to fur will encourage more brands to consider what options are available to them.[33]

Although the International Fur Trade Federation is promoting FurMark, set to launch in 2020—a legal certification process that guarantees animal welfare standards for retailers and consumers—there is no guarantee that all fur farms, including those in China, will take it up. Even then, with increasing environmental and wildlife concerns gaining yet more ground in Western societies, with the continued rise in vegetarianism and veganism, and when the new Generation Z comes of age (the next cohort of people after the Millennials) there is certain to be yet more scrutiny of the ethical practices of the fur trade.

Whatever tighter regulations might be imposed on fur farming in the future, and even if these are enforced effectively, it seems to me to be innately cruel to restrain naturally inquisitive and highly active animals in cages solely for the purpose of producing fashion items of clothing for which there is a very acceptable alternative already adopted by many leading fashion designers.

Likewise, I do not believe that it is acceptable to trap and kill wild-living mammals for the same purpose. Faux fur alternatives exist for both the shtreimel (which is of no religious significance) worn by Hasidic Jewish men and for the bearskin hats so beloved by the Guards' regiments of the British Army. Sadly, tradition appears to transcend responsibility.

In the extreme northern parts of the globe where intense cold demands the very warmest of clothing—and where thousands of years of traditional hunting practices have become an integral component of several Arctic cultures—perhaps there is a case for the continued humane trapping and hunting of some fur-bearing mammals. Albeit not always providing the same degree of heat insulation, synthetic clothing is available in these communities and has in part been adopted by them alongside traditional clothing. But there must be a strong case, too, for considering restricting such indigenous hunting, even if there is no evidence that it is currently causing animal declines. It is, of course, entirely debatable whether long-established practices absorbed over time into the indigenous culture of certain communities trump animal welfare and animal population concerns in today's world.

In his book, *Bringing It to the Table: On Farming and Food*, Wendell Berry (b. 1934), the American novelist, poet, environmental activist, and cultural critic wrote: To husband is to use with care, to keep, to save, to make last, to conserve. Husbandry is the art of keeping tied all the strands in the living network that sustains us.[34] How well we do that is a measure of our care for this planet, its creatures, and all else that it supports.

The IUCN Red List Classification

THE INTERNATIONAL UNION FOR THE CONSERVATION OF NATURE (IUCN) RED LIST OF Threatened Species is the world's most comprehensive inventory of the global conservation status of plants and animals, and IUCN is the world's main authority on the conservation status of species.

The Red List is based on precise criteria to evaluate the extinction risk of thousands of species and subspecies. These criteria are relevant to all species and all regions of the world.

Its aims, according to IUCN, are to provide scientifically based information on the status of species and subspecies at a global level, to draw attention to the magnitude and importance of threatened wildlife, to influence national and international policy and decision-making, and to provide information to guide actions to conserve biological diversity.

The assessments to categorize each species are done by accredited assessors including Bird-Life International, the Institute of Zoology (the research division of the Zoological Society of London), the World Conservation Monitoring Centre, and many Specialist Groups within the IUCN Species Survival Commission.

The IUCN aims to have the category of every species reevaluated every five years if possible, or at least every ten years. This is done in a peer-reviewed manner through IUCN Species Survival Commission Specialist Groups, which are Red List Authorities responsible for a species, group of species, or specific geographic area or, in the case of BirdLife International, an entire class: birds.

The lists are intended to be an easily and widely understood system for classifying species at high risk of global extinction. They aim to provide an explicit, objective framework for the classification of the broadest range of species according to their extinction risk. Extensive consultation and testing in the development of the system strongly suggests that it is robust across most species.

Threatened species, those facing a higher risk of global extinction, are categorized as "critically endangered," "endangered," and "vulnerable." But the Red List also includes information on plants and animals that are categorized as "extinct" or "extinct in the wild" and on plants and animals that are either close to meeting the threatened thresholds or that would be threatened were it not for an ongoing conservation program ("near threatened").

However, it should be noted that although the system places species into the threatened categories with a high degree of consistency, the criteria do not take into account the life histories of every species. Hence, in certain individual cases, the risk of extinction may be under- or over-estimated.

The IUCN Red List is an important indicator of the state of the world's biodiversity, as well as a list of the most up–to-date status and distribution of species. It is a tool widely recognized for catalyzing action where and when it is needed to aid improving the conservation status of threatened species and is used by government agencies, NGOs, and many other institutions worldwide. The website has over 98,500 species listed, of which 27,000 are threatened with extinction, and is intended for regular updating and expansion to include 160,000 species by 2020 in order to provide a larger and better basis for conservation and policy decisions.[1]

The IUCN categories (simplified from their published descriptions) follow.

> **Extinct.** A species is extinct when there is no reasonable doubt that the last individual has died. A species is presumed extinct when exhaustive surveys in known and/or expected habitat, at appropriate times, and throughout its historic range have failed to find it.
>
> **Extinct in the Wild.** A species is extinct in the wild when it is known only to survive in captivity or as a naturalized population (or populations) well outside its past range. It is presumed extinct in the wild when exhaustive surveys in known and/or expected habitat, at appropriate times, and throughout its historic range have failed to record an individual.
>
> **Critically Endangered.** A species is critically endangered when it is considered to be facing an extremely high risk of extinction in the wild.
>
> **Endangered.** A species is endangered when it is considered to be facing a very high risk of extinction in the wild.
>
> **Vulnerable.** A species is vulnerable when it is considered to be facing a high risk of extinction in the wild.
>
> **Near Threatened.** A species is near threatened when it has been evaluated against the criteria but does not qualify for critically endangered, endangered, or vulnerable now but is close to qualifying for, or is likely to qualify for, a threatened category in the near future.
>
> **Least Concern.** A species is of least concern when it has been evaluated against the criteria and does not qualify for critically endangered, endangered, vulnerable, or near threatened. Widespread and abundant species are included in this category.

The definitions of the criteria used by IUCN to determine which category a species fits into are lengthy and complex. The criteria take into account detailed information on the size of a species' population, its geographic range and distribution, the degree of fragmentation of populations, rates of decline, its population structure, an assessment of extinction risk, changes in its habitat, known exploitation, and other factors affecting it.

Notes

INTRODUCTION

1. Robin W. Doughty, *Feather Fashions and Bird Preservation: A Study in Nature Protection* (Berkeley: University of California Press, 1975).

CHAPTER 1. THE EARLIEST HATS AND HAT DECOR

1. From information supplied by the South Tyrol Museum of Archaeology, Bolzano, Italy, where Ötzi's body is preserved in a specially built cold cell.
2. From information supplied by the South Tyrol Museum of Archaeology.
3. From information supplied by the South Tyrol Museum of Archaeology.
4. From information supplied by the South Tyrol Museum of Archaeology.
5. "Bodies of the Bogs: Clothing and Hair Styles of the Bog People," *Archaeology*, 10 December 1997, https://archive.archaeology.org/online/features/bog/.
6. Charlotte Price Persson, "New Method Reveals the Secrets of Bog Bodies," *ScienceNordic*, 12 August 2016.
7. Kai Curry-Lindahl, "The Brown Bear (*Ursus arctos*) in Europe: Decline, Present Distribution, Biology and Ecology," in *Bears: Their Biology and Management; A Selection of Papers from the Second International Conference on Bear Research and Management held at the University of Calgary, Alberta, Canada, 6 to 9 November 1970* (Morges: International Union for Conservation of Nature and Natural Resources, 1972), 2:74–80.
8. Karen Diane Jennett, "Female Figurines of the Upper Paleolithic" (honors thesis, Texas State University, 2008).
9. Olga Soffer, J. M. Adovasio, and D. C. Hyland, "The 'Venus' Figurines: Textiles, Basketry, Gender and Status in the Upper Paleolithic," *Current Anthropology* 41, no. 4 (2000): 511–537.
10. Personal communication from Dr. Olga Soffer, 10 June 2018.
11. Karl H. Schlesier, "More on the 'Venus' Figurines," *Current Anthropology* 42, no. 3 (2001): 410–412.
12. Olga Gertcyk, "World Famous Ancient Siberian Venus Figurines 'are NOT Venuses after all,'" *Siberian Times*, 18 February 2016.
13. Ernest S. Burch, "The Caribou/Wild Reindeer as a Human Resource," *American Antiquity* 37, no. 3 (1972): 339–368.
14. A. Gunn, *Rangifer tarandus*, IUCN Red List of Threatened Species 2016: e.T29742A22167140. http://dx.doi.org/10.2305/IUCN.UK.2016–1.RLTS.T29742A22167140.en.
15. R. Turner Wilcox, *The Mode in Hats and Headdress* (Mineola, NY: Dover Publications, 2008).

16. Frances F. Berdan, "Featherwork as a Commodity Complex in the Late Postclassic Mesoamerican World System" in *Alternative Pathways to Complexity*, ed. Lane F. Fargher and Verenice Y. Heredia Espinoza (Louisville: University Press of Colorado, 2016).

17. "The Resplendent Quetzal in Aztec and Mayan Culture," BirdLife International, http://www.birdlife.org.

18. "The Resplendent Quetzal in Aztec and Mayan Culture."

19. Personal communication from Frances Berdan, 13 August 2018.

20. H. M. Meneses Lozano, "A Forgotten Tradition: The Rediscovery of Mexican Feathered Textiles," in *Historical Technology, Materials and Conservation: SEM and Microanalysis*, ed. N. Meeks et al. (London: Archetype Publications, 2012), 69–75.

21. Walter R. T. Witschey, *Encyclopedia of the Ancient Maya* (Lanham, MD: Rowman & Littlefield, 2016).

22. William H. Prescott, *History of the Conquest of Peru*, vol. 1 (Paris: Baudry's European Library, 1847).

23. Janet Parker and Julie Stanton, *Mythology: Myths, Legends, and Fantasies* (Sydney: Global Book Publishing, 2007).

24. Rayna Green and Melanie Fernandez, *The Encyclopaedia of the First Peoples of North America* (Toronto: Groundwood/Douglas & McIntyre, 1999), 58.

25. K. Aune, D. Jørgensen, and C. Gates, *Bison bison*, IUCN Red List of Threatened Species 2017 (errata version published in 2018): e.T2815A123789863. http://dx.doi.org/10.2305/IUCN.UK.2017–3.RLTS.T2815A45156541.en.

26. Information collated from an exhibit (F85.16.5) of a Shasta Indian Feathered Headdress in the collection of the Bowers Museum, Santa Ana, California.

27. Graham Barwell, *Albatross* (London: Reaktion Books, 2014).

28. BirdLife International, *Pteridophora alberti*, IUCN Red List of Threatened Species 2016: e.T22706229A94057390. http://dx.doi.org/10.2305/IUCN.UK.2016–3.RLTS.T22706229A94057390.en.

29. BirdLife International, *Psittrichas fulgidus*, IUCN Red List of Threatened Species 2017: T22685025A118772050. http://dx.doi.org/10.2305/IUCN.UK.2017–3.RLTS.T22685025A118772050.en.

30. Josep del Hoyo et al., eds., *Handbook of the Birds of the World*, vol. 6 (Barcelona: Lynx Edicions, 2001).

31. Barwell, *Albatross*.

32. Barwell, *Albatross*.

33. David M. Welch, "Aboriginal Adornment—3," Aboriginal Culture, http://www.aboriginalculture.com.au/body_adornment3.html.

34. Josep del Hoyo et al., eds., *Handbook of the Birds of the World*, vol. 4 (Barcelona: Lynx Edicions, 1997).

35. "Feathers Have Always Been Used by Humans as Decoration and Status Symbols," BirdLife International, http://www.birdlife.org.

36. Paul R. Ehrlich, David Dobkin, and Darryl Wheye, *Birds in Jeopardy: The Imperiled and Extinct Birds of the United States and Canada* (Stanford: Stanford University Press, 1992).

37. Information from the Bernice Pauahi Bishop Museum, the Hawai'i State Museum of Natural and Cultural History, Honolulu, Hawaii.

CHAPTER 2. A DEADLY FELT REVOLUTION

1. Stephanie Bunn, *Nomadic Felts: Artistic Traditions in World Cultures* (London: British Museum Press, 2011).
2. Information compiled from "The Danbury Hatters," Connecticut History, 1 August 2014, https://connecticuthistory.org; and from John Pirro, "The Rise and Fall of Hatting in Danbury," *NewsTimes*, 1 February 2011.
3. Detail of the manual felt-making and hat-making processes commonplace in the eighteenth and nineteenth century in the United Kingdom (but similar wherever felt hats were made) is derived mainly from discussions at the Hatworks, a museum funded by Stockport Metropolitan Borough Council, England, which re-creates the felt-hat-making process from rabbit pelts to the finished hat. An award-winning tourist attraction, it is housed in a Victorian former cotton mill.
4. Maths Berlin, Rudolfs K. Zalups, and Bruce A. Fowler, "Mercury," in *Handbook on the Toxicology of Metals* (Cambridge, MA: Academic Press, 2007).
5. T. H. Lloyd, *The English Wool Trade in the Middle Ages* (Cambridge: Cambridge University Press, 1977).
6. Roger Lovegrove, *Silent Fields: The Long Decline of a Nation's Wildlife* (Oxford: Oxford University Press, 2007).
7. Charles E. Kellogg, *Utility of Jackrabbit and Cottontail Skins*, USDA Misc. Publication no. 289 (Washington, DC: U.S. Department of Agriculture, 1937).
8. Elspeth M. Veale, *The English Fur Trade in the Later Middle Ages* (London: London Record Society, 2003), British History Online, http://www.british-history.ac.uk.
9. Madeleine Ginsburg, *The Hat: Trends and Traditions* (New York: Barrons, 1988).
10. Ginsburg, *The Hat*.
11. From information collated by the Welsh Beaver Project managed by the Wildlife Trust Wales, 2012–2016. The project has examined the demise and recent reintroductions of Eurasian beavers in each country in Europe including the United Kingdom, including best estimates for extinctions country by country.
12. Veale, *The English Fur Trade*.
13. J. Batbold et al., *Castor fiber*, IUCN Red List of Threatened Species 2016 (errata version published in 2017): e.T4007A115067136. http://dx.doi.org/10.2305/IUCN.UK.2016-3.RLTS.T4007A22188115.en.
14. Carolyn Merchant, *Ecological Revolutions: Nature, Gender and Science in New England* (Chapel Hill: University of North Carolina Press, 2010).
15. Ann M. Carlos and Frank D. Lewis, *Commerce by a Frozen Sea: Native Americans and the European Fur Trade* (Philadelphia: University of Pennsylvania Press, 2010).
16. Carlos and Lewis, *Commerce by a Frozen Sea*.
17. Carlos and Lewis, *Commerce by a Frozen Sea*.
18. "Section 2: Beaver," North Dakota: People Living on the Land, State Historical Society of North Dakota, https://www.ndstudies.gov/gr8/content/unit-ii-time-transformation-1201-1860/lesson-1-changing-landscapes/topic-4-fur-bearing-animals/section-2-beaver.
19. Ginsburg, *The Hat*, 44.
20. The Proceedings of the Old Bailey, London's Central Criminal Court, 1674–1913, proceedings of 31 August 1688, https://www.oldbaileyonline.org. This is a fully searchable edition of the largest body of texts detailing the lives of nonelite people ever published, containing 197,745 criminal trials held at London's central criminal court.

21. Carlos and Lewis, *Commerce by a Frozen Sea*.

22. Ann M. Carlos and Frank D. Lewis, "Indians, the Beaver, and the Bay: The Economics of Depletion in the Lands of the Hudson's Bay Company, 1700–1763," *The Journal of Economic History* 53, no. 3 (1993): 465–494.

23. Carlos and Lewis, *Commerce by a Frozen Sea*.

24. Carlos and Lewis, *Commerce by a Frozen Sea*.

25. Carlos and Lewis, *Commerce by a Frozen Sea*.

26. Ginsburg, *The Hat*, 45.

27. Alan Axelrod, *Little-Known Wars of Great and Lasting Impact* (Beverly, MA: Fair Winds Press, 2009).

28. Axelrod, *Little-Known Wars*.

29. Dietland Müller-Schwarze and Lixing Sun, *The Beaver: Natural History of a Wetlands Engineer* (New York: Comstock Publishing Associates, 2003).

CHAPTER 3. WHEN THE FUR FLIES

1. Gintarė Skyrienė and Algimantas Paulauskas, "Distribution of Invasive Muskrats (*Ondatra zibethicus*) and Impact on Ecosystem," *Ekologika* 58, no. 3 (2012): 357–367.

2. "Ondatra zibethicus (Muskrat)," *Invasive Species Compendium*, CABI, last modified 19 November 2018, https://www.cabi.org/isc. Up to twenty-eight inches in length—with its tail half of that— the muskrat has short, thick fur that is mid-brown to black. They spend most of their time in water and can dive for several minutes. Vegetation eaters, they have a reputation for denuding wetland habitats of many of their typical plants.

3. Max Bachrach, *Fur: A Practical Treatise* (New York: Prentice-Hall, 1953).

4. David Campbell, *Finnish Soldier vs Soviet Soldier: Winter War 1939–40* (Oxford: Osprey Publishing, 2016).

5. Raisa Kirsanova, "Russia: A History of Dress," in *Encyclopedia of Clothing and Fashion*, ed. Valerie Steele (Farmington Hills, MI: Gale Group, 2005), 121–127.

6. Louise Edwards, "Military Celebrity in China: The Evolution of 'Heroic and Model Servicemen,'" in *Celebrity in China*, ed. Elaine Jeffreys and Louise Edwards (Hong Kong: Hong Kong University Press, 2010), 21–44.

7. J. D. Murdoch, *Vulpes corsac*, IUCN Red List of Threatened Species 2014: e.T23051A59049446. http://dx.doi.org/10.2305/IUCN.UK.2014-2.RLTS.T23051A59049446.en. The corsac fox, pale yellow-brown in color, is confined to a large land area of southern Russia and northern Asia where it inhabits vast arid steppes. Generally common and widespread, the intensity of trapping or shooting for its fur varies between regions and is intense enough to substantially reduce populations at least locally. Hunting for their fur has long been a traditional and commercial activity; hunting bans have been implemented periodically in Mongolia and Russia to allow their populations to recover following intense periods of hunting, although for many years after the collapse of the USSR controls there were poorly implemented.

8. Jill Oakes et al., "Comparison of Traditional and Manufactured Cold Weather Ensemble," *Climate Research* 5 (1995): 83–90.

9. Aline J. Cotel et al., "Effect of Ancient Inuit Fur Parka Ruffs on Facial Heat Transfer," *Climate Research* 26 (2004): 77–84.

10. Betty Kobayashi Issenman, Sinews of Survival: The Living Legacy of Inuit Clothing (Vancouver: University of British Columbia Press, 1998).

11. "The Inuit," Canada's First Peoples, 2007, https://firstpeoplesofcanada.com/fp_groups/fp_inuit3. html.

12. Information supplied by Anni Guttorm, curator at the Sámi Museum Siida, Inari, Finland.

13. Issenman, Sinews of Survival.

14. James W. Vanstone, Nunivak Island Eskimo (Yuit) Technology and Material Culture (Chicago: Field Museum of Natural History, 1989).

15. Fran Reed, "Embellishments of the Alaska Native Gut Parka," *Textile Society of America Symposium Proceedings* 127, 2008, http://digitalcommons.unl.edu/tsaconf/127.

16. Reed, "Embellishments."

17. Joseph J. Gross and Sigrid Khera, *Ethnohistory of the Aleuts* (Fairbanks: University of Alaska, 1980).

18. John A. Love, *Sea Otters* (Golden, CO: Fulcrum Publishing, 1992). With the densest fur of any animal, sea otters survive in the cold inshore waters of the North Pacific where they dive to the sea floor to forage for small fish and invertebrates. One of the very few mammals to use tools, they use rocks to dislodge prey and to open shells.

19. Charles A. Simenstad et al., "Aleuts, Sea Otters, and Alternate Stable-State Communities," *Science*, n.s. 200 (1978): 403–411.

20. Adele Ogden, *The California Sea Otter Trade, 1784–1848* (Berkeley: University of California Press, 1975).

21. Roland M. Nowak, *Walker's Mammals of the World*, vol. 2, 6th ed. (Baltimore: Johns Hopkins University Press, 1999).

22. A. Doroff and A. Burdin, *Enhydra lutris*, IUCN Red List of Threatened Species 2015: e.T7750A21939518. http://dx.doi.org/10.2305/IUCN.UK.2015-2.RLTS.T7750A21939518.en.

23. Nowak, *Walker's Mammals*.

24. Nowak, *Walker's Mammals*.

25. Michael Wallis, *David Crockett: The Lion of the West* (New York: W. W. Norton, 2011), 82.

26. Richard Knötel et al., *Uniforms of the World: A Compendium of Army, Navy and Air Force Uniforms, 1700–1937* (London: Charles Scribner's Sons, 1980).

27. "Bearskin Hats in Danger," *New York Times*, 3 August 1888.

28. Preben Kannick, *Military Uniforms of the World in Color* (Basingstoke: MacMillan, 1968).

29. D. L. Garshelis, B. K. Scheick, D. L. Doan-Crider, J. J. Beecham, and M. E. Obbard, *Ursus americanus*, IUCN Red List of Threatened Species 2016 (errata version published in 2017): e.T41687A114251609. http://dx.doi.org/10.2305/IUCN.UK.2016-3.RLTS. T41687A45034604 .en. Black bears are North America's smallest but most widely distributed bear. Omnivorous forest-dwellers, they often leave tree cover to find food. Their largest populations tend to be in heavily forested mountainous regions.

30. Kannick, *Military Uniforms*.

31. Wendy Skilton, *British Military Band Uniforms: Cavalry Regiments* (London: Midland Publishing, 1992).

32. A. E. Haswell Miller and John Mollo, *Vanished Armies: A Record of Military Uniform Observed and Drawn in Various European Countries during the Years 1907 to 1914* (London: Shire Publications, 2009).

33. James J. Boulton, *Head-dress of the Canadian Mounted Police, 1873–2000* (Calgary: Bunker to Bunker Publications, 2000).

34. Information supplied by Royal Canadian Mounted Police National Communication Services, September 2018.

35. Ester Muchawsky-Schnapper, *A World Apart Next Door: Glimpses into the Life of Hasidic Jews* (Jerusalem: The Israel Museum, 2012).

36. Dan Arnon, *A Hat for All Seasons* (Tel Aviv: Am Oved, 1995).

37. Muchawsky-Schnapper, *A World Apart Next Door.*

38. Raphael Straus, "The 'Jewish Hat' as an Aspect of Social History," *Jewish Social Studies* 4, no. 1 (1942): 59–72.

39. W. Bruce Lincoln, *The Conquest of a Continent: Siberia and the Russians* (Ithaca: Cornell University Press, 1994), 38.

40. Benson Bobrick, *East of the Sun: The Epic Conquest and Tragic History of Siberia* (New York: Poseidon Press,1992).

41. Lincoln, *The Conquest of a Continent.*

42. Robert G. Hodgson, *Fisher Farming* (Toronto: Fur Trade Journal of Canada, 1937).

43. K. Helgen and F. Reid, *Martes pennanti*, IUCN Red List of Threatened Species 2018 (amended version of 2016 assessment): e.T41651A125236220. http://dx.doi.org/10.2305/IUCN. UK.2016-2.RLTS.T41651A125236220.en. Fishers are small, dark-furred, forest-dwelling mustelids, related to stoats and weasels. They spend more time on the forest floor than in trees. Dark in color and larger than martens, they are capable of killing quite large prey such as snowshoe hares and porcupines but will also eat a range of vegetable food such as nuts and berries.

CHAPTER 4. EUROPEAN FLAMBOYANCE

1. Madeleine Ginsburg, The Hat: Trends and Traditions (New York: Barron's, 1990).

2. Ginsburg, The Hat.

3. Ginsburg, The Hat.

4. R. Turner Wilcox, The Mode in Hats and Headdress (Mineola, NY: Dover Publications, 2008).

5. Wilcox, The Mode in Hats, 70.

6. Alan D. Mansfield, *Ceremonial Costume: Court, Civil, and Civic Costume from 1660 to the Present Day* (New York: Barnes & Noble Books, 1980).

7. Gianluigi Arca, "Bersaglieri Infantry: Heroes in Italian History," *NATO Armies and Their Traditions* 13 (2009): 23–25.

8. Ostriches are closely related to the emu, cassowaries, rheas, and kiwis, all flightless and mostly large birds (the exception being the much smaller kiwis) mainly found in the Southern Hemisphere. It is likely that they evolved in predator-free environments where energy-expensive flight was unnecessary. This group of birds, known as ratites, consists of just ten species worldwide, of which half are considered vulnerable or endangered. Two species have become extinct since 1600.

9. Edgar Williams, Ostrich (London: Reaktion Books, 2013).

10. William Smellie, A Natural History, General and Particular (London: Richard Evans, 1817).

11. Sarah Abrevaya Stein, Plumes: *Ostrich Feathers, Jews and a Lost World of Global Commerce* (New Haven: Yale University Press, 2008). Sarah Abrevaya Stein is professor of history and the Maurice Amado Chair in Sephardic Studies at the University of California, Los Angeles. Her book is an economic and social history of the ostrich feather market boom in the latter decades of the nineteenth century and early twentieth century.

12. Williams, Ostrich.

13. Stein, Plumes.

14. Chicken-like, ground-living birds, there are over 150 species of pheasant and partridge worldwide of which at least forty are vulnerable or endangered. The males of those found in the Old World, especially pheasants, are some of the most visually attractive larger birds. They include Asia's red junglefowl, the wild ancestor of domestic chickens, and the Indian peafowl, the male of which (the peacock) spreads its massive, "eye-dotted," multicolored fan of a tail in the gardens of many a stately home.

15. Michael Shrubb, *Feasting, Fowling and Feathers* (London: T. & A. D. Poyser, 2013).

16. Shrubb, *Feasting*.

17. The nineteen species of stork in the world are closely related to herons, ibises, and spoonbills but are generally heavier with more massive bills. All are somewhat ungainly looking wading birds and are found in both tropical and temperate regions worldwide. Africa's marabou—the largest—stands up to five feet tall. Of the two species of adjutant stork found in India and adjacent regions, the greater adjutant is only slightly smaller and the lesser adjutant attains a height of four feet. The three are very similar and closely related; their genus name *Leptoptilos* derives from the Greek words for fine (*leptos*) and feather (*ptilos*).

18. *The Asiatic Journal and Monthly Register for British and Foreign India, China and Australasia*, vol. 15 (London: Parbury Allen and Co, 1834), 311.

19. "The Adjutant," *Scientific American* 39, no. 4 (1878), 57.

20. *Reports by the Juries on the Subjects in the Thirty Classes into which the Exhibition Was Divided: Exhibition of the Works of Industry of All Nations* (London: William Clowes & Sons, 1851).

21. Robin W. Doughty, *Feather Fashions and Bird Preservation: A Study in Nature Protection* (Berkeley: University of California Press, 1975).

22. Josep del Hoyo et al., eds., *Handbook of the Birds of the World*, vol. 14 (Barcelona: Lynx Edicions, 1995).

23. Clifford B. Frith and Bruce M. Beehler, *Birds of Paradise* (Oxford: Oxford University Press, 1998). There is confusion over which species were the first preserved birds of paradise to arrive in Britain from New Guinea as a result of Magellan's expedition.

24. The greater and lesser birds of paradise are two of the forty-four species of birds of paradise, tropical rainforest birds occurring mainly in New Guinea with a few of the species also found on nearby islands and the extreme northeast of Australia. Not all are brilliantly colored or sport flamboyant male plumage. Feeding mainly on fruits, berries, and insects, they are mainly confined to mountain forest though some will venture into savanna and gardens. Only four are regarded by the IUCN as currently threatened, but eight others are classified as "near threatened"; forest clearance is the main threat they face today.

25. Alfred Russel Wallace, *The Malay Archipelago* (London: Macmillan, 1869), 419–420.

26. Stuart Kirsch, "History and the Birds of Paradise," *Expedition Magazine* 48, no. 1 (2006): 16–21.

27. Wallace, *The Malay Archipelago*, 423.

28. Doughty, *Feather Fashions and Bird Preservation*, 19.

29. BirdLife International, *Goura victoria*, IUCN Red List of Threatened Species 2016: e.T22691874A93326799. http://dx.doi.org/10.2305/IUCN.UK.2016-3.RLTS. T22691874A93326799.en.

30. Ginsburg, The Hat.

31. Mark Cocker and Richard Mabey, *Birds Britannica* (London: Chatto & Windus, 2005), 49.

32. Cocker and Mabey, *Birds Britannica*, 49–50.

33. Doughty, *Feather Fashions and Bird Preservation*.

34. Doughty, *Feather Fashions and Bird Preservation*.

35. Ginsburg, The Hat.

36. Ginsburg, The Hat, 73.

37. Ginsburg, The Hat, 92.

CHAPTER 5. A FEATHER IN LONDON'S CAP

1. William T. Hornaday, *Our Vanishing Wildlife: Its Extermination and Preservation* (New York: Charles Scribner's Sons, 1913). William Temple Hornaday (1854–1937) was an American zoologist and author, an early pioneer of wildlife conservation, and the first director of the then New York Zoological Park, now the Bronx Zoo.

2. R. J. Moore-Colyer, "Feathered Women and Persecuted Birds: The Struggle against the Plumage Trade, 1860–1922," *Rural History* 11, no. 1 (2000): 57–73.

3. Tessa Boase, *Mrs Pankhurst's Purple Feather* (London: Aurum Press, 2018).

4. Moore-Colyer, "Feathered Women and Persecuted Birds."

5. Superb lyrebirds are one of two lyrebird species, both large ground birds found only in Australia. With two long, gently curved, mottled guard plumes on either side of the tail and a set of lace-like, delicately filamentous feathers inside them, the rather drab grey and brown body plumage of these unusual birds was of no value. They were trapped and killed solely for their tail plumes.

6. James Beattie, Edward Melillo, and Emily O'Gorman, *Eco-Cultural Networks and the British Empire: New Views on Environmental History* (London: Bloomsbury Academic, 2014).

7. Hornaday, *Our Vanishing Wildlife*.

8. H. A. Macpherson, *History of Fowling* (Edinburgh: David Douglas, 1897), 151.

9. Mark Cocker and Richard Mabey, *Birds Britannica* (London: Chatto & Windus, 2005), 49.

10. Michael Shrubb, *Feasting, Fowling and Feathers* (London: T. & A. D. Poyser, 2013).

11. Josep del Hoyo et al., eds., *Handbook of the Birds of the World*, vol. 1 (Barcelona: Lynx Edicions, 1995).

12. Del Hoyo et al., *Handbook*, vol. 1.

13. James Hancock and Hugh Elliott, *The Herons of the World* (London: Harper Collins, 1978).

14. Anonymous, *Fowls of the Air*, Society for the Protection of Birds Leaflet 23 (London, 1896), 5–6.

15. Robin W. Doughty, *Feather Fashions and Bird Preservation: A Study in Nature Protection* (Berkeley: University of California Press, 1975).

16. George Reid, "Addenda to the Birds of the Lucknow Civil Division," *Stray Feathers* 10, no. 6 (1887): 444–453.

17. P. T. L. Dodsworth, "Protection of Wild Birds in India," *Journal of the Bombay Natural History Society* 20, no. 4 (1910): 1103–1114.

18. Anonymous, "England's Plumage Bill," *Bird-lore* 76–79 (1914), 77–78.

19. Josep del Hoyo et al., eds., *Handbook of the Birds of the World*, vol. 14 (Barcelona: Lynx Edicions, 2009). Found only in New Guinea, some nearby islands, and part of eastern Australia, birds of paradise are some of the most extravagantly colored birds in the world known for the fantastic, sometimes almost unbelievable, displays of the males. There are forty-four different species.

20. William T. Cooper and Joseph M. Forshaw, *Birds of Paradise and Bower Birds* (London: Collins, 1978).

21. Doughty, *Feather Fashions and Bird Preservation*.
22. Josep del Hoyo et al., eds., *Handbook of the Birds of the World*, vol. 16 (Barcelona: Lynx Edicions, 2010).
23. Josep del Hoyo et al., eds., *Handbook of the Birds of the World*, vol. 5 (Barcelona: Lynx Edicions, 1999).
24. Graeme Gibson, *The Bedside Book of Birds* (London: Bloomsbury Publishing. 2005).
25. Gibson, *Bedside Book*.
26. Doughty, *Feather Fashions and Bird Preservation*, 25.
27. Edgar Williams, *Ostrich* (London: Reaktion Books, 2013).
28. Amelia Opie, *The Father and Daughter with Dangers of Coquetry*, ed. Shelley King and John B. Pierce (Peterborough, ON: Broadview Press, 2003), 226.
29. Sarah Abrevaya Stein, *Plumes: Ostrich Feathers, Jews and a Lost World of Global Commerce* (New Haven: Yale University Press, 2008).
30. Thomas Abler, *Hinterland Warriors and Military Dress: European Empires and Exotic Uniforms* (London: Bloomsbury, 1999).
31. Personal communication from Louis Chalmers. Chalmers is the owner of The Plumery in Whitehall Gardens, London.
32. Charles Blanc, *Art in Ornament and Dress* (London: Chapman and Hall, 1877), 128.
33. Boase, *Mrs Pankhurst's Purple Feather*.
34. Del Hoyo et al., *Handbook*, vol. 1.
35. Doughty, *Feather Fashions and Bird Preservation*.
36. *The Auk* is a prestigious weekly, peer-reviewed journal established in 1884 that covers the anatomy, behavior, and distribution of birds. It is the official publication of the American Ornithological Society.
37. Shrubb, *Feasting*, 197.
38. Shrubb, *Feasting*.
39. Shrubb, *Feasting*.
40. J. Penry-Jones, "Feathers," *Port of London Authority Monthly* 33 (1958): 91–94.
41. Del Hoyo et al., *Handbook*, vol. 1.
42. Graham Barwell, *Albatross* (London: Reaktion Books, 2014).
43. One of nineteen grebe species worldwide, great crested grebes are serene water birds that dive regularly and have a striking courtship display. Breeding across most of the southern half of Europe including the United Kingdom, they are pale grey on the back with a white neck but with remarkable auburn and black ear and head feather tufts in breeding plumage.
44. Cocker and Mabey, *Birds Britannica*.
45. Carl C. Gaither and Alma E. Cavazos-Gaither, eds., *Gaither's Dictionary of Scientific Quotations* (New York: Springer, 2008), 7.
46. Simon Holloway, *The Historical Atlas of Breeding Birds in Britain and Ireland, 1875–1900* (London: T. & A. D. Poyser, 1996).
47. Shrubb, *Feasting*.
48. Cocker and Mabey, *Birds Britannica*.
49. Cocker and Mabey, *Birds Britannica*.
50. Cocker and Mabey, *Birds Britannica*.
51. Christopher Perrins, ed., *The Encyclopedia of Birds* (Oxford: Oxford University Press, 2009).
52. Cocker and Mabey, *Birds Britannica*.
53. Jeremy Gaskill, *Who Killed the Great Auk?* (Oxford: Oxford University Press, 2000), 171–172.

54. Shrubb, *Feasting.*
55. Cocker and Mabey, *Birds Britannica.*
56. Jeremy Gaskill, *Who Killed the Great Auk?*, 186–187.
57. Doughty, *Feather Fashions and Bird Preservation.*
58. A. H. E. Mattingley, "A Visit to Heronries," *The Emu* 7 (1907): 65–73.

CHAPTER 6. AN AMERICAN TRAGEDY UNFOLDS

1. Paul Ehrlich and David S. Dobkin, *The Birder's Handbook: A Field Guide to the Natural History of North American Birds* (New York: Simon & Schuster, 1988).
2. *Forest and Stream*, founded in 1873, was published in New York City until 1930 when it merged with *Field and Stream*. It promoted outdoor life, canoeing, and camping, and it was dedicated to wildlife conservation, helping to launch the National Audubon Society.
3. Carolyn Merchant, "George Bird Grinnell's Audubon Society: Bridging the Gender Divide in Conservation," *Environmental History* 15, no. 1 (2010): 12.
4. Jennifer Price, *Flight Maps: Adventures with Nature in Modern America* (New York: Basic Books, 1999), 59.
5. Jennifer Farley Gordon and Colleen Hill, *Sustainable Fashion: Past, Present and Future* (London: Bloomsbury, 2015), 136.
6. Jeanmarie Tucker, "The Bird Hat: Murderous Millinery," Maryland Historical Society, 2017, http://blog.mdhs.org/costumes/the-bird-hat-murderous-millinery. The 1868 edition of Harper's Bazaar announced the emergence of feather-decorated hats as fashion items in the United States, thereby following the European trend.
7. Paul Ehrlich, David Dobkin, and Darryl Wheye, *Birds in Jeopardy: The Imperiled and Extinct Birds of the United States and Canada* (Stanford: Stanford University Press, 1992).
8. Gary G. Gray, *Wildlife and People: The Human Dimensions of Wildlife Ecology* (Chicago: University of Illinois Press, 1993), 35.
9. Anonymous, *The Destruction of Our Native Birds*, Bulletin no.1 of the Committee on the Protection of Birds, Special Publication, Supplement to Science, 26 February 1887, American Ornithologists' Union. Founded in 1883, the AOU merged in 2016 with the Cooper Ornithological Society to form the American Ornithological Society.
10. William Dutcher, "Destruction of Birdlife in the Vicinity of New York." *Science* 7 1886, 197.
11. Thomas E. Dahl and Gregory G. Allord, *History of Wetlands in the Coterminous United States*, U.S. Geological Survey Water Supply Paper 2425, National Water Summary on Wetland Resources, 1997.
12. Thomas Gilbert Pearson was an American conservationist, a founder of the National Audubon Society, and one of the first faculty members at the University of North Carolina. The quote is taken from a paper read by Pearson at the World Congress on Ornithology, Chicago, 1897, in Robin W. Doughty, *Feather Fashions and Bird Preservation: A Study in Nature Protection* (Berkeley: University of California Press, 1975), 64–65.
13. *San Francisco Call* 83, no. 124, 3 April 1898.
14. Josep del Hoyo et al., eds., *Handbook of the Birds of the World*, vol. 1 (Barcelona: Lynx Edicions, 1995).
15. Gray, *Wildlife and People.*

16. W. E. D. Scott, "The Present Condition of Some of the Bird Rookeries of the Gulf Coast of Florida," *The Auk* 4 (1887): 135–144.

17. W. E. D. Scott, *The Story of a Bird Lover* (New York: Outlook, 1904), 256–257.

18. Del Hoyo et al., *Handbook*, vol. 1.

19. William T. Hornaday, *Our Vanishing Wildlife: Its Extermination and Preservation* (New York: Charles Scribner's Sons, 1913).

20. Ehrlich and Dobkin, *The Birder's Handbook*.

21. Closely allied with gulls, terns—of which there are forty-four species worldwide—are generally smaller than gulls and more delicate in appearance. Many have forked tails, most are light in color, and all have long, pointed wings. Mostly coastal birds, some species breed at inland lakes. Feeding on fish, squid, and crustaceans, they mainly plunge-dive into the water to catch them. Many fly long distances on migration and most rarely rest on water, preferring to stand on shorelines. Communal breeders, they nest on the ground near water, which makes them vulnerable both to mammalian predators and to human disturbance.

22. Ehrlich and Dobkin, The Birder's Handbook.

23. Ehrlich, Dobkin, and Wheye, Birds in Jeopardy.

24. *Forest and Stream*, 7 August 1884, 24.

25. Michael Shrubb, *Feasting, Fowling and Feathers* (London: T. & A. D. Poyser, 2013), 196.

26. Ehrlich, Dobkin, and Wheye, *Birds in Jeopardy*.

27. Celia Thaxter, *Woman's Heartlessness* (Boston: repr. for the Audubon Society of the State of New York, 1899), in National Audubon Society records, 1883–1991, Manuscript and Archives Division, Humanities and Social Library of the New York Public Library, Section C, Box C32, New York State Audubon Society folder.

28. James Reed was a Democratic senator for Missouri from 1911 to 1929. In Lisa Wade, "How the Bird Hat Craze Almost Killed the Dinosaurs," *Sociological Images* (blog), 27 December 2014, https://thesocietypages.org/socimages/.

29. Carolyn Merchant, *Ecological Revolutions: Nature, Gender and Science in New England* (Chapel Hill: University of North Carolina Press, 2010).

30. Merchant, *Ecological Revolutions*.

31. Jeffrey B. Snyder, *Stetson Hats & the John B Stetson Company:1865–1970* (Atglen, PA: Schiffer Publishing, 1997).

32. Hornaday, *Our Vanishing Wildlife*, 126.

33. What Women Are Wearing, *New York Times*, 25 September 1904, quoted in "1. Birds of Paradise," Fashioning Feathers, https://fashioningfeathers.info/birds-of-paradise/.

34. "Edwardian Hats—Winter 1903," *Victoriana Magazine*, http://www.victoriana.com/EdwardianHats/edwardian-hats-1903.html.

35. T. Eaton Company Limited, known as "Eaton's," was founded in 1869 and was once Canada's largest department store chain. It had buying offices worldwide, perfect for the feather trade. Its catalog was once to be found in most Canadian homes. It filed for bankruptcy in 1999.

36. Doughty, *Feather Fashions and Bird Preservation*.

37. Hornaday, *Our Vanishing Wildlife*, 130.

38. Gordon and Hill, *Sustainable Fashion*.

39. Gordon and Hill, *Sustainable Fashion*, 137.

40. Doug Alderson, *The Ghost Orchid Ghost and Other Tales from the Swamp* (Sarasota: Pineapple Press, 2007).

41. The Florida Audubon Society, the first state-based Audubon, was formed in 1886 by George Bird

Grinnell in response to widespread killing of birds in the state, especially egret colonies.

42. Gail Clement, "Everglades Biographies: Guy Bradley Biography," *Reclaiming the Everglades: South Florida's Natural History, 1884–1934* (Miami: Everglades Digital Library, Publication of Archival Library and Museum Materials, Florida International University, 2014).

43. Stuart B. McIver, *Death in the Everglades: The Murder of Guy Bradley, America's First Martyr to Environmentalism* (Gainesville: University Press of Florida, 2003) is one of several published accounts of Bradley's murder.

44. Jesse Greenspan, "The History and Evolution of the Migratory Bird Treaty Act," Audubon, 22 May 2015, https://www.audubon.org/news/the-history-and-evolution-migratory-bird-treaty-act.

45. Sarah Abrevaya Stein, *Plumes: Ostrich Feathers, Jews and a Lost World of Global Commerce* (New Haven: Yale University Press, 2008).

46. Stein, *Plumes.*

47. Adee Braun, "Fine-Feathered Friends," *Lapham's Quarterly*, 28 June 2013.

CHAPTER 7. LADIES WITH INFLUENCE

1. Kathryn Lasky, *She's Wearing a Dead Bird on Her Head* (New York: Meadowdale Books, 1997).

2. William Souder, "How Two Women Ended the Deadly Feather Trade," *Smithsonian Magazine*, March 2013, 2.

3. Robin W. Doughty, *Feather Fashions and Bird Preservation: A Study in Nature Protection* (Berkeley: University of California Press, 1975).

4. "Massachusetts Audubon Society Collection Guide Complete," Massachusetts Historical Society News, 7 January 2013, https://www.masshist.org.

5. Jennifer Price, *Flight Maps: Adventures with Nature in Modern America* (New York: Basic Books, 1999).

6. Doughty, *Feather Fashions and Bird Preservation.*

7. Tessa Boase, *Mrs Pankhurst's Purple Feather* (London: Aurum Press, 2018).

8. Molly Baer Kramer, "Williamson [née Bateson], Emily (1855–1936)," *Oxford Dictionary of National Biography*, Oxford University Press, doi:10.1093/ref:odnb/54568.

9. Jonathan Burt, "Phillips [née Barron], Eliza [known as Mrs Edward Phillips] (1822/3–1916)," *Oxford Dictionary of National Biography*, Oxford University Press.

10. *Punch* magazine was established in 1841; specializing in humor and satire, it helped to coin the term "cartoon" as a humorous illustration. Most influential in the 1840s and 1850s, after the 1940s when its circulation peaked, it declined, closing finally in 2002.

11. Boase, *Mrs Pankhurst's Purple Feather*, 65.

12. Boase, *Mrs Pankhurst's Purple Feather.*

13. Boase, *Mrs Pankhurst's Purple Feather.*

14. Boase, *Mrs Pankhurst's Purple Feather*, 70.

15. Price, *Flight Maps*, 86.

16. Price, *Flight Maps*, 82–83.

17. Mary Thatcher, "The Slaughter of the Innocents," *Harper's Bazaar* 8, no. 21 (22 May 1875): 338, repr. in Wildbirds Broadcasting, http://wildbirdsbroadcasting.blogspot.com/2012/01/slaughter-of-innocents.html.

18. Doughty, *Feather Fashions and Bird Preservation.*

19. Doughty, *Feather Fashions and Bird Preservation*, 113.

20. Doughty, *Feather Fashions and Bird Preservation*.

21. Doughty, *Feather Fashions and Bird Preservation*.

22. "Migratory Bird Treaty Act," U.S. Fish and Wildlife Service, last updated 26 September 2018, https://www.fws.gov.

23. Merle Patchett, "From Sexual Selection to Sex and the City: The Biogeographies of the Blue Bird of Paradise," *Journal of Social History*, 4 October 2018.

24. Boase, *Mrs Pankhurst's Purple Feather*, 226.

25. Boase, *Mrs Pankhurst's Purple Feather*, 73.

26. Boase, *Mrs Pankhurst's Purple Feather*, 86–87.

27. Boase, *Mrs Pankhurst's Purple Feather*.

28. Doughty, *Feather Fashions and Bird Preservation*.

29. Doughty, *Feather Fashions and Bird Preservation*, 68.

30. "Birds of a Feather: The Female Founders of the RSPB," History Press, https://www.thehistorypress.co.uk.

31. Boase, *Mrs Pankhurst's Purple Feather*.

32. "Birds of a Feather," History Press.

33. R. J. Moore-Colyer, "Feathered Women and Persecuted Birds: The Struggle against the Plumage Trade, c. 1860–1922," *Rural History* 11, no.1 (2000): 57–73.

34. Moore-Colyer, "Feathered Women and Persecuted Birds."

35. Boase, *Mrs Pankhurst's Purple Feather*.

36. Doughty, *Feather Fashions and Bird Preservation*.

37. Josep del Hoyo et al., eds., *Handbook of the Birds of the World*, vol. 1 (Barcelona: Lynx Edicions, 1995).

38. Josep del Hoyo et al., eds., *Handbook of the Birds of the World*, vol. 9 (Barcelona: Lynx Edicions, 2004).

39. Moore-Colyer, "Feathered Women and Persecuted Birds."

40. James A. Rimbach. "The Judeo-Christian Tradition and the Human–Animal Bond," *International Journal for the Study of Animal Problems* 3 no. 3 (1982): 206.

41. Robin Attfield, "Christian Attitudes to Nature," *Journal of the History of Ideas* 44, no. 3 (1983): 369.

42. Boase, *Mrs Pankhurst's Purple Feather*, 289.

43. Moore-Colyer, "Feathered Women and Persecuted Birds."

44. Doughty, *Feather Fashions and Bird Preservation*, 96.

45. Personal communication from Robin Doughty, August 2018.

46. "The Women of the Early Florida Audubon Society," University of Florida, http://users.clas.ufl.edu/davisjac/courses/environmental/PooleAudubonWomen.html.

47. "The Conservation (Natural Habitats, &c.) Regulations 1994," The National Archives, http://www.legislation.gov.uk/uksi/1994/2716/contents/made.

48. Robert S. Anderson, *The Lacey Act: America's Premier Weapon in the Fight Against Unlawful Wildlife Trafficking* (East Lansing: Michigan State University Animal Legal and Historical Center, 1995).

CHAPTER 8. THE DAVY CROCKETT REVIVAL

1. Up to twenty-eight inches in length and grey in color, northern raccoons have a black-and-white facial mask and a ringed tail. Extremely agile and intelligent, they are forest mammals that have adapted to a wide range of habitats including urban areas where they are usually considered as pests. Raccoons have been introduced to parts of Europe and Japan.

2. Michael Wallis, *David Crockett: The Lion of the West* (New York: W.W. Norton, 2011).

3. Dwight Blocker Bowers, "The Saga of Davy Crockett's Coonskin Cap," Stories from the National Museum of American History, Smithsonian American History, 17 November 2014, http://americanhistory.si.edu.

4. Richard Severo, "Fess Parker" (obituary), *New York Times*, 19 March 2010.

5. Bowers, "The Saga of Davy Crockett's Coonskin Cap."

6. Wallis, *David Crockett*.

7. Wallis, *David Crockett*.

8. The Boone Society (https://www.boonesociety.com/pages/) is an association of descendants, genealogists, and historians set up to study the lives and times of Daniel Boone and his family. One of its principal goals is to identify and preserve Boone-related documents and artifacts.

9. Dorcas MacClintock, *A Natural History of Raccoons* (New York: Charles Scribner's Sons, 1981).

10. Glenn Hinson and William Ferris, eds., Folklife, vol. 14 of The New Encyclopedia of Southern Culture (Chapel Hill: University of North Carolina Press, 2009).

11. Samuel I. Zeveloff, *Raccoons: A Natural History* (Vancouver: University of British Columbia Press, 2002).

12. Zeveloff, *Raccoons*.

13. June Swan et al., *Birds of Paradise: Plumes and Feathers in Fashion* (Tielt: Lannoo Publishers, 2014).

14. R. Turner Wilcox, The Mode in Hats and Headdress (Mineola, NY: Dover Publications, 2008).

15. Madeleine Ginsburg, The Hat: Trends and Traditions (New York: Barron's, 1990).

16. Ginsburg, The Hat, 115.

17. Robin W. Doughty, *Feather Fashions and Bird Preservation: A Study in Nature Protection* (Berkeley: University of California Press, 1975).

18. Ginsburg, The Hat.

19. Doughty, *Feather Fashions and Bird Preservation*.

20. Ginsburg, The Hat.

CHAPTER 9. THE SURVIVORS' STORY

1. Josep del Hoyo et al., eds., *Handbook of the Birds of the World*, vol. 1 (Barcelona: Lynx Edicions, 1995).

2. BirdLife International, *Struthio camelus*, IUCN Red List of Threatened Species 2016: e.T45020636A95139620. http://dx.doi.org/10.2305/IUCN.UK.2016-3.RLTS.T45020636A95139620.en.

3. BirdLife International, *Struthio molybdophanes*, IUCN Red List of Threatened Species 2016: e.T22732795A95049558. http://dx.doi.org/10.2305/IUCN.UK.2016-3.RLTS.T22732795A95049558.en.

4. Del Hoyo et al., *Handbook of the Birds of the World*, vol. 1.

5. BirdLife International, *Ardea alba*, IUCN Red List of Threatened Species 2016: e.T22697043A86468751. http://dx.doi.org/10.2305/IUCN.UK.2016-3.RLTS. T22697043A86468751.en.

6. Robin W. Doughty, *Feather Fashions and Bird Preservation: A Study in Nature Protection* (Berkeley: University of California Press, 1975).

7. BirdLife International, *Egretta thula*, IUCN Red List of Threatened Species 2016: e.T22696974A93595536. http://dx.doi.org/10.2305/IUCN.UK.2016-3.RLTS. T22696974A93595536.en.

8. James A. Kushlan et al., *Waterbird Conservation for the Americas: The North American Waterbird Conservation Plan, Version 1* (Washington, DC: U.S. Fish and Wildlife Service, 2002).

9. Dawn Balmer et al., *Bird Atlas, 2007–2011: The Breeding and Wintering Birds of Britain and Ireland* (Thetford: BTO Books, 2013).

10. BirdLife International, *Egretta rufescens*, IUCN Red List of Threatened Species 2016: e.T22696916A93592693. http://dx.doi.org/10.2305/IUCN.UK.2016-3.RLTS. T22696916A93592693.en.

11. Del Hoyo et al., *Handbook of the Birds of the World*, vol. 1.

12. BirdLife International, *Leptoptilos dubius*, IUCN Red List of Threatened Species 2016: e.T22697721A93633471. http://dx.doi.org/10.2305/IUCN.UK.2016-3.RLTS. T22697721A93633471.en. BirdLife International, *Leptoptilos javanicus*, IUCN Red List of Threatened Species 2017 (amended version of 2016 assessment): e.T22697713A110481858. http://dx.doi.org/10.2305/IUCN.UK.2017-1.RLTS.T22697713A110481858.en.

13. BirdLife International, *Platalea ajaja*, IUCN Red List of Threatened Species 2016: e.T22697574A93621961. http://dx.doi.org/10.2305/IUCN.UK.2016-3.RLTS. T22697574A93621961.en.

14. "Species factsheet: Scarlet Ibis *Eudocimus ruber*," BirdLife International, 2018, http://www. birdlife.org.

15. Del Hoyo et al., *Handbook of the Birds of the World*, vol. 1.

16. Jan Betlem and Ben H. J. de Jong, "De rode ibis-moord in Frans-Guiana," *Vogeljaar* 31, no. 4 (1983): 192–198.

17. Balmer et al., *Bird Atlas*.

18. Del Hoyo et al., *Handbook of the Birds of the World*, vol. 1.

19. Del Hoyo et al., *Handbook of the Birds of the World*, vol. 1.

20. Del Hoyo et al., *Handbook of the Birds of the World*, vol. 1.

21. Del Hoyo et al., *Handbook of the Birds of the World*, vol. 1.

22. "Species factsheet: Black-legged Kittiwake *Rissa tridactyla*," BirdLife International, 2018, http://www.birdlife.org.

23. BirdLife International, *Sterna dougallii*, IUCN Red List of Threatened Species 2017 (amended version of 2017 assessment): e.T22694601A118624109. http://dx.doi.org/10.2305/IUCN. UK.2017-3.RLTS.T22694601A118624109.en.

24. BirdLife International, *Sternula antillarum*, IUCN Red List of Threatened Species 2016: e.T22694673A93462098. http://dx.doi.org/10.2305/IUCN.UK.2016-3.RLTS. T22694673A93462098.en.

25. Josep del Hoyo et al., eds., *Handbook of Birds of the World*, vol. 3 (Barcelona: Lynx Edicions, 2004).

26. Les Beletsky, *Birds of the World* (London: Harper Collins, 2006).

27. BirdLife International, *Paradisaea rubra*, IUCN Red List of Threatened Species 2016:

e.T22706241A94057735. http://dx.doi.org/10.2305/IUCN.UK.2016-3.RLTS. T22706241A94057735.en.

28. BirdLife International, *Paradisornis rudolphi*, IUCN Red List of Threatened Species 2016: e.T22706266A94059137. http://dx.doi.org/10.2305/IUCN.UK.2016-3.RLTS. T22706266A94059137.en.

29. Julian P. Hume and Michael Walters, *Extinct Birds* (London: T. & A. D. Poyser, 2012).

30. BirdLife International, *Pavo cristatus*, IUCN Red List of Threatened Species 2016: e.T22679435A92814454. http://dx.doi.org/10.2305/IUCN.UK.2016-3.RLTS. T22679435A92814454.en.

31. BirdLife International, *Menura novaehollandiae*, IUCN Red List of Threatened Species 2016: e.T22703605A93929511. http://dx.doi.org/10.2305/IUCN.UK.2016-3.RLTS. T22703605A93929511.en.

32. BirdLife International, *Chrysolophus pictus*, IUCN Red List of Threatened Species 2016: e.T22679355A92812162. http://dx.doi.org/10.2305/IUCN.UK.2016-3.RLTS. T22679355A92812162.en.

33. Josep del Hoyo et al., eds., *Handbook of the Birds of the World*, vol. 2: *New World Vultures to Guineafowl* (Barcelona: Lynx Edicions, 2001).

34. BirdLife International, *Lophophorus impejanus*, IUCN Red List of Threatened Species 2016: e.T22679182A92806166. http://dx.doi.org/10.2305/IUCN.UK.2016-3.RLTS. T22679182A92806166.en.

35. "Species factsheet: Reeves's Pheasant *Syrmaticus reevesii*," BirdLife International, 2018, http://www.birdlife.org.

36. Josep del Hoyo et al., eds., *Handbook of the Birds of the World*, vol. 4 (Barcelona: Lynx Edicions, 1997).

37. Beletsky, *Birds of the World*.

38. BirdLife International, *Chrysolampis mosquitus*, IUCN Red List of Threatened Species 2016: e.T22687160A93142952. http://dx.doi.org/10.2305/IUCN.UK.2016-3.RLTS. T22687160A93142952.en.

39. Josep Del Hoyo et al., eds., *Handbook of Birds of the World*, vol. 6 (Barcelona: Lynx, 2001).

40. BirdLife International, *Halcyon smyrnensis*, IUCN Red List of Threatened Species 2017 (amended version of 2016 assessment): e.T22725846A119289544. http://dx.doi.org/10.2305/IUCN. UK.2017-3.RLTS.T22725846A119289544.en.

41. BirdLife International, *Pharomachrus mocinno*, IUCN Red List of Threatened Species 2016: e.T22682727A92958465. http://dx.doi.org/10.2305/IUCN.UK.2016-3.RLTS. T22682727A92958465.en.

42. Bruce W. Baker and Edward P. Hill, "Beaver (*Castor canadensis*)," in *Wild Mammals of North America: Biology, Management, and Conservation*, ed. G. A. Feldhamer, B. C. Thompson, and J. A. Chapman (Baltimore, MD: Johns Hopkins University Press, 2003), 288–310.

43. H. Bryant White et al., "Trapping and Furbearer Management in North American Wildlife Conservation," *International Journal of Environmental Studies* 72, no. 5 (2015): 756–769.

44. F. Cassola, *Castor canadensis*, IUCN Red List of Threatened Species 2016: e.T4003A22187946. http://dx.doi.org/10.2305/IUCN.UK.2016-3.RLTS.T4003A22187946.en.

45. J. Batbold et al., *Castor fiber*, IUCN Red List of Threatened Species 2016 (errata version published in 2017): e.T4007A115067136. http://dx.doi.org/10.2305/IUCN.UK.2016-3.RLTS. T4007A22188115.en.

46. J. Carter and B. P. Leonard, "A Review of the Literature on the Worldwide Distribution, Spread of,

and Efforts to Eradicate the Coypu," *Wildlife Society Bulletin* 30, no. 1 (2002): 162–175.

47. R. Ojeda, C. Bidau, and L. Emmons, *Myocastor coypus*, IUCN Red List of Threatened Species 2016 (errata version published in 2017): e.T14085A121734257.

48. F. Lebas et al., "The Rabbit: Husbandry, Health and Production," FAO Animal Production and Health Series No. 21, 1997, http://www.fao.org.

49. A. T. Smith, and A. F. Boyer, *Oryctolagus cuniculus*, IUCN Red List of Threatened Species 2008: e.T41291A10415170. http://dx.doi.org/10.2305/IUCN.UK.2008.RLTS.T41291A10415170.en.

50. A. T. Smith, and C. H. Johnston, *Lepus europaeus*, IUCN Red List of Threatened Species 2008: e.T41280A10430693. http://dx.doi.org/10.2305/IUCN.UK.2008.RLTS.T41280A10430693.en.

51. Mexican Association for Conservation and Study of Lagomorphs (AMCELA), F. J. Romero Malpica, and H. Rangel Cordero, *Lepus californicus*, IUCN Red List of Threatened Species 2008: e.T41276A10412537. http://dx.doi.org/10.2305/IUCN.UK.2008.RLTS.T41276A10412537.en. A. T. Smith, and C. H. Johnston, *Lepus townsendii*, IUCN Red List of Threatened Species 2008: e.T41288A10413649. http://dx.doi.org/10.2305/IUCN.UK.2008.RLTS.T41288A10413649.en.

52. D. Murray, and A. T. Smith, *Lepus arcticus*, IUCN Red List of Threatened Species 2008: e.T41274A10410937. http://dx.doi.org/10.2305/IUCN.UK.2008.RLTS.T41274A10410937.en.

53. A. T. Smith and C. H. Johnston, *Lepus timidus*, IUCN Red List of Threatened Species 2008: e.T11791A3306541. http://dx.doi.org/10.2305/IUCN.UK.2008.RLTS.T11791A3306541.en.

54. A. Angerbjörn and M. Tannerfeldt, *Vulpes lagopus*, IUCN Red List of Threatened Species 2014: e.T899A57549321. http://dx.doi.org/10.2305/IUCN.UK.2014-2.RLTS.T899A57549321.en.

55. M. Hoffmann, and C. Sillero-Zubiri, *Vulpes vulpes*, IUCN Red List of Threatened Species 2016: e.T23062A46190249. http://dx.doi.org/10.2305/IUCN.UK.2016-1.RLTS.T23062A46190249.en.

56. J. D. Murdoch, *Vulpes corsac*, IUCN Red List of Threatened Species 2014: e.T23051A59049446. http://dx.doi.org/10.2305/IUCN.UK.2014-2.RLTS.T23051A59049446.en.

57. White et al., "Trapping and Furbearer Management."

58. V. G. Monakhov, *Martes zibellina*, IUCN Red List of Threatened Species 2016: e.T41652A45213477. http://dx.doi.org/10.2305/IUCN.UK.2016-1.RLTS.T41652A45213477.en.

59. K. Helgen and F. Reid, *Martes americana*, IUCN Red List of Threatened Species 2016: e.T41648A45212861. http://dx.doi.org/10.2305/IUCN.UK.2016-1.RLTS.T41648A45212861.en.

60. J. Herrero et al., *Martes martes*, IUCN Red List of Threatened Species 2016: e.T12848A45199169. http://dx.doi.org/10.2305/IUCN.UK.2016-1.RLTS.T12848A45199169.en.

61. A. V. Abramov, *Gulo gulo*, IUCN Red List of Threatened Species 2016: e.T9561A45198537. http://dx.doi.org/10.2305/IUCN.UK.2016-1.RLTS.T9561A45198537.en.

62. F. Cassola, *Urocitellus parryii*, IUCN Red List of Threatened Species 2016: e.T20488A22262403. http://dx.doi.org/10.2305/IUCN.UK.2016-3.RLTS.T20488A22262403.en.

63. R. Timm et al., *Procyon lotor*, IUCN Red List of Threatened Species 2016: e.T41686A45216638. http://dx.doi.org/10.2305/IUCN.UK.2016-1.RLTS.T41686A45216638.en.

64. A. V. Abramov et al., *Martes foina*, IUCN Red List of Threatened Species 2016:

e.T29672A45202514. http://dx.doi.org/10.2305/IUCN.UK.2016-1.RLTS.T29672A45202514. en.

65. G. Roemer, B. Cypher, and R. List, *Urocyon cinereoargenteus*, IUCN Red List of Threatened Species 2016: e.T22780A46178068. http://dx.doi.org/10.2305/IUCN.UK.2016-1.RLTS. T22780A46178068.en.

66. K. Helgen and F. Reid, *Martes pennanti*, IUCN Red List of Threatened Species 2018 (amended version of 2016 assessment): e.T41651A125236220. http://dx.doi.org/10.2305/IUCN. UK.2016-2.RLTS.T41651A125236220.en.

67. A. Gunn, *Rangifer tarandus*, IUCN Red List of Threatened Species 2016: e.T29742A22167140. http://dx.doi.org/10.2305/IUCN.UK.2016-1.RLTS.T29742A22167140.en.

68. D. L. Garshelis et al., *Ursus americanus*, IUCN Red List of Threatened Species 2016 (errata version published in 2017): e.T41687A114251609. http://dx.doi.org/10.2305/IUCN.UK.2016-3.RLTS.T41687A45034604.en.

69. A. Doroff and A. Burdin, *Enhydra lutris*, IUCN Red List of Threatened Species 2015: e.T7750A21939518. http://dx.doi.org/10.2305/IUCN.UK.2015-2.RLTS.T7750A21939518.en.

70. K. M. Kovacs, *Erignathus barbatus*, IUCN Red List of Threatened Species 2016: e.T8010A45225428. http://dx.doi.org/10.2305/IUCN.UK.2016-1.RLTS.T8010A45225428.en.

71. L. Lowry, *Odobenus rosmarus*, IUCN Red List of Threatened Species 2016: e.T15106A45228501. http://dx.doi.org/10.2305/IUCN.UK.2016-1.RLTS.T15106A45228501.en.

CHAPTER 10. TODAY'S HATS

1. Personal communication from Ellen Colon-Lugo, 15 October 2018.
2. Personal communication from Lindsay Whitehead, 22 October 2018.
3. Personal communication from Phil Sykes, 15 October 2018.
4. Charlotte Mackaness, "Feathers Are the Milliner's Friend, Put One in Your Hat," *The Field*, 14 July 2014.
5. Personal communication from Benjamin Jaffé, 1 November 2018.
6. Personal communication from Louis Chalmers, 5 November 2018.
7. Personal communication from the director of the Museo Bersaglieri, Rome.
8. "Species factsheet: Western Capercaillie *Tetrao urogallus*," BirdLife International, 2018, http://www.birdlife.org.
9. Personal communication from Peter O'Donoghue. Peter J. Begent and Hubert Chesshyre, *The Most Noble Order of the Garter: 650 Years* (London: Spink, 1999).
10. Personal communication from Peter O'Donoghue, 7 November 2018.
11. Personal communication from Anni Guttorm, 10 September 2018.
12. Personal communication from Bernadette Driscoll Engelstad, 23 August and 6 September 2018.
13. Alison Crawford, "Wanted by the Mounties: 4,470 Muskrat Hats," *CBC News*, 4 October 2017, https://www.cbc.ca.
14. E-mail from Army Secretariat, 13 September 2018.
15. Chloe Pantazi, "A BBC Reporter Got a Startling Look Inside a Russian Fur Farm," *Business Insider UK*, 27 April 2016.
16. Ester Muchawsky-Schnapper, *A World Apart Next Door: Glimpses into the Life of Hasidic Jews* (Jerusalem: The Israel Museum, 2012).

17. Yori Yanover, "Haredi Leader: Wearing a Shtreimel Is Chilul Hashem," *The Jewish Press*, 22 August 2013.

18. Muchawsky-Schnapper, *A World Apart Next Door*.

19. Beverly Chico, "History of Women's Hats," Lovetoknow, https://fashion-history.lovetoknow.com/fashion-history-eras/history-womens-hats.

20. Meeting with Craig Sallis, Christys' factory, 15 May 2018.

21. The International Fur Federation was established in 1949 and claims that it is the only organization to represent the international fur industry and regulate its practices and trade. The federation promotes the business of fur, establishing certification and traceability programs on welfare and the environment. It is also committed to supporting young designers and retailers who intend to go into fur and fashion. It represents fifty-six members' associations in over forty countries. The members encompass all parts of the fur trade including farmers, trappers, dressers, manufacturers, brokers, auction houses, retailers, and designers. Each of these members has signed a strict code of conduct committing them to upholding the industry-relevant laws they fall under in their home countries.

22. Don E. Wilson and Russell A. Mittermeier, eds., *Handbook of the Mammals of the World*, vol. 1 (Barcelona: Lynx Edicions, 2009).

23. Wilson and Mittermeier, *Handbook*.

24. PETA focuses its attention on the four areas in which the largest numbers of animals suffer the most intensely for the longest periods of time: in laboratories, in the food industry, in the clothing trade, and in the entertainment industry. They also work on a variety of other issues including the cruel killing of rodents, birds, and other animals that are often considered "pests" as well as cruelty to domesticated animals. PETA works through public education, cruelty investigations, research, animal rescue, legislation, special events, celebrity involvement, and protest campaigns.

25. Andrey Kolokolnikov, "International Fur Trade Trends, Challenges, Prospects" (bachelor of Business Administration International Business and Logistics thesis, Helsinki Metropolia University, 2013).

26. Kolokolnikov, "International Fur Trade Trends."

27. Kolokolnikov, "International Fur Trade Trends."

28. European Commission Scientific Committee on Animal Health and Animal Welfare, "The Welfare of Animals Kept for Fur Production," 2001.

29. European Commission Scientific Committee on Animal Health and Animal Welfare, "The Welfare of Animals Kept for Fur Production."

30. H. Bryant White et al., "Trapping and Furbearer Management in North American Wildlife Conservation," *International Journal of Environmental Studies* 72, no. 5 (2015): 756–769.

31. Lesley A. Peterson, *Detailed Discussion of Fur Animals and Fur Production* (East Lansing: Michigan State University College of Law, 2010).

32. Harriet Brown, "Real versus Fake: The Next Battleground in the Fur Debate." *Drapers Magazine*, 10 April 2018.

33. Scarlett Conlon, "London Fashion Week Vows to Be Fur-Free," *The Guardian*, 7 September 2018, https://www.theguardian.com/fashion/2018/sep/07/london-fashion-week-vows-to-be-fur-free.

34. Wendell Berry, *Bringing It to the Table: On Farming and Food* (Indore, India: Banyan Tree, 2013), 96.

APPENDIX. THE IUCN RED LIST CLASSIFICATION

1. The IUCN Red List of Threatened Species, https://www.iucnredlist.org.

Bibliography

Abler, Thomas. *Hinterland Warriors and Military Dress: European Empires and Exotic Uniforms*. London: Bloomsbury, 1999.

"The Adjutant." *Scientific American* 39, no. 4 (1878), 57.

Alderson, Doug. *The Ghost Orchid Ghost and Other Tales from the Swamp*. Sarasota: Pineapple Press, 2007.

Anderson, Robert S. *The Lacey Act: America's Premier Weapon in the Fight Against Unlawful Wildlife Trafficking*. East Lansing: Michigan State University Animal Legal and Historical Center, 1995.

Anonymous. *The Destruction of Our Native Birds*. Bulletin no.1 of the Committee on the Protection of Birds, Special Publication, Supplement to Science, 26 February 1887, American Ornithologists' Union.

Anonymous. "England's Plumage Bill." *Bird-lore* (1914), 76–79.

Arca, Gianluigi. "Bersaglieri Infantry: Heroes in Italian History." *NATO Armies and Their Traditions* 13 (2009): 23–25.

Arnon, Dan. *A Hat for All Seasons*. Tel Aviv: Am Oved, 1995.

The Asiatic Journal and Monthly Register for British and Foreign India, China and Australasia, vol. 15. London: Parbury Allen and Co, 1834.

Attfield, Robin. "Christian Attitudes to Nature." *Journal of the History of Ideas* 44, no. 3 (1983): 369–386.

Axelrod, Alan. *Little-Known Wars of Great and Lasting Impact*. Beverly, MA: Fair Winds Press, 2009.

Bachrach, Max. *Fur: A Practical Treatise*. New York: Prentice-Hall, 1953.

Baker, Bruce W., and Edward P. Hill. "Beaver (*Castor canadensis*)." In *Wild Mammals of North America: Biology, Management, and Conservation*, edited by G. A. Feldhamer, B. C. Thompson, and J. A. Chapman, 288–310. Baltimore, MD: Johns Hopkins University Press, 2003.

Balmer, Dawn, et al. *Bird Atlas, 2007–2011: The Breeding and Wintering Birds of Britain and Ireland*. Thetford: BTO Books, 2013.

Barwell, Graham. *Albatross*. London: Reaktion Books, 2014.

Beattie, James, Edward Melillo, and Emily O'Gorman. *Eco-Cultural Networks and the British Empire: New Views on Environmental History*. London: Bloomsbury Academic, 2014.

Begent, Peter J., and Hubert Chesshyre. *The Most Noble Order of the Garter: 650 Years*. London: Spink, 1999.

Beletsky, Les. *Birds of the World*. London: Harper Collins, 2006.

Berdan, Frances F. "Featherwork as a Commodity Complex in the Late Postclassic Mesoamerican World System." In *Alternative Pathways to Complexity*, edited by Lane F. Fargher and Verenice Y. Heredia Espinoza, 131–154. Louisville: University Press of Colorado, 2016.

Berlin, Maths, Rudolfs K. Zalups, and Bruce A. Fowler. "Mercury." In *Handbook on the Toxicology of Metals*, 676–718. Cambridge, MA: Academic Press, 2007.

Berry, Wendell. *Bringing It to the Table: On Farming and Food*. Berkeley: Counterpoint, 2009.

Betlem, Jan, and Ben H. J. de Jong. "De rode ibis-moord in Frans-Guiana." *Vogeljaar* 31, no. 4 (1983): 192–198.

The IUCN Red List of Threatened Species. https://www.iucnredlist.org.

BirdLife International. "Species factsheet: Western Capercaillie *Tetrao urogallus*." 2018. http://www. birdlife.org.

Birdsall, Amelia. "A Woman's Nature: Attitudes and Identities of the Bird Hat Debate at the Turn of the 20th Century." Senior thesis, Haverford College, Pennsylvania, 2002.

Blanc, Charles. *Art in Ornament and Dress*. London: Chapman and Hall, 1877.

Boase, Tessa. *Mrs Pankhurst's Purple Feather*. London: Aurum Press, 2018.

Bobrick, Benson. *East of the Sun: The Epic Conquest and Tragic History of Siberia*. New York: Poseidon Press,1992.

"Bodies of the Bogs: Clothing and Hair Styles of the Bog People." *Archaeology*, 10 December 1997. https://archive.archaeology.org/online/features/bog/.

Boulton, James J. *Head-dress of the Canadian Mounted Police, 1873–2000*. Calgary: Bunker to Bunker Publications, 2000.

Bowers, Dwight Blocker. "The Saga of Davy Crockett's Coonskin Cap." Stories from the National Museum of American History, Smithsonian American History, 17 November 2014. http:// americanhistory.si.edu.

Braun, Adee. "Fine-Feathered Friends." *Lapham's Quarterly*, 28 June 2013.

Brown, Harriet. "Real versus Fake: The Next Battleground in the Fur Debate." *Drapers Magazine*, 10 April 2018.

Bunn, Stephanie. *Nomadic Felts: Artistic Traditions in World Cultures*. London: British Museum Press, 2011.

Burch, Ernest S. "The Caribou/Wild Reindeer as a Human Resource." *American Antiquity* 37, no. 3 (1972): 339–368.

Burt, Jonathan. "Phillips [née Barron], Eliza [known as Mrs Edward Phillips] (1822/3–1916)." *Oxford Dictionary of National Biography*, Oxford University Press. https://doi.org/10.1093/ ref:odnb/50752.

CABI. "Ondatra zibethicus (Muskrat)." *Invasive Species Compendium*. Last modified 19 November 2018. https://www.cabi.org/isc.

Campbell, David. *Finnish Soldier vs Soviet Soldier: Winter War 1939–40*. Oxford: Osprey Publishing, 2016.

Canada's First Peoples. "The Inuit." 2007. https://firstpeoplesofcanada.com/fp_groups/fp_inuit3.html.

Carlos, Ann M., and Frank D. Lewis. *Commerce by a Frozen Sea: Native Americans and the European Fur Trade*. Philadelphia: University of Pennsylvania Press, 2010.

———. "Indians, the Beaver, and the Bay: The Economics of Depletion in the Lands of the Hudson's Bay Company, 1700–1763." *The Journal of Economic History* 53, no. 3 (1993): 465–494.

Carter, J., and B. P. Leonard. "A Review of the Literature on the Worldwide Distribution, Spread of, and Efforts to Eradicate the Coypu," *Wildlife Society Bulletin* 30, no. 1 (2002): 162–175.

Chico, Beverly. "History of Women's Hats." Lovetoknow. https://fashion-history.lovetoknow.com/ fashion-history-eras/history-womens-hats.

Clement, Gail. "Everglades Biographies: Guy Bradley." *Reclaiming the Everglades: South Florida's Natural History, 1884–1934*. Miami: Everglades Digital Library, Publication of Archival Library and Museum Materials, Florida International University, 2014.

Cocker, Mark, and Richard Mabey. *Birds Britannica*. London: Chatto & Windus, 2005.

Conlon, Scarlett. "London Fashion Week Vows to Be Fur-Free." *The Guardian*, 7 September 2018.

https://www.theguardian.com/fashion/2018/sep/07/london-fashion-week-vows-to-be-fur-free.

Connecticut History. "The Danbury Hatters." 1 August 2014. https://connecticuthistory.org.

Cooper, William T., and Joseph M. Forshaw. *Birds of Paradise and Bower Birds*. London: Collins, 1978.

Cotel, Aline J., et al. "Effect of Ancient Inuit Fur Parka Ruffs on Facial Heat Transfer," *Climate Research* 26 (2004): 77–84.

Crawford, Alison. "Wanted by the Mounties: 4,470 Muskrat Hats." *CBC News*. 4 October 2017. https://www.cbc.ca.

Curry-Lindahl, Kai. "The Brown Bear (*Ursus arctos*) in Europe: Decline, Present Distribution, Biology and Ecology." In *Bears: Their Biology and Management; A Selection of Papers from the Second International Conference on Bear Research and Management held at the University of Calgary, Alberta, Canada, 6 to 9 November 1970*, 2:74–80. Morges: International Union for Conservation of Nature and Natural Resources, 1972.

Dahl, Thomas E., and Gregory G. Allord. *History of Wetlands in the Coterminous United States*. U.S. Geological Survey Water Supply Paper 2425, National Water Summary on Wetland Resources, 1997.

del Hoyo, Josep, et al., eds. *Handbook of the Birds of the World*. Vols. 1–6, 9, 14, 16. Barcelona: Lynx Edicions, 1992–2010.

Dodsworth, P. T. L. "Protection of Wild Birds in India." *Journal of the Bombay Natural History Society* 20, no. 4 (1910): 1103–1114.

Doughty, Robin W. *Feather Fashions and Bird Preservation: A Study in Nature Protection*. Berkeley: University of California Press, 1975.

Dutcher, William. "Destruction of Birdlife in the vicinity of New York." *Science* 7 (1886), 197.

Edwards, Louise. "Military Celebrity in China: The Evolution of 'Heroic and Model Servicemen.'" In *Celebrity in China*, edited by Elaine Jeffreys and Louise Edwards, 21–44. Hong Kong: Hong Kong University Press, 2010.

Ehrlich, Paul R., and David S. Dobkin. *The Birder's Handbook: A Field Guide to the Natural History of North American Birds*. New York: Simon and Schuster, 1988.

Ehrlich, Paul R., David Dobkin, and Darryl Wheye. *Birds in Jeopardy: The Imperiled and Extinct Birds of the United States and Canada*. Stanford: Stanford University Press, 1992.

European Commission Scientific Committee on Animal Health and Animal Welfare, "The Welfare of Animals Kept for Fur Production," 2001.

Frith, Clifford B., and Bruce M. Beehler. *Birds of Paradise*. Oxford: Oxford University Press, 1998.

Gaither, Carl C., and Alma E. Cavazos-Gaither, eds. *Gaither's Dictionary of Scientific Quotations*. New York: Springer, 2008.

Gaskill, Jeremy. *Who Killed the Great Auk?* Oxford: Oxford University Press, 2000.

Gertcyk, Olga. "World Famous Ancient Siberian Venus Figurines 'are NOT Venuses after all.'" *Siberian Times*, 18 February 2016.

Gibson, Graeme. *The Bedside Book of Birds*. London: Bloomsbury Publishing. 2005.

Ginsburg, Madeleine. *The Hat: Trends and Traditions*. New York: Barrons, 1990.

Gordon, Jennifer Farley, and Colleen Hill. *Sustainable Fashion: Past, Present and Future*. London: Bloomsbury, 2015.

Gray, Gary G. *Wildlife and People: The Human Dimensions of Wildlife Ecology*. Chicago: University of Illinois Press, 1993.

Green, Rayna, and Melanie Fernandez. *The Encyclopaedia of the First Peoples of North America*. Toronto: Groundwood/Douglas & McIntyre, 1999.

Gross, Joseph J., and Sigrid Khera. *Ethnohistory of the Aleuts*. Fairbanks: University of Alaska, 1980.

Hancock, James, and Hugh Elliott. *The Herons of the World*. London: Harper Collins, 1978.

Henry, Alexander. *Alexander Henry's Travels and Adventures in the Years 1760–1776.* Edited by Milo Milton Quaife. Chicago: R. R. Donnelley & Sons, 1921.

Hinson, Glenn, and William Ferris, eds. *Folklife.* Vol. 14 of *The New Encyclopedia of Southern Culture.* Chapel Hill: University of North Carolina Press, 2009.

History Press. "Birds of a Feather: The Female Founders of the RSPB." https://www.thehistorypress.co.uk.

Hodgson, Robert G. *Fisher Farming.* Toronto: Fur Trade Journal of Canada, 1937.

Holloway, Simon. *The Historical Atlas of Breeding Birds in Britain and Ireland, 1875–1900.* London: T. & A. D. Poyser, 1996.

Hornaday, William T. *Our Vanishing Wildlife: Its Extermination and Preservation.* New York: Charles Scribner's Sons, 1913.

Hume, Julian P., and Michael Walters. *Extinct Birds.* London: T. & A. D. Poyser, 2012.

Issenman, Betty Kobayashi. *Sinews of Survival: The Living Legacy of Inuit Clothing.* Vancouver: University of British Columbia Press, 1998.

Jennett, Karen Diane. "Female Figurines of the Upper Paleolithic." Honors thesis, Texas State University, 2008.

Kannick, Preben. *Military Uniforms of the World in Color.* Basingstoke: MacMillan, 1968.

Kellogg, Charles E. *Utility of Jackrabbit and Cottontail Skins.* USDA Misc. Publication no. 289. Washington, DC: U.S. Department of Agriculture, 1937.

Kirsanova, Raisa. "Russia: A History of Dress." In *Encyclopedia of Clothing and Fashion*, edited by Valerie Steele, 121–127. Farmington Hills, MI: Gale Group, 2005.

Kirsch, Stuart. "History and the Birds of Paradise," *Expedition Magazine* 48, no.1 (2006): 16–21.

Knötel, Richard, et al. *Uniforms of the World: A Compendium of Army, Navy and Air Force Uniforms, 1700–1937.* London: Charles Scribner's Sons, 1980.

Kolokolnikov, Andrey. "International Fur Trade Trends, Challenges, Prospects." Bachelor of Business Administration International Business and Logistics Thesis, Helsinki Metropolia University, 2013.

Kramer, Molly Baer. "Williamson [née Bateson], Emily (1855–1936)." *Oxford Dictionary of National Biography.* Oxford University Press. doi:10.1093/ref:odnb/54568.

Kushlan, James A., et al. *Waterbird Conservation for the Americas: The North American Waterbird Conservation Plan, Version 1.* Washington, DC: U.S. Fish and Wildlife Service, 2002.

Lasky, Kathryn. *She's Wearing a Dead Bird on Her Head.* New York: Meadowdale Books, 1997.

Lebas, F., P. Coudert, H. de Rochambeau, and R. G. Thébault. "The Rabbit: Husbandry, Health and Production." FAO Animal Production and Health Series No. 21, 1997. http://www.fao.org.

Lincoln, W. Bruce. *The Conquest of a Continent: Siberia and the Russians.* Ithaca: Cornell University Press, 1994.

Lloyd, T. H. *The English Wool Trade in the Middle Ages.* Cambridge: Cambridge University Press, 1977.

Love, John A. *Sea Otters.* Golden, CO: Fulcrum Publishing, 1992.

Lovegrove, Roger. *Silent Fields: The Long Decline of a Nation's Wildlife.* Oxford: Oxford University Press, 2007.

MacClintock, Dorcas. *A Natural History of Raccoons.* New York: Charles Scribner's Sons, 1981.

Mackaness, Charlotte. "Feathers Are the Milliner's Friend, Put One in Your Hat." *The Field*, 14 July 2014.

Macpherson, H. A. *History of Fowling.* Edinburgh: David Douglas, 1897.

Mansfield, Alan D. *Ceremonial Costume: Court, Civil, and Civic Costume from 1660 to the Present Day.* New York: Barnes & Noble Books, 1980.

Massachusetts Historical Society News. "Massachusetts Audubon Society Collection Guide Complete." 7 January 2013. https://www.masshist.org.

Mattingley, A. H. E. "A Visit to Heronries," *The Emu* 7 (1907): 65–73.

Maxwell, Herbert. *Fowls of the Air*. Society for the Protection of Birds Leaflet 23 (London, 1896).

McIver, Stuart B. *Death in the Everglades: The Murder of Guy Bradley, America's First Martyr to Environmentalism*. Gainesville: University Press of Florida, 2003.

Meneses Lozano, H. M. "A Forgotten Tradition: The Rediscovery of Mexican Feathered Textiles." In *Historical Technology, Materials and Conservation: SEM and Microanalysis*, edited by N. Meeks et al., 69–75. London: Archetype Publications, 2012.

Merchant, Carolyn. *Ecological Revolutions: Nature, Gender and Science in New England*. Chapel Hill: University of North Carolina Press, 2010.

Merchant, Carolyn. "George Bird Grinnell's Audubon Society: Bridging the Gender Divide in Conservation." *Environmental History* 15, no. 1 (2010): 3–30.

Miller, A. E. Haswell, and John Mollo. *Vanished Armies: A Record of Military Uniform Observed and Drawn in Various European Countries during the Years 1907 to 1914*. London: Shire Publications, 2009.

Moore-Colyer, R. J. "Feathered Women and Persecuted Birds: The Struggle against the Plumage Trade, c. 1860–1922." *Rural History* 11, no. 1 (2000): 57–73.

Muchawsky-Schnapper, Ester. *A World Apart Next Door: Glimpses into the Life of Hasidic Jews*. Jerusalem: The Israel Museum, 2012.

Müller-Schwarze, Dietland, and Lixing Sun. *The Beaver: Natural History of a Wetlands Engineer*. New York: Comstock Publishing Associates, 2003.

Nowak, Roland M. *Walker's Mammals of the World*. Vol. 2, 6th ed. Baltimore: Johns Hopkins University Press, 1999.

Oakes, Jill, et al. "Comparison of Traditional and Manufactured Cold Weather Ensemble." *Climate Research* 5 (1995): 83–90.

Ogden, Adele. *The California Sea Otter Trade, 1784–1848*. Berkeley: University of California Press, 1975.

Opie, Amelia. *The Father and Daughter with Dangers of Coquetry*. Edited by Shelley King and John B. Pierce. Peterborough, ON: Broadview Press, 2003.

Pantazi, Chloe. "A BBC Reporter Got a Startling Look Inside a Russian Fur Farm." *Business Insider UK*, 27 April 2016.

Parker, Janet, and Julie Stanton. *Mythology: Myths, Legends, and Fantasies*. Sydney: Global Book Publishing, 2007.

Patchett, Merle. "From Sexual Selection to Sex and the City: The Biogeographies of the Blue Bird of Paradise." *Journal of Social History*, 4 October 2018.

Penry-Jones, J. "Feathers." *Port of London Authority Monthly* 33 (1958): 91–94.

Perrins, Christopher, ed. *The Encyclopedia of Birds*. Oxford: Oxford University Press, 2009.

Persson, Charlotte Price. "New Method Reveals the Secrets of Bog Bodies." *ScienceNordic*, 12 August 2016.

Peterson, Lesley A. *Detailed Discussion of Fur Animals and Fur Production*. East Lansing: Michigan State University College of Law, 2010.

Pirro, John. "The Rise and Fall of Hatting in Danbury." *NewsTimes*, 1 February 2011.

Prescott, William H. *History of the Conquest of Peru*, vol. 1. Paris: Baudry's European Library, 1847.

Price, Jennifer. *Flight Maps: Adventures with Nature in Modern America*. New York: Basic Books, 1999.

Reed, Fran. "Embellishments of the Alaska Native Gut Parka." *Textile Society of America Symposium Proceedings* 127. 2008. http://digitalcommons.unl.edu/tsaconf/127.

Reid, George. "Addenda to the Birds of the Lucknow Civil Division." *Stray Feathers* 10, no. 6 (1887): 444–453.

Reports by the Juries on the Subjects in the Thirty Classes into which the Exhibition Was Divided: Exhibition of the Works of Industry of all Nations. London: William Clowes & Sons, 1851.

Rimbach, James A. "The Judeo-Christian Tradition and the Human–Animal Bond." *International Journal for the Study of Animal Problems* 3 no. 3 (1982): 198–207.

Roberts, Emma. *Scenes and Characteristics of Hindostan, with Sketches of Anglo-Indian Society.* London: W. H. Allen, 1835.

Schlesier, Karl H. "More on the 'Venus' Figurines." *Current Anthropology* 42 no. 3 (2001): 410–412.

Scott, W. E. D. *The Story of a Bird Lover.* New York: Outlook, 1904.

Severo, Richard. "Fess Parker" obituary. *New York Times*, 19 March 2010.

Shrubb, Michael. *Feasting, Fowling and Feathers.* London: T. & A. D. Poyser, 2013.

Simenstad, Charles A., et al. "Aleuts, Sea Otters, and Alternate Stable-State Communities." *Science*, n.s., 200 (1978): 403–411.

Skilton, Wendy. *British Military Band Uniforms: Cavalry Regiments.* London: Midland Publishing, 1992.

Skyrienė, Gintarė, and Algimantas Paulauskas, "Distribution of Invasive Muskrats (*Ondatra zibethicus*) and Impact on Ecosystem." *Ekologika* 58, no. 3 (2012): 357–367.

Smellie, William. *A Natural History, General and Particular.* London: Richard Evans, 1817.

Snyder, Jeffrey B. *Stetson Hats & the John B Stetson Company: 1865–1970.* Atglen, PA: Schiffer Publishing, 1997.

Soffer, Olga, J. M. Adovasio, and D. C. Hyland. "The 'Venus' Figurines: Textiles, Basketry, Gender and Status in the Upper Paleolithic." *Current Anthropology* 41 no. 4 (2000): 511–537.

Souder, William. "How Two Women Ended the Deadly Feather Trade," *Smithsonian Magazine*, March 2013. https://www.smithsonianmag.com/science-nature/how-two-women-ended-the-deadly-feather-trade-23187277/.

Stein, Sarah Abrevaya. *Plumes: Ostrich Feathers, Jews and a Lost World of Global Commerce.* New Haven: Yale University Press, 2008.

Straus, Raphael. "The 'Jewish Hat' as an Aspect of Social History." *Jewish Social Studies* 4, no. 1 (1942): 59–72.

Swan, June, et al. *Birds of Paradise: Plumes and Feathers in Fashion.* Tielt: Lannoo Publishers, 2014.

Thaxter, Celia. *Woman's Heartlessness.* Boston: repr. for the Audubon Society of the State of New York, 1899.

Tucker, Jeanmarie. "The Bird Hat: Murderous Millinery." Maryland Historical Society, 2017, http://blog.mdhs.org/costumes/the-bird-hat-murderous-millinery.

U.S. Fish and Wildlife Service. "Migratory Bird Treaty Act." Last updated 26 September 2018. https://www.fws.gov.

Vanstone, James W. *Nunivak Island Eskimo (Yuit) Technology and Material Culture.* Chicago: Field Museum of Natural History, 1989.

Veale, Elspeth M. *The English Fur Trade in the Later Middle Ages.* London: London Record Society, 2003. British History Online. http://www.british-history.ac.uk.

Wade, Lisa. "How the Bird Hat Craze Almost Killed the Dinosaurs." *Sociological Images* (blog), 27 December 2014. https://thesocietypages.org/socimages/.

Wallace, Alfred Russel. *The Malay Archipelago.* London: Macmillan, 1869.

Wallis, Michael. *David Crockett: The Lion of the West.* New York: W. W. Norton, 2011.

White, H. Bryant, et al. "Trapping and Furbearer Management in North American Wildlife Conservation." *International Journal of Environmental Studies* 72, no. 5 (2015): 756–769.

Wilcox, R. Turner. *The Mode in Hats and Headdress.* Mineola, NY: Dover Publications, 2008.

Williams, Edgar. *Ostrich*. London: Reaktion Books, 2013.

Wilson, Don E., and Russell A. Mittermeier, eds. *Handbook of the Mammals of the World*. Vol. 1. Barcelona: Lynx Edicions, 2009.

Witschey, Walter R. T. *Encyclopedia of the Ancient Maya*. Lanham, MD: Rowman & Littlefield, 2016.

Wood, J. G. *Wood's Illustrated Natural History*. London: Routledge, 1852.

Yanover, Yori. "Haredi Leader: Wearing a Shtreimel Is Chilul Hashem." *The Jewish Press*, 22 August 2013.

Zeveloff, Samuel I. *Raccoons: A Natural History*. Vancouver: University of British Columbia Press, 2002.

Index